TOWARDS
A
RADICAL
DEMOCRACY

The Political Economy of the
Budapest School

TOWARDS
A
RADICAL
DEMOCRACY

The Political Economy of the
Budapest School

DOUGLAS M. BROWN
Northern Arizona University

London
UNWIN HYMAN
Boston   Sydney   Wellington

Published by the Academic Division of
Unwin Hyman Ltd
15/17 Broadwick Street, London W1V 1FP, UK

Allen & Unwin Inc.,
8 Winchester Place, Winchester, Mass. 01890, USA

Allen & Unwin (Australia) Ltd,
8 Napier Street, North Sydney, NSW 2060, Australia

Allen & Unwin (New Zealand) Ltd in association with the Port
Nicholson Press Ltd,
60 Cambridge Terrace, Wellington, New Zealand

First published in 1988

British Library Cataloguing in Publication Data

Brown, Douglas, 1947–
Towards a radical democracy: the political economy of the
Budapest school.
1. Mixed economy
I. Title
330.12'6   HD3611
ISBN 0-04-330408-7

Library of Congress Cataloging in Publication Data

Brown, Douglas, 1947–
Towards a radical democracy: the political economy of the
Budapest school/Douglas Brown.
Bibliography: p.
Includes index.
ISBN 0-04-330408-7 (alk. paper)
1. Socialism and society. 2. Mixed economy – Hungary.
3. Hungary-Economic conditions – 1945– I. Title.
HX542.B7167   1988
335.43'4 – dc19

Typeset in 10 on 12 point Sabon by Computape (Pickering) Ltd
and printed in Great Britain by
Billing and Sons, London and Worcester

For My Parents

Betty Thoma Brown and Melvin R. Brown

whose genuine love for humanity is
the inspiration for this book

Contents

Acknowledgements

There are numerous people to whom I owe an immeasurable debt for helping me to complete this book. I want to thank, first, Ron Stanfield for his critical and very creative role in bringing the book to fruition. When we initially discussed the Budapest School's writings it was he who commented that their work suggests a defence of the mixed economy. It was with this pivotal insight that I began to view the mixed economy defence as an organizing principle. In addition, his thorough reading of the manuscript yielded invaluable insights and constructive suggestions. I owe much to his creative talent for synthesizing diverse ideas. I owe much to his friendship and his commitment to a liberated world. Secondly, I want to thank Agnes Heller and Ferenc Feher for their helpful comments and supportive interest in this project.

I also want to thank Chuen-mei Fan, Bob Keller and Dave Crocker at Colorado State University. Each of them read the manuscript and provided me with much needed suggestions and commentary. Cheryl Tyler typed the original manuscript, and I want to express special thanks to her for her help and co-operation. In addition, Toni Ohrn did the word processing for the final draft, taught me how to use a computer and most importantly offered me her friendship and emotional support without which this probably would not have been completed. For this I owe her heartfelt thanks. I also want to thank the Northern Arizona University Business College for supporting me in completion of the final draft, and I want to thank Linda Stratton, who helped me prepare this draft. Lastly, I will remain forever indebted to my wife, Cheryl, and my children, Mathieu and Sierra. It is an indebtedness that I genuinely cherish, because as they have been there for me, I too want to return the kind of care and support they have shown me.

Douglas M. Brown

xi

Introduction

The Budapest School is a group of Hungarian scholars and dissidents, formerly students of the Marxist philosopher Georg Lukacs. The major figures in this grouping are Ferenc Feher, Agnes Heller, Georg Markus and Mihaly Vajda. The commonly used appellation 'the Budapest School' is used here to refer to this group of writers. Although I have avoided the issue of whether the Budapest School constitutes a school of thought, I have analysed the writings of these individuals with the understanding that they share a common neo-Marxian heritage. Given their differing circumstances and interests, especially within the last ten years, to argue that they constitute a 'school of thought' makes little sense. However, this study argues that within the Budapest School's neo-Marxism there exists a defence of a mixed economy characterized by both planning and markets as well as by mixed forms of property ownership. I have attempted to provide an interpretation of the Budapest School's work that draws from key themes and issues they have developed. It is by no means the only or the correct interpretation, but one that I would hope contributes to the overall objective of, as Agnes Heller states, 'making the world a home for humanity'.

What I believe to be some of the essential features of the Budapest School's thought are elaborated in this study by examining these writers' conceptions of both Western capitalism and existing socialism. Moreover, their view of these two types of social formation, which I have loosely labelled neo-Marxist, is premised upon the Budapest School's understanding of Marx. Although I would argue that the Budapest School writers have gone well beyond Marx, as they have understood him in their analysis of Western capitalism and existing socialism, I have consciously

1

avoided the issue of whether their understanding of Marx is correct.

My essential purpose in this study is to demonstrate that in the thought of the Budapest School there exists a novel and unique defence of the mixed economy providing the basis for a realizable society that transcends the undemocratic character of both capitalism and existing socialism. I consider their approach to Western capitalism as neo-Marxian because it rejects the orthodox Marxian view that the essence and driving force of capitalism is reducible to its class dichotomy of capitalist and proletariat. Their approach to Eastern European societies is also considered neo-Marxian in as much as they argue that because these societies are neither capitalist nor socialist they are clearly inexplicable within orthodox Marxian categories. Yet if the essence of Marxism is primarily its method, as Lukacs and Korsch suggested, then the Budapest School has retained enough of Marx's approach to be considered neo-Marxian.

The Budapest School's conception of industrial capitalism draws heavily on Karl Polanyi's work, and argues that capitalism never became the class-constituted society Marx believed it was. What orthodox Marxism understood to be the essence of capitalism, that is, its class dichotomy, was primarily a 'tendency' subject to 'countertendencies'. The Budapest School's neo-Marxian conception suggests that capitalism is a stratified society in which control over social decision-making is not fully democratic.

The Budapest School's understanding of existing socialism interprets these societies as political societies, because capitalism's autonomous economic sphere has been assimilated by a totalitarian form of state. Because of the totalitarian character of the state and the elimination of capitalism's civil society, these writers view soviet society (that is, what can now be labelled a generic form of socialism first introduced in the Soviet Union) as having relatively less freedom than industrial capitalism. Additionally, according to the Budapest School, the Bolshevik Revolution that founded these societies was ideologically based on orthodox Marxism's misconception of capitalism.

The Budapest School writers propose an alternative model to both Western capitalism and existing socialism. Their model, which they call radical democracy, represents the precondition for the full and free development of the individual. It is characterized by many features of capitalist constitutional democracy, including political pluralism, constitutionally guaranteed civil liberties and separation

2

of state and civil society. Additionally, it includes the demand for collective self-management and the formal recognition of all needs. In what follows I argue that the model of radical democracy not only requires the democratizing of the stratified social decision-making mechanisms of both capitalism and existing socialism, but moreover necessitates a type of mixed economy that includes the separation of state and civil society, the use of markets and diverse forms of property ownership.

Stated differently, in capitalism the state and civil society are separate spheres. Although this serves to preserve the freedom and liberty of the individual, the autonomous economic sphere of civil society dominates the state. The stratification of power over social decision-making is grounded in civil society where the profit interests of the top strata dominate social decision-making processes. Consequently, the separation of polity and economy in capitalism preserves both individual liberty and an unequal distribution of power based upon property ownership. In existing socialism, on the contrary, the Marxist, anti-capitalist revolutions were premised on the notion that the capital–labour dichotomy, in which capitalists exploit workers, could only be transcended by abolishing civil society. The sphere of civil society was absorbed by the state, and consequently one of bourgeois society's major achievements, that is, the preservation of the liberty of the individual, was sacrificed.

The Budapest School's model of radical democracy implies that the value of individual self-determination can best be advanced in a society where the state and civil society remain as separate spheres with mixed ownership forms but where the mechanisms of capitalism's stratified power distribution have been democratized – where the state exercises greater control over civil society. Consequently the social democratic (welfare state) economies of the West and the Budapest School's radical democracy are both mixed economies, but in the latter democracy has been carried one step further – a radical step further – by eliminating the stratified power system through a series of radical reforms including self-management and public supervision of the market.

One motivation for this study derives from my belief that the Budapest School through both its political and academic experiences has been able to articulate a realistic model of a society that in its realization would constitute human progress as measured by the Enlightenment values of individual freedom and social progress.

3

The model of radical democracy is unique and deserves attention not so much because of its constituent features of self-management, political pluralism and constitutional democracy, but because it is a direct by-product of a novel but logically consistent analysis of *both* capitalism and existing socialism. It is the Budapest School's unique approach to both of these societies that precipitates the radical democracy model. An additional motivation is that since the Budapest School articulates and derives the model of radical democracy theoretically and at a rather high level of abstraction, it becomes necessary to flesh out the details and specifics of this model beyond what the writers have done themselves. The argument in this study – that the Budapest School's radical democracy implies a mixed economy form – is intended to do this. It is an attempt to make more concrete as well as to contribute to the actualization of a radicalized democracy.

A Note of Clarification on Neo-Marxism

Although I have made no thematic effort to specify the neo-Marxian character of the Budapest School, a preliminary clarification of the term 'neo-Marxian' is necessary. Early Western Marxists such as Labriola, Gramsci, Korsch and Lukacs tried to emphasize that Marxism was much more than a set of criticisms of capitalist society. For them, if it was to be useful, Marxism needed to be an approach or perspective one could apply to any type of society. Consequently they tried to reorient orthodox Marxism towards Marx's philosophical foundation in Hegel and German speculative philosophy. The neo-Marxian interpretation given to the Budapest School falls within this same tradition, as it has accepted Lukacs's claim that Marxism is above all a method.

There are some general comments that can be made about the Budapest School's relation to Marx and the group's own use of the term 'neo-Marxian'. First, there is little value in attempting to pin one correct or appropriate label on the Budapest School's thought. Whether the Budapest School is best characterized as neo-Marxian, post-Marxian, leftist, or radical democratic is clearly not essential to understanding its contribution. One reason the neo-Marxian label has been adopted is because these writers have referred to them-

Introduction

selves in this way (see Feher and Heller, 1982a, p. 23). More
recently they have sought to define the term 'leftist' and would
therefore also consider themselves leftists (see Feher and Heller,
1986b). The extent to which they are or are not neo-Marxian leftists
is, again, largely irrelevant for the purposes of this study.
Additionally, neo-Marxism is equivalent to the literature of Western
Marxism, and it is unquestionably true that the Budapest School is
very close to this tradition since both are derived from philosophical
opposition to Second International, deterministic Marxism.[1]

Secondly, although the spirit and influence of Marx continues to
reside in the Budapest School's writings, there is a good deal of
Marx's method that they have sought to go beyond as well. In this
respect Vajda states:

It took quite a time for me to understand that the idea of the
renaissance of Marxism was not for me anymore. It would
either lead once again to a leftist radical vanguardism, something such as the communist movement originally was, or it
would serve simply as an impotent intellectual dream, as a drug
to calm and quieten our conscience. I did not want to choose
any of these alternatives, so I had no choice but to admit that *it
was precisely Marx's method that one has to give up* and not
just the results of his investigations, not just the belief in this or
that thesis. (Vajda, 1981, p. 6, my emphasis)

Marx's materialist method is founded on what the Budapest
School calls the paradigm of production. This is essentially the idea
that the forces and relations of production form a dialectic based on
economically determined classes all of which reside in the economic
base of society (as distinguished from the superstructure). For Marx
the growth of the forces of production under capitalism was
supposed to create an awareness in the proletariat that its own
liberation required the transcendence of capitalist relations of
production. Here the Budapest School agrees with Habermas that
the growth of productive forces no longer implies emancipatory
results (Markus, 1980a).

The fact that the theory of a dialectical relationship between
productive forces and relations of production has lost its
critical-emancipatory potential, only makes evident its original
inadequacy. Marx succeeded in evading the trap of historical

5

relativism only because he identified in a positivistic manner technical evolution with social progress. (Markus, 1980a, p. 5; see also Markus, 1979, p. 260)

The paradigm of production implies 'determination by the economic in the last instance' and describes Marx's reduction of social phenomena to economic factors. Neo-Marxism in the sense used here disputes this form of reduction.

Thirdly, neo-Marxism, as it applies to going beyond the paradigm of production and the relevance of the base-superstructure dichotomy, also calls into question Marx's 'class' type of analysis. Classes as determined by property relations in the economic base are not the most fundamental category. Even though the Budapest School rejects Marx's dictum that all history is the history of class struggle (since it 'overgeneralizes'), it does refer to the term as a tendency. Furthermore, 'there is one major point which we retain in common with Marx in our definition of class: the emphasis on the *conflictual* character of history' (Feher and Heller, 1983a, p. 214, original emphasis).

The Budapest School's neo-Marxism with respect to class analysis can be summarized in this fashion:

the explanatory value of the concept of class is crucial but *not universal* (all-embracing) as required by any consistent structuralist conception. We consider the well-known Marxian-Lukacsian predilection for such a class a myth ... [T]here is no such social ensemble which could serve as the universal basis of the interpretation of all social phenomena. (Feher and Heller, 1983a, pp. 214–15, original emphasis)

Fourthly, neo-Marxian as it applies to the analysis of existing socialism also refers to going beyond basic Marxian categories and revising his method of class struggle. As Markus has stated:

Clearly, these systems represent a social formation, the ominous possibility of which was not only unforeseen by Marxian theory, but *could* not have been predicted by it. Therefore, to give a critical account of these societies demands significant revisions and modifications in the basic conceptual framework of Marxist theory. (Markus, 1982, p. 295, original emphasis)

Mihaly Vajda has stated similarly that Marx's method is too 'one-sided' when applied to soviet societies.

Property relations cannot illuminate this social structure; more precisely stated, we are compelled in this instance to take note of a fact: we are confronted here by a society in which the property-relations – the real not legally sanctioned ones – were created by the political relations of power. (Vajda, 1981, p. 66)

In general, the individuals of the Budapest School have gradually but continuously drifted further from their Marxian roots. In certain respects they might also be called post-Marxists. The Budapest School has used the term 'post-Marxian' appreciatively in reference to Cornelius Castoriadis and Claude Lefort, who they state are now 'at the centre of post-Marxist radical discourse' (Feher and Heller, 1983b, p. 48). By briefly looking at the current approach of these former French Trotskyists one realizes that what the Budapest School writers consider post-Marxian about Lefort and Castoriadis is also applicable to themselves and is consistent with the interpretation I have given to the Budapest School in what follows.[2]

As in the Budapest School, self-management is a key democratic principle and major social goal for Lefort and Castoriadis, and this began to split them from the Trotskyist Party. By the late 1940s they questioned the meaning of socialism.

It ended with the definition of socialism as worker management of production and the collective management of all social activities by everyone who participated in them. This was a long way from the Trotskyists' conception of 'nationalization' and 'planning' as central objectives of the revolution. (Castoriadis, 1975, p. 133)

Castoriadis and Lefort reject the belief that the proletariat is now a meaningful category in the social analysis of capitalism and, additionally, they do not consider it the universal agent for revolutionary change.

The only criterion of differentiation within the mass of wage-earners which is still relevant for us is their attitude toward the established system. This amounts to saying that it is necessary to abandon 'objective criteria', whatever they may be. With the exception of a small minority at the top, the entire population is equally open – or closed – to a revolutionary perspective. (Castoriadis, 1975, p. 150)

7

The objective criteria that Lefort and Castoriadis have rejected are Marx's class-based categories, especially as they are used by Marxists to identify the essence of capitalism. Similar to the Budapest School's approach, this also implies a rejection of Marx's economic determinism because it makes ideology, rather than class position, the primary constituent of reality.

Like the Budapest School, Castoriadis and Lefort challenge Marx's paradigm of production: 'The political privilege of the proletariat in Marxism was homologous to the theoretical and philosophical privilege accorded the sphere of production. We have seen that the latter cannot be maintained' (Castoriadis, 1975, p. 151).

The similarities in approach are also striking with respect to the analysis of soviet societies. Lefort now argues against the Trotskyist view that bureaucracy exists *within* soviet society, and states instead that soviet society *is* bureaucratic society. However it is here that Marxism is of little help because 'its conception of society as completely regulated by the class struggle does not encourage a study of bureaucracy for its own sake' (Lefort, 1975, p. 35). In general,

> an examination of the Russian regime challenges nothing less than the definition of social reality and, with it the distinction between base and superstructure. Even if one notes that social relations are generated at the level of production, and that property relations are only their juridical expression – as Castoriadis has shown – one still remains too close to the Marxist problematic. (Lefort, 1975, p. 63)

Like the neo-Marxism here attributed to the Budapest School, Lefort and Castoriadis view both East and West as bureaucratic societies, the major feature of which is stratification of social decision-making mechanisms and processes. Thus this calls into question the usefulness of the capital-labour dialectic itself.

> In examining these phenomena, it is futile to maintain that the proletarianization of society spreads, according to the scheme outlined by Marx, for the mass of men separated from the means of production do not resemble the image that he had of them. (Lefort, 1975, p. 61)

Castoriadis draws the conclusion from this that 'Being a wage-earner is the practically general condition in modern capitalist society; it is no longer a situation of "class" ' (Castoriadis, 1975,

p. 150). There are diffuse and diverse forms of opposition in stratified societies, but 'it becomes impossible to make everything converge toward a single revolutionary focus to preserve the image of society centered around the praxis of a class' (Lefort, 1975, p. 63).

Given this perspective one càn question whether the Budapest School, Lefort and Castoriadis might be better considered non-Marxists rather than either post-Marxists or neo-Marxists. However, the following comment by Castoriadis clarifies this and reveals the Marxian inspiration they continue to rely on:

> In fact, it is true that Marx's work, according to his spirit and even his intention, stands or falls within this assertion: the proletariat is, and is manifest as, the revolutionary class which is on the point of changing the world. If such is not the case – as it is not – then Marx's work again becomes what it really always was, *an attempt ... to think society and history in the perspective of their revolutionary transformation* – and we have to take it all up again on the basis of our own situation, which certainly includes as components both Marx himself and the history of the proletariat. (Castoriadis, 1975, p. 151, my emphasis)

In general, what is Marxian about the Budapest School is, as Castoriadis says, its desire to analyse both capitalism and existing socialism from the perspective of these societies' transformation. They would maintain that Marx still offers a useful point of departure in understanding industrial societies and social change. Based on Polanyi, the Budapest School's neo-Marxism suggests that Marx's categories help to explain a *tendency* in capitalism but not its essentials. The essence of the neo-Marxian view in this study is that neither capitalism nor soviet society can be understood as dichotomized class societies in Marx's sense of the term.

A Note of Clarification on Mixed Economies

The defence of the mixed economy developed in this study is not an apology for the political economic structures as they now exist in the United States and Western Europe. In other words, the term 'mixed economy' as I have used it is not intended to be identified exclusively with nations such as Sweden, Great Britain, or the United States. The Budapest School's defence of the mixed economy is not an acritical acceptance of these nations' existing policies and allocative mechanisms. Consequently, 'mixed economy' as it is used here requires some clarification.

The literature on the mixed economy is so diverse that I can identify no consistent definition of it. Some authors, such as Smith (1979) and Shonfield (1980) argue that the mixed economy cannot be adequately defined. On the other hand, there are others, for example, Lieberman (1977) and Young (1974), who maintain that 'mixed economy' is a generic term that requires no definition.

Hjern and Hull (1983, p. 295) have also referred to the mixed economy as a 'metaphor' to denote the 'growing conflation between "the economic" and "the political" in modern societies'. They also state that it is 'rarely defined with clarity'. Furthermore, they say 'a literature review of mixed economy is easy if one concludes, truthfully, if laconically, that there is as good as no literature addressed specifically to "mixed economy" ' (Hjern and Hull, 1983, p. 296).

There are in general two broad yet distinguishable definitions of 'mixed economy': a political definition and an apolitical definition. The political definition refers to the degree of state intervention in what is basically a capitalist market economy (see Preston, 1982; Galan, 1980; and Rowley, 1982). Thus this definition 'portray[s] the phenomenon in terms of state encroaching upon market and thereby suggest[s] that market is the natural or preferable mechanism for allocating resources, which state has come to supplant' (Hjern and Hull, 1983, p. 295). The political definition of 'mixed economy' precludes extending it to non-capitalist systems. The mixed economy is then primarily a hybrid form of capitalism in which an autonomous economic sphere is subjected to various degrees of penetration by the state or political sphere.

The apolitical definition of 'mixed economy' generally refers to the mix of public and private ownership forms, or public versus private enterprise. Following this approach, Kaldor says that a mixed economy exists in soviet societies (for example, state versus small private enterprise in agriculture, and state versus agricultural co-operatives) as well as in the West. Consequently one can talk about socialist mixed economies, capitalist mixed economies, or

10

social democratic mixed economies. Here 'mixed economy' itself does not specify a political form (see Kaldor, 1980). It means an economy characterized by a combination of public and private ownership as well as planning and markets.

Roll (1982, p. 3) has described this distinction between the political and apolitical definitions by stating that the latter 'relates to ownership and to the management of the economic activity of a society' while the former 'is concerned with the instruments of economic policy, that is, the means used by the state to influence a generally privately owned and managed economy'. The limits in the apolitical definition

> are set on the one side by collective ownership of what are traditionally called the means of production; on the other side by the institution of private property in the means of production, by the exclusive reliance on individual interest and private enterprise as the motive force in putting these to use. (Roll, 1982, p. 3)

'Mixed economy', as it is used in what follows, refers to the apolitical definition. Therefore the defence of the mixed economy in the Budapest School's neo-Marxism is *not* a defence of state intervention in the capitalist economy of the West because it is not a defence of capitalism. This study argues that the features of a 'radical democracy', if it is to be actualized, would necessitate a mixed economy. Mixed economy in this sense means a mix of public and private ownership, a mix of state (the political sphere) with civil society (the economic sphere), and a mix of public planning with private market mechanisms.

Consequently by using the apolitical definition what has to be distinguished is the precise difference between the social democratic mixed economy of the West and the radical democratic mixed economy of the Budapest School. The primary difference between the two has to do with the political form that each takes. What will be argued is that the social democratic mixed economies (and this term is used here to include the USA, the UK and Western Europe in general) are characterized by a stratified distribution of power, and as a result the transition to radical democracy means democratizing this stratified power system. The radical democratic mixed economy has democratic social decision-making processes, which the social democratic economies lack, even though both have mixed forms of economic organization and resource allocation.

One difficulty with the mixed economy literature is that it either ignores or obscures the stratified nature of social decision-making. Chapter 2 of this study attempts to theorize the evolution of the social democratic mixed economy and its stratified power system. In effect, the social democratic mixed economy is a result of the state's response to disaffected social groups whose security and interests are threatened by self-regulating markets. As Polanyi has shown, diverse social groups sought protection against the vagaries and disruption of the unfolding of the self-regulating market economy. The formally democratic state was the vehicle accessible to these groups. Their advances and gains acted as a counter-tendency to that of market forces and prevented the creation of a dichotomized capitalism composed of homogeneous proletariat and capitalists. What was created instead was a mixed economy characterized by the stratified distribution of power over social decision-making mechanisms. Thus the social democratic mixed economy, in which the state has both expressed the interests of subordinate groups and countered the complete depoliticization of the economic sphere, is one that is best understood as a stratified society rather than a class society. The transition to a radical democracy becomes radical in the sense that it is precisely social democracy's stratified power distribution that is challenged and abolished. However, because radical democracy is itself a mixed economy, many of the changes in economic policy are reform oriented, not radical. The Budapest School's radical democracy is a mixed economy because the needed reforms, although they would strengthen the public sector of social democracy and provide for greater worker participation, would retain a strong private sector. The reform-oriented character of the policies notwithstanding, the transition to a fully democratized mixed economy cannot be imagined without realizing that it requires the force of a majoritarian, popular movement. Thus it is the necessity of a grass-roots and undoubtedly coalition-based democratic movement that also makes the transition radical in nature.

Notes

1 See, for example, Russell Jacoby, *Dialectic of Defeat: Contours of Western Marxism* (New York: Cambridge University Press, 1981), and David McLellan, *Marxism after Marx* (Boston: Houghton Mifflin, 1979).

2 Castoriadis is Greek and fought in the Greek resistance during the Second World War. He then emigrated to Paris, where he met Lefort in the French Trotskyist Party in 1946.

[1]

The Philosophical Foundation of the Budapest School

> The chief goal is not merely the replacement of the existing social forms with new ones, but the establishment of more fully human individuals and social relations.
>
> Agnes Heller and Mihaly Vajda

The Budapest School's critique of capitalism and existing socialism has an ethical and philosophical foundation, and any effort aimed at interpreting this critique would be incomplete without recognizing it. This chapter provides some of the philosophical background that necessarily informs these writers' critique. Additionally, I have provided a biographical sketch indicating that one cannot divorce the evolution of the Budapest School's philosophy from the writers' experiences as political dissidents in Hungary. Much of their thought has been shaped by both the political repression they suffered in Hungary and the experience of political democracy several of the Budapest School have had since they left Hungary. Moreover, their work cannot be considered as positive science or value-free research but is grounded instead on the values of individual freedom and equal self-determination. In this respect an understanding of their epistemology and notions of human essence and alienation are essential in situating their neo-Marxian approaches to capitalism and existing socialism. Much of their

14

philosophical framework is inherited from Lukacs and his Marxism, so their relation to Lukacs is described as well.

Biographical Sketch of the Budapest School

The Budapest School is in a formal sense a creation of Georg Lukacs and for him it represented the best and brightest of his students and intellectual companions. The Budapest School was never an organizational entity that had any recognized existence apart from Lukacs. Lukacs coined the term in an interview shortly before his death in 1971. In the interview he stated that he considered his work 'more a matter of the establishment of a line of thinking, a school' (Lukacs, 1971b, p 663). Subsequently, by implication, those who worked with him and studied his thought became his Budapest School. The challenge Lukacs brought to the Budapest School 'was to test and put over the effectiveness of such methods [Marx's and Lukacs's], by their concrete application to all-important problems of social life' (Lukacs, 1971b, p. 663). In the interview Lukacs mentions Agnes Heller, her husband Ferenc Feher, Georg Markus and Mihaly Vajda as those of his students with significant academic contributions and thus by implication comprising the Budapest School. He suggests that as a school these members share a common concern not only for the application of Marxian social theory to contemporary issues but also for the elimination of alienation and making 'the distance between the potentialities of the human species and its individual richness the smallest' (Lukacs, 1971b, p. 664). One purpose of this study is to elaborate and assess the contribution of the Budapest School in the light of Lukacs's praise for the group's work and his conviction that 'works like these are the forerunners of the philosophical literature of the future' (Lukacs, 1971b, p. 664).

The term 'Budapest School' should not, however, be misunderstood. It does not imply or constitute a monolithic organization or an elite club of Lukacs's closest confidants, but rather a loosely knit group of former Lukacs students and fellow travellers, now separated by great physical distances, who appreciated Lukacs's commitment to a revitalized Marxism. Those individuals mentioned by Lukacs in the London *Times* interview are the most significant contributors in this study. By virtue of the fact that this group continues to collaborate on and co-author many publications, there is also reason, for purposes of this analysis, to view it as a school. However, Maria Markus, Sandor Radnoti, Andras Hegedus, Ivan Szelenyi, Georg Bence, Janos Kis and Georg Konrad are considered by some to be members of the school. One should note, for instance, that the only edition of collected articles bearing the name Budapest School in its title, *The Humanization of Socialism: Writings of the Budapest School*, includes articles by Andras Hegedus, Maria Markus, Ferenc Feher, Agnes Heller and Mihaly Vajda but excludes any of Georg Markus's works.

Prior to Lukacs's death in 1971 most of these individuals, now in their 50s, had been identified by the Hungarian government as dissident intellectuals. The evolution of their dissenting views began with the Hungarian Revolution in 1956. As their critique of soviet socialism became increasingly acute throughout the 1960s, fuelled by the 1968 Soviet invasion of Czechoslovakia, they finally chose to leave Budapest in the late 1970s. Georg and Maria Markus as well as Feher, Heller and Szelenyi emigrated to Australia, where they were able to find academic positions at Australian universities. Feher and Heller, however, have since emigrated to the United States and are currently at the New School for Social Research in New York. Georg Markus is Senior Lecturer in General Philosophy at the University of Sydney; Ivan Szelenyi has left Flinders University in Australia and is currently at the City University of New York. Mihaly Vajda was a guest lecturer at Bremen University in West Germany from 1978 to 1979 but returned to Budapest in 1980. Georg Konrad and Andras Hegedus (who is a generation older than the others and has been labelled Hungary's last Stalinist premier [Vardys, 1979]) continue to live in Budapest.

In the 1950s and at the time of the Hungarian Revolution the Budapest School writers considered themselves 'reform communists' and most were members of Hungary's Communist Party. By the late 1950s, Imre Nagy, a resolute anti-Stalinist and charismatic leader of the Hungarian Revolution, had been executed (1958) and Janos Kadar quickly consolidated power and set about directing Hungary on a de-Stalinized course of national development. Kadar essentially took up what was initiated in the 1946–8 period, prior to Rakosi's regime. Rakosi's unbridled Stalinism and regime of terror had brought Hungary close to economic collapse by 1955. During the early 1960s, although their hopes were dashed by the Soviet invasion in 1956, reform communists were still willing to believe that there was actually something socialist about the soviet system and hoped that they could help transform Kadar's economic reforms into positive social reforms (Hegedus, 1976a). Among reform communists

> Yugoslavia was *then* the model state, and for that objective our generation was ready to overlook obvious deficiencies in the Yugoslav political system, and we uncritically adored its resolute stance against Stalin; its (relative) internal rationality and liberty. (Feher and Heller, 1983b, p. 51, original emphasis)

In the 1960–8 period their Marxist humanism was not perceived as a significant threat to the Hungarian political apparatus, and in fact their humanist critique of existing socialism actually united political liberals and economic reformists. They were engaged during these years not in a structural critique of existing socialism but rather in a 'moralistic negation of state socialism' (Szelenyi, 1977, pp. 62–6). In effect Kadar offered intellectuals a compromise: if they accepted the party dictatorship and the de-Stalinized Soviet model, life would be made easier for them (Boella, 1979).

The 1960–8 period was one in which the Budapest School was concerned about the 'humanization of socialism'.[1] More precisely it began to attack the Kadarist economic reforms as a harbinger of an impending technocratic take-over of Hungarian life. At the same time Hegedus began to address the issue of bureaucratic domination within soviet society. Thus by the late 1960s they increasingly alienated themselves from both liberal reformers and bureaucratic conservatives (Szelenyi, 1977, p. 64; Tökés, 1979, p. 195).

The period of relative tolerance by the government ended in 1968. After the August 1968 Soviet invasion of Czechoslovakia the Markuses and Heller signed the 'Korcula protest letter' while attending the Korcula summer school in Yugoslavia. For this they received an official reprimand from the Hungarian government. Hegedus for his protest was removed from his position at the Academy of Sciences (Tökés, 1979). At this time Georg Markus published in *Kortars* (a Budapest monthly of wide circulation) 'Trends and Tendencies within Marxist Philosophy', which argued for a 'plurality within Marxism'. It was officially condemned by the Secretary of the Central Committee in September 1968 and Markus was censored (Feher, 1976, p. 162; Tökés, 1979, pp. 149–50). For

17

their imprudent protest of Soviet aggression Hegedus, Heller, Vajda and the Markuses were subsequently expelled from the Communist Party (Boella, 1979; Szelenyi, 1977).

Between 1968 and 1973, when the next major confrontation with the government occurred, the 'humanization of socialism' theme took on new meaning and their critique of soviet society intensified. In the 1960–8 period they functioned as the loyal opposition, but their willingness to support consumerist economic reforms was undermined by their experience with the government in 1968. Yet there was another reason for rejecting Kadar's consumerist economic reforms. Lukacs had challenged them to carry out what he called a Marx renaissance,

> one of the main tenets of which consisted just in the rediscovery and 'rehabilitation' of the young Marx ... this in turn was motivated partly by a desire to demolish the completely petrified framework of the official Marxisms [diamat and histmat], to find in the tradition itself elements which can serve as starting points to face theoretically the changed realities of our own time. (Markus, 1980b, p. 79)

The Marx renaissance led them to the young Marx of the *Early Manuscripts* and the problem of transcending alienation in both the East and the West. Under this influence consumerist reforms appeared increasingly sterile. The counter-culture movement and the new left in the West had a definite influence on the Budapest School writers in these years, as they had strong sympathies for the new left rejection of consumerism. They equated the technocratic economic reform movement in Hungary (for example, the New Economic Mechanism of 1968) with an attempt by the apparatus to assuage the Hungarian people with increased consumer goods as a substitute for substantive political reforms. The new left represented a protest against the consumerist equation of the goods life with the good life. According to Feher, 'the mainstream of the New Left which articulated a new system of needs [what could be called qualitative needs as opposed to quantitative needs], a radical system of needs, was one of the most important impacts in our ideological life' (Feher, 1976, p. 163). During this period the humanization of socialism came to be translated as the need for the 'revolution of everyday life'. For Hegedus the ideas of humanization meant simply 'closer adjustment of social conditions to human needs' (Hegedus, 1976a, p. 174).

However, in existing socialism the structure of needs was alienated for much the same reason that needs were alienated in capitalism. Accordingly, because of the social division of labour in which workers are denied satisfying work in both existing socialism and capitalism, workers' needs tend to be reduced to the need to possess. Needs become quantified. In capitalism, and to a lesser extent in soviet society, satisfaction comes primarily from the purchase of goods in the market. In both systems alienation and its alienated need structure are then manifested as consumerism. The solution to this problem was the emergence of 'radical needs' – needs that commodities cannot satisfy – and this took the form of the 'revolution of everyday life'. The counter-culture movement of the West appeared to be an incipient revolution of this form, and the Budapest School began analysing its implications for structural reform in Eastern Europe.

The technocratic view in Hungary as well as in the West believed 'that the problems of human destiny can be solved simply by means of the development of productive capacity, science, and the increased satisfaction of people's everyday needs' (Heller, 1976b, p. 44). Since these are alienated needs that derive from everyday life, the end of alienation implied 'the radical restructuring of everyday life' (Heller, 1976b, p. 43). In other words, progress cannot be measured by the increased ability of an economic system to fulfil needs if the needs themselves are left unexamined. This is a theme traceable not only to the Frankfurt School writers (for example, Marcuse and Horkheimer) but also to Thorstein Veblen a generation earlier. The increased rationalization of the means used to fulfil irrational needs does not constitute a rational system. The Budapest School, in a manner echoing Galbraith's *Affluent Society* and *New Industrial State*, concluded that needs are produced by the very same system designed to fulfil them. The system and its need structure form a totality that, if relations of subordination and domination exist, cannot be said to be rational. Restructuring everyday life meant democratizing it.

Furthermore the problem of everyday life leads ultimately to the workplace.

Largely because of the atomization of life, ways in which man can express and develop his personality must generally be looked for in the world of work, not only directly as part of his working activity, but also in the field of self-management and social control that is connected with it. (Hegedus and Markus, 1976b, p. 93)

Thus the humanization of socialism and the revolution of everyday life that is necessary to transcend alienated needs require inevitably that one must embrace the values of 'equality, mutuality, freedom of choice, and the refusal to treat others as means' (Heller, 1976b, p. 38).

Thus if the sort of social mechanism could be brought into being which really permits workers to have their say in and to exercise control over decisions concerning production and distribution, this would provide much greater incentives for increasing the general cultural level and for changing consumption in a corresponding direction than any sort of propaganda, however intensive it may be, in favour of cultural values. (Hegedus and Markus, 1976a, p. 160)

The humanization of socialism was premised on the idea that there was something essentially socialist about the soviet system that simply needed to be humanized. Ultimately reasoning of this sort led the Budapest School to conclude that humanization required revolution in everyday life, yet this implied the need for basic structural changes. Consequently what started out as a humanist and moral critique of existing socialism in the 1960s, by 1973 had undermined its basic premiss and concluded that there was nothing socialist about the soviet system.

Gyorgy Aczel was the cultural delegate for the Hungarian Socialist Workers' Party (the Communist Party) at the Regional Conference on Agitation, Propaganda and Culture held in Budapest in January 1973. Aczel set out to denounce the Budapest School as 'revisionists of the "New Left"' (Frankel and Martin, 1973, p. 123). Moreover this was a major turning point in the evolution of the Budapest School writers' thinking on Eastern Europe, because the political character of their criticism not only resulted in Aczel's condemnation but cost them their academic positions. According to Aczel's indictment, the Budapest School programme

is aimed at the revision of basic principles of Marxism-Leninism. Its leading motives are foggy and generally humanistic phrases, petit-bourgeois utopias about communities that will transform the structure of needs and guarantee the self-realization of the free self-expression of individuals. Such communities will allegedly be able to control both the state bureaucracy and the market. We are supposed to see the prototype of these communities in the counter-culture and communal movements of the industrially most developed capitalist countries. (Hungarian Party Document, 1973, p. 140)

Although put forward as a condemnation of the Budapest School, it is in fact a fairly accurate statement of the group's work in the 1968–73 period, and one with which the Budapest School might well have agreed. For the Hungarian Communist Party, however, it not only was a 'new variety of revisionist backsliding' but also represented a 'reverse convergence theory' in that the West and the East were converging towards a common point of equal depravity: administered societies of engineered needs and contrived fulfilments. In other words, both societies were tending towards systems of centralized authority in which life-styles were administered through manipulation and control of the individual's realm of choice in work and leisure.

Not only did the Budapest School writers lose their jobs in May 1973 (except for Ferenc Feher, who resigned in protest and solidarity with the others), but they were banned from publishing and from public life. Their passports were also revoked. At this same time a young Hungarian poet, Miklos Haraszti, who had drafted a manuscript of his experiences as a wage-labourer in a tractor factory, was arrested and tried for subversion. His manuscript stood as a first-hand account of the dehumanization and alienating conditions typical of the Eastern European workplace, and supported empirically the theoretical critique of the Budapest School (see Haraszti, 1978; also Haraszti, 1975). After his trial the authorities issued a law banning the sending of manuscripts abroad. At the end of July 1974 Feher was arrested and jailed for several days for allegedly attempting to send Haraszti's manuscript out of Hungary for publication.[2]

Between 1973 and 1976 most of the Budapest School writers were unemployed and isolated from public life in general. Although Kadarism may have appeared liberal to Western observers, for Lukacs's students the 'unlimited tyranny of Stalinism' had been replaced by an 'enlightened absolutism' of which they were the unfortunate victims (Boella, 1979). By 1977, when they were able to leave Hungary, they no longer believed there was much possibility for them to contribute to reform of the system from within. Additionally, formal democracy (meant to include political pluralism and civil liberties) in Western capitalist nations took on new meaning.

Their emigration to the West has given them the chance to evaluate critically and from personal experience both capitalism and existing socialism. They remain dissidents inspired by Marx and Lukacs, but their analysis of Eastern Europe has shifted towards a structural critique in which they have been compelled to transcend orthodox Marxian categories in an effort to come to terms with soviet society.

From within their evolving framework, which I have labelled neo-Marxian, existing socialism appears as a wholly new social formation that is definitely Marxian but not at all socialist. Furthermore the theoretical transcendence of both existing socialism and capitalism must go beyond Marx's categories and revive Enlightenment values of individual freedom and democracy.

Their project has become the theoretical elaboration of an alternative model to what exists in the West and the East. Their model, which they refer to as radical democracy, emerges out of their neo-Marxian critiques of both capitalism and existing socialism.

> To put it in plain English, we do not believe that socialism is the substance, and democracy is only a kind of decoration. We believe that socialism and democracy are two inseparable entities. No combination of civil rights constitutes socialism, but socialism in the genuine sense cannot exist without the entirety of civil rights. (Feher, 1976, p. 163)

The Critical Theory Paradigm
of the Budapest School

In general the work of the Budapest School writers should be considered as critical theory, and as such it rejects the attempt implicit in the neo-positivist paradigm to theorize society in a valueless fashion. Vajda has argued that their work draws from the anti-positivist positions of both Husserl and Lukacs. They accept Husserl's argument that

22

Merely fact-minded sciences make fact-minded people. In our vital need – so we are told – this science has nothing to say to us. It excludes in principle precisely the questions which man, given over in our unhappy times to the portentous upheavals, finds the most burning: questions of the meaning or meaninglessness of the whole of this human existence. (Edmund Husserl, quoted in Vajda, 1983, p. 108)

Likewise Feher notes that 'every significant innovation in political theory has confronted the question concerning what man is', yet only recently has this been considered 'value-free' science (Feher, 1980c, p. 56). Lukacs, Husserl and the Budapest School would agree that today's sciences cannot provide complete and convincing answers to the questions of existence. Furthermore this incapacity is due to the fact that the scientific view of the world is fundamentally a dualistic view and as such ignores the phenomenal world of existence that grounds dualistic consciousness. The scientific view does not capture the whole picture of life, in other words.

In 'Truth or Truths' Vajda (1975), following Husserl, argues that scientific and philosophical truth are distinguishable. The Budapest School, like Marx, is concerned with philosophical truth – that is, with the reflective and liberating knowledge of critical theory. This is truth and knowledge as a 'human constitution' (Vajda, 1975, p. 32).

The truth of philosophy of Marx, is not *the truth of the given*, not a reflection of what already exists [that is, scientific truth], but the truth of a relative, i.e., not closed, 'totality': the truth of revolutionary, social *praxis*, the truth of a practice which, besides utilizing existing possibilities, *creates* new ones in order to realize the fulfillment of 'human essence'. (Vajda, 1975, p. 34, original emphasis)

Adopting critical theory as the epistemological paradigm for all of their work, the Budapest School writers do not reject scientific truth but seek to go beyond this form of positivist knowledge. They apply the term 'critical theory'

in the broadest way possible, designating by it negatively the rejection by Marx of all the previous philosophical ideologies as necessarily reproducing the false alternative of an acritical acceptance or an unreal criticism of the given social reality. On the other hand, positively, this idea involves the programme of a theory which in reality itself finds the tendencies pointing to, and striving towards, its radical transformation, since social reality is conceived in it not only in the form of an object to be described and explained but also as a subject who reaches through the theory his own self-consciousness, the consciousness of its latent radical needs, induced and developed under the impact of the existing social relations but unsatisfiable, or even unarticulable within their system. (Markus, 1980b, p. 80)

The critical theory context of the Budapest School's research is also derived from Marx's materialist method. 'It means a relentless criticism of the hypostatisation of ideas into independent social forces, a denial of their autonomy and autarchy' (Markus, 1979, p. 255). For Markus this kind of materialism simply refers to the truism that people change their lives not only by changing their consciousness but by changing their material world as well. Thus their method

only attempts to articulate the conditions under which historical life can now be transformed into a *meaningful task* measured to people. But it can only 'evoke' the subjects able and ready to undertake this task. Whether it will be actually undertaken, is a judgment not upon humankind but upon the 'truth' and 'rightness' of the theory. (Markus, 1980a, p. 26, original emphasis)

Through their mutual acceptance of a critical theory paradigm, notwithstanding their disagreement on certain issues, they have evolved a common perspective on several others:

They were the natural precondition of the practical-social orientation of Marxist philosophy, the recognition of the central role of the category of 'labour', the treatment of ideology as an actual force (not merely as a 'superstructural reflex') and the careful treatment of the central categories of alienation. (Feher, Heller, Markus and Vajda, 1983, p. 132)

With respect to the 'practical-social orientation of Marxist philosophy' they remain indebted to him. However, as elaborated in what follows, they not only rejected the mechanistic, Second International Marxism of Soviet orthodoxy, but began to question central tenets of Marx's method as well.

Although we remain unshaken in our demand to transcend the bourgeois state of the world and convinced that this transcendence can and should be achieved with Marx as a starting-point, since the middle 1950s (i.e., the time when we began to regard ourselves as philosophically independent, thinking human beings), we experienced more and deeper doubts, problems and questions concerning the 'traditional' Marxist philosophical framework. (Feher, Heller, Markus and Vajda, 1983, p. 129)

In general what the Budapest School has come to understand along with numerous other Western Marxists is that the best of what Marxism has to offer is in the critical theory methodology. Heller has developed this with the theme of 'radical philosophy' (see Heller, 1984). A critical theory of society offers a type of reflective knowledge that allows people to understand the forces and interests that shape their ideas and values. It is knowledge that when put to use provides people with the means to carry out their own emancipation and liberation. As Heller suggests, such knowledge goes beyond simply 'giving the world a norm', because as radical philosophy it is also aimed at giving the norm a world that conforms to it. What is most essential, then, in the Budapest School's philosophical foundation is the historical objective of 'making the world a home for humanity'. The obvious question is, what are the essential values that determine the extent to which the world is (or can be) a home for humanity?

The Value Premises:
Freedom and Equal Self-Determination

As critical theorists the Budapest School writers found their analysis on the acceptance of certain values derived from Marx and the Enlightenment tradition. In order to understand and evaluate the thought of the Budapest School and, additionally, to interpret their thought as a defence of the mixed economy, these values must be clearly defined. The Enlightenment said, 'I am a human being and nothing else', and this conviction creates the inseparable and coterminous values of life, human freedom and individuality (Heller, 1983a). As a 'human' being, this is the 'individual rich in needs, capabilities, enjoyments, and productive forces' that informs much of the Budapest School's thought (Heller, 1982a, p. 349). However, for the abstract individual, that is, for *any* individual in general, to actualize his or her powers and capabilities and to determine the direction of his or her life in general, *all* individuals must have equal opportunity and access to decision-making power over the basic conditions of their lives (see Feher and Heller, 1986a, pp. 6–35). This is the value of democracy. Democracy in this sense means the right of equal self-determination, and furthermore it establishes the need for ethics.[3] A society premised on the values of freedom and equal self-determination necessitates an ethics that, for the Budapest School, implies the acceptance of a common set of values as self-evident. These fundamental values are freedom, justice and an end to human suffering (Heller, 1981c).

Moreover, the principle of equal self-determination derives from the transcendent character of being itself. We determine ourselves, *within a set of social institutions*, because what we are is fundamentally the potentiality to become as 'rich in needs and capabilities' as we desire. What makes equal self-determination a yardstick by which to measure societies is that self-determination is itself an existential part of our being. It is fundamental to being and corresponds to the concept of existential freedom. To think otherwise is simply Sartre's idea of 'bad faith'. To preface and qualify self-determination with the word 'equal' means that we give existential freedom a material foundation. Consequently all forms of social domination, oppression and exploitation become inconsistent with this principle. What Heller has stated about the value of human potentiality applies at least as well to the value-standard of equal self-determination. Thus we can say that equal self-determination

> establishes a norm against which we can measure the reality and value of our ideas, and with which we can determine the limitedness of our actions: it expresses the most beautiful aspiration of mature humanity, an aspiration that belongs to our being. (Heller, 1974b, p. 130)

In other words, the value-premiss of equal self-determination implies that all people have a transcendent character in that they can become more in needs and capabilities than they are at any given time. Thus self-determination 'belongs to our being' because our being is open-ended. It is that which is to be determined. 'For man is never an inert being, his active character is part of his essence ...

26

Man is a being of intentionality, oriented towards the future, is essentially a "longing" being' (Heller, 1979e, p. 47). A 'longing' being is then one of needs and desires. This ontology of Becoming, which is the Budapest School's idea of human essence adopted from Marx, implies that if *any* given individual is to control this process of Becoming, than *all* must have equal control over their own Becoming. This is what is meant by freedom.

> Our leading value is freedom: we regard the sense of life as more important than mere living. More importantly, only a combination of freedom and life as values yields the good life, and there are potentials in this direction in all 'progressive' movements. (Feher and Heller, 1984, p. 44; see also Feher and Heller, 1986a, p. 7)

Freedom then makes possible 'the universal unfolding of the creativity of the individuals' in a society where 'all forms of subordination' have been eliminated (Heller, 1981d, p. 19). Lukacs's use of the term 'soul' was synonymous with the Budapest School's conception of the process of Becoming. Soul implies

> the maximum development, the highest possible intensification of the powers of an individual's *will*, his capabilities and his 'psychical energies', those unique potentialities that every human being is capable of developing, and ought to develop, in order to become a real personality. (Markus, 1983b, p. 81, original emphasis)

Thus the task for the Budapest School, which has to be clarified and understood in order to evaluate its contributions, is to 'construct theoretical positions with the help of analyses made on the basis of the Marxist value-system [equal self-determination and freedom] and constantly confronted with social reality' (Hegedus and Markus, 1976c, p. 126). Thus it is the principle of equal self-determination that best captures the essence of the Budapest School's value-standards.

Human Essence and Alienation

If in the most general terms human essence in the Budapest School philosophy is associated with the particularly human quality for

27

self-determination, more specifically these writers have a Marxian definition of essence that is composed of three features. Their concept of essence requires some elaboration because alienation, a key category in their approach, is defined as separation from this essence. The difficulty with alienation is that, defined in this fashion, the Budapest School considers its elimination to be unrealistic even in the model of radical democracy. To understand the reason for this, that is, for why the school's neo-Marxian view of capitalism and existing socialism implies that alienation cannot be completely transcended, its view of human essence has to be understood.

First of all human essence is not considered a form of 'abstraction inherent in each single individual' and common to all people at all times (Markus, 1978, p. 37). Rather, it is historically determined and, as Marx put it, in its reality is the ensemble of social relations' (Markus, 1978, p. 37). It is potentiality that is embodied in society rather than in each individual. Thus Markus disputes Eric Fromm's thesis that there is an 'essence' embedded in each person that is 'human' but distorted and alienated by capitalist institutions (Markus, 1978). On the other hand the Budapest School rejects the Althusserian framework in which the individual is only a 'bearer of structures' – that is, that there is no essence.

Accordingly, Heller states:

> regarding the constituent parts of the essence of man I have accepted the position of Marx, according to which: sociality, work (objectification), freedom, consciousness, universality constitute the essence of man. (Heller, 1979e, p. 63)

'These are what characterize humanity since its formation, as opposed to the world of animals, *hence these are the potentials of man*' (Heller, 1979d, p. 18; my emphasis).

The three constituents of essence are: (1) work, (2) sociality and (3) consciousness; universality and freedom are here considered not as additional, separate constituents but as aspects of the first three. Work, as distinguished from labour, refers to self-creative life activity, which for humans becomes the object of will and intentions. 'Work constitutes the real historical relation of man to nature and at the same time it determines the fundamental relation between man and man, so it forms the basis of whole human life' (Markus, 1978, p. 5).

Sociality simply refers to the fact that people as self-creative beings always objectify their existence in a social context. The real core of the 'self' is itself constituted socially, 'for everything that is specifically human in man's biological makeup has evolved socially and is socially determined, even if the ever "given" social environment seems to be a "natural" circumstance' (Heller, 1979d, p. 1). Consciousness implies conscious life activity or the reflexivity of human consciousness. However, 'the conception of consciousness as an inner, non-communicable experience and feeling of pure subjectivity is totally alien to Marx' as well as to the Budapest School (Markus, 1978, pp. 26–27). Thus, like Husserl and phenomenologists in general, consciousness always has an object – consciousness is always consciousness of something. This is a conception of consciousness that is at odds with Cartesian dualism. Consciousness means that as a human being one is a 'teleological being who realizes set objectives and selects the appropriate means for their realization' (Heller, 1979d, p. 19).

These three features of human essence imply that people are self-conscious, objectifying social beings and thus 'the principal characteristic, the "true essence" of man, *lies precisely in the presence of this self-activity whereby he creates and forms his own subjectivity*' (Markus, 1978, p. 40; my emphasis). This is a concept of essence in which people are defined existentially as self-determining beings who therefore have potentiality. However, full potentiality is 'carried by mankind, whereas the individual person carries only the consciousness of this "species character" [essence], and the consciousness of his relation to it' (Heller, 1979d, p. 86). Essence in this sense is not an inherent element of each person whereby identification with it creates 'authentic' being and alienation from it creates 'inauthentic' being. It is *not* what unfolds from within each person, yet it does allow for 'openness' and 'plasticity' of human nature, that is, the potentiality that makes the rich-in-needs person a real possibility. Human essence is then the potentiality in human beings to develop all kinds of new capabilities based upon new needs. People are their developmental possibilities. Equal self-determination is then the value-principle that is logically consistent with this definition of human essence.

Alienation is therefore the separation of the individual's developmental possibilities from what is embodied in the historical development of the species – in the development of the society. Thus alienation in capitalism means that the human powers for people in general are raised to new heights by the dynamics of the forces of production, but they are not raised to new heights for all individuals in particular.

Alienation is the discrepancy between human essence and existence: it is the development of mankind's material powers at the expense of the human essence of individuals and that of whole social classes and strata. (Heller, 1976c, p. 29; see also Markus, 1978, p. 46)

Alienation exists when the 'historical progress of mankind is separated from the development of single individuals, whereby the self-formative and creative aspects of human activity appear only in the larger context of the social whole' (Markus, 1978, p. 46). Of course a separation of this nature, in which the social whole develops at the expense of the individual, is a human phenomenon – only individuals or their institutions can alienate other individuals or social groups. Thus separation of existence and essence can only come about if people and institutions use others as a means.

Marx felt that through the course of historical development the 'human essence becomes the nature of men, becomes "natural" for men, and this process only gains adequate realization in communism' (Markus, 1978, p. 37). Drawing on Lukacs, Heller has modified this Marxian notion of 'essence becoming nature' by reference to 'second nature'. According to her:

This second nature has developed historically and finds incarnation in the objectivations, and in the individuals of the present world, as a matter of reciprocal influence. The concrete potentials contained in the present are part and parcel of this 'nature', both in the direction of the negative and of the positive alternatives. I claim that the 'building-in' of the 'species essence' into the 'second nature' is both possible and desirable; and this belief is derived not from my 'optimism', but from my choice. (Heller, 1979d, pp. 96–7)

Although the 'building-in' of essence to the second nature of existence is more realistic than the ahistorical view that humane institutions will reunite essence and existence, it does not solve another problem. Eliminating alienation, that is, reuniting essence, as the potentiality for the rich-in-needs individual, and existence means 'the creation of such social conditions under which it will become possible to judge the general level of societal development, of human progress, by the developmental level of single individuals' (Markus, 1978, p. 46). However, it is precisely with this deduction that the Budapest School's view of capitalism argues that alienation can never be *completely* transcended. This problem will be subsequently elaborated in conjunction with the group's analysis of capitalism.

The Budapest School's Relation to Lukacs

Before examining the Budapest School's unique contribution to a defence of the mixed economy it is necessary to identify briefly the extent to which these individuals are distinguishable from their intellectual predecessor, Georg Lukacs. In effect in their effort to come to terms with Eastern European societies they found themselves in a problematic relation, not to Lukacs himself as their close friend and comrade, but to his Marxism in general. Their neo-Marxian view, to be elaborated in this study, is one that is filtered through Lukacs. In questioning Lukacs's distinction between imputed and empirical class consciousness they came to the conclusion that it was Marx's concept of class itself that was really at issue, rather than the presence or absence of a class's imputed consciousness.

What unites Lukacs with his students is the Marxian commitment to the creation of a truly democratic society. In this respect Feher states:

> I would not deny that he [Lukacs] was against plurality in Marxism. But, on the other hand, I would say that, whenever he said that socialism is only realizable together with democracy, this is the position which we claim legitimately as ours. (Feher, 1976, p. 163)

Similarly, Lukacs stated that

> the essence of socialist development ... is known by a name: workers' councils. To express this on a theoretical plane, we could say that it is the *democracy of everyday life*. Democratic self-government unfolds at the most elementary levels of everyday life, reaching upwards until it becomes the decision of the

people as a whole over all important public issues. (Lukacs, 1973, p. 316, original emphasis)

Most Western Marxists and certainly the Budapest School would prefer to broaded Lukacs's definition of the essence of socialist development to include more than the factory council movement (whose historical significance cannot be denied). However, like Lukacs they would agree that democracy in the form of equal self-determination is what socialism *should* be about.

The real issue between Lukacs and his students was not about the commitment to the 'democracy of everyday life', which is essentially equivalent to the Budapest School's model of radical democracy, but about how such a model would be realized. Much of this disagreement originates in Lukacs's *History and Class Consciousness*, where

> Lukacs wanted to find a way out of the vicious circle of universal festishism: how can one attain to a true and correct consciousness in an alienated, reified society? His answer at the time of *History and Class Consciousness* was that the consciousness *imputed* to the being of a certain class represented true consciousness itself. (Heller, 1983c, p. 1984, my emphasis)

Lukacs, although he was concerned with the role of consciousness and rejected Second International determinism, remained orthodox in another sense. Like deterministic Marxism, Lukacs distinguished between base and superstructural elements regardless of the fact that he awarded a greater significance to the superstructure. For him the capital–labour dichotomy of the base, from which the proletariat should derive its consciousness, was still the point of departure in understanding the evolution of capitalism. Unlike Second International economism (economic determinism), he did not view the superstructure as an epiphenomenon of the base, but on the other hand he did presume the existence of a proletariat whose imputed consciousness was largely to be derived from its economically determined position in the base.

Laclau and Mouffe have argued that Lukacs suffered from a more subtle type of economic determinism than that associated with Kautsky, Plekhanov and the Second International. Lukacs did not view consciousness as a simple reflex of the class struggle. He realized that consciousness shaped the material world, that ideas

32

could be a material force and that consciousness could not be considered an epiphenomenon of the economic base. On the other hand, Laclau and Mouffe argue that Lukacs embraced a concept that derived all ideas constituting consciousness from economic status. Thus for Lukacs consciousness is a key variable in the class struggle, yet it is a consciousness whose make-up is ultimately traceable to what he believed to be the class basis of all ideas (see Laclau, 1979; Mouffe, 1979). In other words, Lukacs maintained that the ideological constituents of consciousness generally had their origin in the class structure of society. As Vajda states,

> Lukacs's concept of history in general is purely an economistic-deterministic one. As regards the history of the bourgeois world, he accepts an economically determined determinism, even if he does so through the mediator of imputed class consciousness, whose unfolding, equivalent to the revolution itself – is necessary. (Vajda, 1981, p. 49)

The category of economically determined 'class' was fundamental to Lukacs, and even though he did not view its consciousness as an epiphenomenon it was still his belief that all ideological elements have a 'class-belonging'. Thus the ideas that make up the consciousness of the proletariat may mystify reality but have their origin in the economic structure of the society.

The proletariat in *History and Class Consciousness* is the agent of change and potentially the revolutionary subject. Lukacs made class consciousness a 'deductive construction', and to this extent he was incorrect. By contrast Vajda states that consciousness is determined by a 'composite of diverse concrete circumstances such as living standards, historically shaped needs, traditions and so forth' (Vajda, 1981, p. 50).

The Budapest School has referred to Lukacs's view as the 'myth of the proletariat' (Vajda, 1981, p. 5).

> If the proletariat itself ... 'consists' of isolated individuals acting according to their private interests or at least intending to act thus, and if therefore the proletariat disintegrates into different interest-groups, then the proletarian class consciousness cannot be the class consciousness of any *real proletariat*, or at best it can only be the consciousness of a particular group within the proletariat as a whole. (Vajda, 1981, pp. 23–4, original emphasis)

Lukacs did not question Marx's idea that capitalism's essence can be adequately understood through the economically determined concept of class. Lukacs attempted to frame the problem of the absence of revolutionary consciousness by distinguishing empirical from imputed consciousness and by arguing

> that the *actual* consciousness of individuals belonging to a certain class which becomes manifest through their actions is not the same as the class consciousness which the individuals of the class in question *ought* to possess as an inevitable consequence of their class affiliation (Vajda, 1976, pp. 7–8).

Lukacs's students have rejected this framework. They state: 'we categorically reject the Marxian-Lukacsian distinction between the *empirical* and the *imputed* consciousness of the working class' (Feher and Heller, 1983a, p. 223).

In general the Budapest School's neo-Marxism is a by-product of an evolving post-Lukacsian view. 'Lukacs's ideas cannot be transcended without a critical reconsideration of Marx's concept of class' (Vajda, 1976, p. 8). In other words, what Lukacs struggled with was the missing consciousness of a class whose existence he did not question. His students came to realize that it was not the consciousness that was missing so much as the class itself. What the Budapest School began to question was an analysis of capitalism premised on the existence of an economically determined, homogeneous proletariat objectively and dialectically related to a capitalist class.

Ultimately it was Lukacs's charge for the renaissance of Marxism and his conviction that Marx's method was still absolute that led his students beyond his Marxian economism.

> In his last period, however, the absolute had changed: it was only Karl Marx, as source and prophecy, that had to be regarded as absolute. *Diamat* [Soviet Marxism] appeared no longer as the continuation of the theoretical legacy but as the opposite, its distortion. The 'genuine' Marx had to be uncovered and the *real* succession to his ideas, in the form of a philosophical construction, had to be found; that was the 'assignment'. The fact that he kept accepting the source as absolute, however, made him still captive to his prejudices of the 1930s, 1940s, and 1950s. Non-Marxist philosophy after

1848 could be understood only as 'bourgeois decadence' in all its manifestations, since it was blind to the prophecy. Lukacs could not see what was obvious: the fact that great philosophy in the twentieth century is no longer bourgeois, since for him the non-bourgeois was identical with the acceptance of Karl Marx as *the* absolute. (Heller, 1983c, p. 189, original emphasis)

The Budapest School, like Lukacs, subscribes to a critical theory paradigm founded upon the search for a holistic view – that is, a form of self-knowledge that implies grasping the totality.

For Lukacs the holistic perspective is the standpoint of the proletariat. In the light of this discussion, the most important questions of our time seem to be whether we need a total reorientation to overcome the crisis of our era, and whether such a reorientation – be it total or partial – must represent the standpoint of *one* sociologically and concretely delimitable social group (or whether it is attainable independent of such particularity). (Vajda, 1983, p. 117, original emphasis)

Lukacs's students affirm the need for comprehending the totality of social existence but reject the idea that this totality is represented by one social group – the proletariat. They reject Lukacs's notion in *History and Class Consciousness* that the proletariat is both the object and the subject of history.

The Budapest School's neo-Marxism is clearly inspired by Lukacs's statement that it is necessary to 'undertake an economic and social analysis of *what has been achieved under capitalism*: an analysis which we Marxists have not made and lacking which we are unable to isolate the concrete problems which demand solutions' (Lukacs, 1973, p. 321). Thus an essential component of the Budapest School's neo-Marxian view is that capitalism has made considerable achievements with respect to defending the value of the individual through both market and formal democracy, especially when compared to soviet societies. Furthermore it is the formal democracy of the West, as well as its market system, that is largely responsible for the creation of a stratified society rather than a class society constituted by homogeneous proletariat and capitalists. To grasp the totality of capitalist social relations therefore involves going beyond orthodox Marxism's capital–labour dichotomy.

Lukacs maintained that the essence of Marxian orthodoxy was its method, yet for him it was a method ultimately premised upon a dialectic of capital versus labour. The Budapest School's neo-Marxism is post-Lukacsian, because although it accepts Marx's critical theory methodology, it has gone beyond Lukacs's class-constituted dialectic.

To summarize, the Budapest School's neo-Marxism is an effort to transcend Marx's understanding of capitalism. Yet these writers have evolved from a mould cast in orthodox Marxism and Lukacsian Marxism, and they do acknowledge a substantial philosophical debt to both Marx and Lukacs. They have accepted both of their intellectual predecessors' commitment to the fundamental values of human self-development and freedom and argue, like them, that the purpose of their theories is to offer explanations of the world that lead ultimately to its transformation. Theirs is not a value-free science but a project that contributes to the universalization of the material conditions necessary for obtaining equal self-determination. Thus they have adopted Marx's and Lukacs's value commitment and philosophical materialism but in other ways have been compelled to transcend their economically determined materialism.

Like Marx and Lukacs, the Budapest School is committed to a belief that there continues to be in modern society a substantial gap between what people are and what they can become. In going beyond Marx and Lukacs it questions the role that Marx's concept of economic class plays in the historical activity and process of closing this gap. The Budapest School has developed a conception of capitalism that diverges from both Lukacs's and Marx's conception, because it rejects their reduction of capitalism to an essential antagonism between economically determined classes. The writers' life experiences in both soviet societies and Western capitalism have helped give them a different vision of the good society than those of Marx and Lukacs. More specifically, as leftists all of them share a common vision of a socially just society in which all members have equal power and the right of equal participation in the conditions that determine their lives. However, the Budapest School's vision differs from that of Marx and Lukacs with respect to the exact nature of the economic and political institutions that ground the just and free society. The Budapest School's vision is derived in part from its conception and critique of capitalism, to which we turn in the next chapter. It is a conception of capitalism premised upon acceptance of the value-standards of freedom and equal self-determination. These values become the yardstick by which we measure the performance of capitalist society, and by which we compare this performance to that of existing socialist societies.

Notes

1 See Heller, A. (ed.), *The Humanization of Socialism: Writings of the Budapest School* (New York: St. Martin's Press, 1976).
2 Although no author was credited, a statement regarding this incident was published in *Critique*, no. 3 (1974), p. 108, under the title 'Repression against the Marxist in Hungary'.
3 The idea of democracy as equal self-determination has been defined and discussed in detail by Mihailo Markovic in *Democratic Socialism: Theory and Practice* (New York: St. Martin's Press, 1982). There is little theoretical divergence between Markovic and the Budapest School with respect to this concept.

[2]

A Neo-Marxian Conception of Industrial Capitalism

> If political questions (decision-making, political power) and not
> the relations of production are now in the centre of my views
> concerning society, if I do not think in social formations any
> more ... but in social decision-making mechanisms, if I believe
> that the goal or ideal to be attained in each society is simply the
> maximum of democracy possible under given conditions, then
> this does not mean ... that the democratization of the relations
> of production ... has become unimportant for me.
>
> Mihaly Vajda

This chapter develops and elaborates the Budapest School's neo-
Marxian interpretation of capitalism. Drawing on Karl Polanyi, the
basic thesis is that when Marx reduced the essence of the capitalist
system to the capital–labour dialectic, that is, to the social relations
of production in the economic base of society, this dialectic was not
the 'essence' of capitalism, as he thought, but only a 'tendency' in the
unfolding of the self-regulating market economy. Thus the capital–
labour dialectic was, in fact, not the essence of capitalism but, more
precisely, the 'essence of a tendency' in the total unfolding of
capitalism. This is what accounts for Marx's economism, that is, the
'determination by the economic in the last instance', and it is this
expression of economism that the Budapest School disputes. For
Marx the essence of capitalism – its driving force – is reducible to the

autonomous economic sphere where the class struggle of capital and labour is constituted. The class struggle that Marx took to be capitalism's essence would have been more accurately described as a dominant tendency subject to countertendencies. The historical conjuncture of market forces, which tended to create a dichotomous class society (the economic sphere) with the countertendencies of social groups victimized by these market forces (the political sphere), produced the stratified social democratic mixed economy. Additionally, because it was the state and political democracy that were the primary vehicles in manifesting countertendencies, the state cannot be considered an epiphenomenon of capitalist property relations, as is suggested by Marx's base–superstructure framework. Relegation of the state to the superstructure, thus making it an epiphenomenon of the base, is another aspect of Marx's economism. The state has been constitutive of the fundamental social relations of capitalism. With this understanding one realizes that formal, or political, democracy has had a much greater role in the evolution of industrial capitalism than many Marxists have been willing to recognize.

The relation of market forces (in civil society) to the state reveals not only a more pluralistic distribution of power than Marxism has suggested, but also shows that throughout its evolution capitalism has continued to preserve a sphere of individual autonomy that is largely a consequence of political democracy and the separation of state and civil society. The problem, then, in actualizing the conditions for equal self-determination is to retain and perpetuate the ideas of individual freedom and self-development as they have been preserved in capitalism and simultaneously to transcend capitalism by democratizing its stratified system of social decision-making.

Can capitalism be transcended without sacrificing the notion and objective basis for the free individual? In answering this question we are led to a reassessment of what Marx thought was possible in transcending bourgeois society. Therefore the Budapest School's view of capitalism implies some revisions of what Marx understood socialism to achieve. If it was bourgeois society itself, that is, the market coupled with political democracy, that gave birth to the *idea* of individual self-determination, to what extent can bourgeois society be transcended without destroying the conditions for the self-determined individual? Thus the Budapest School's neo-Marxian view of capitalism also yields a different conception of the future from what Marx envisioned.

Budapest School Opposition to Economism

The Budapest School's approach to capitalism begins with the understanding, as indicated in the epigraph to this chapter, that general political questions take precedence over the relations of production, and this leads one beyond Marx's categories of class analysis. Marx's reductionism and economism are essentially two ways to refer to the same thing – the reduction of the totality of social forces to those of economically determined classes. Vajda describes this economism as

> the reduction of power relations, the relations of subordination and superordination, to the relations of economic exploitation, the reduction of social formations to socio-economic formations expressing economic dependence relations, the reduction of the formation of social groups to classes, and of the corresponding social conflict to class conflicts. (Vajda, 1981, p. 6)

This economism treats all social groups and relations that are not directly those of production relations as subsidiary to or derivative of production relations, and, as will be developed, this results in a serious weakness when examining the stratification of modern social democratic societies.

The Budapest School, however, does not reject the importance of the economic sphere. More precisely, it de-emphasizes the exaggerated role that economics takes in Marx. In the school's view,

> If one states that it is, in all societies, a social necessity to produce at least on subsistence level, one is not obliged to say at the same time that the development of the forces of production is *the* independent variable in *all* cultures. (Heller, 1982d, p. 295, original emphasis)

Moreover, Marx's base–superstructure dichotomy is a fundamental expression of his economism, and Heller states:

> But I strongly disagree with the opinion that the base–superstructure distinction did not belong to the core of Marx's theory. Even if one disregards the strong version of this theory (that in the *Preface to the Critique of Political Economy*), it remains undeniable that the primacy of economic (property)

relations as compared to the political and legal expression is the very essence of Marxian historical materialism. (Heller, 1981b, p. 74)

In contrast to Marx, the Budapest School views the historical development of bourgeois society not so much from a broader angle as from a less economically determined one.

We state simply, without historical analyses of any kind, the fact of the more or less simultaneous emergence and later symbiosis of democracy, capitalist organization of socio-economic life and industrialization. We do not call this symbiosis either 'historically necessary' or 'historically contingent'. From the above it follows as well that we explicitly reject the customary historical materialist conception according to which one of these factors (the capitalist market organization of the allegedly eternal separate sphere) would determine the other two – 'in the last instance'. (Feher and Heller, 1983a, p. 211)

The Budapest School is not the first to reject the economistic interpretation of Marx, largely inherited from Engels and the Second International. However, in the tradition of Western Marxism beginning with Lukacs, Korsch and Gramsci, much concern has focused on the absence of class consciousness and, along with this, a rejection of the economistic view that conscious-ness is itself an epiphenomenon of class struggle. Although the Budapest School's thought falls within the tradition of Western Marxism, these writers are not so much at odds with an *interpreta-tion* of Marx as with Marx himself. As they began to realize from their studies of Lukacs, what may be the most important reason in accounting for the absence of class consciousness is the absence of the class itself.

The Polanyi Thesis and Neo-Marxism

The Budapest School's neo-Marxian approach to capitalism is founded on one essential premise: Marx's economism resulted from the fact that he mistook a tendency of capitalism for its essence. The basis for this belief is Polanyi's *Great Transformation*. Polanyi and Lukacs, although they never collaborated on any of their work, were friends and mutual participants with Leo Popper in the Galilei

41

Circle. The Galilei Circle was initiated by left-leaning students in Budapest just prior to the First World War (see Fekete and Karadi, 1981). Because the Budapest School has been so strongly influenced by both of these thinkers, the Galilei Circle, which brought Polanyi and Lukacs together, has been referred to as the 'first Budapest School' (see Szelenyi, 1977). In certain respects the Budapest School's intellectual affinity to Polanyi increased as a result of its scepticism of Lukacs's class consciousness thesis and his reliance on the category of class itself.

Yet both Polanyi and particularly the young Lukacs shared the feeling that bourgeois society had destroyed the organic bonds between people that existed in precapitalist societies. Furthermore, they viewed this new freedom of the individual as problematic because it also meant subordination to 'a whole series of more abstract and complex bonds' (Lukacs, quoted in Markus, 1983a, p. 17). Lukacs spent his life in the Marxian paradigm with the hope that someday the working class would come to understand these bonds. Polanyi is neo-Marxian in the sense that he did not see these bonds as solely class determined, and at this point in its thinking the Budapest School owes at least as much to Polanyi as it does to Lukacs. The fact that the Budapest School first became conscious of and then rejected Marx's economism is a debt it owes Polanyi, since he too rejected this.

Polanyi's thesis in *The Great Transformation* is essentially that the emergence, at least in embryonic form, of a self-regulating market economy was not at all an organic process and that its destructive ramifications for the social fabric of society were so great that it was met simultaneously with protest and reaction by victimized social groups (Polanyi, [1944] 1957, p. 35). The process Polanyi describes takes place primarily in the nineteenth century and can also be viewed as the process by which a separate, depoliticized economic sphere was carved out of what had previously been political societies (feudalism and mercantilism) 'Nineteenth century civilization alone was economic in a different and distinctive sense, for it chose to base itself on a motive only rarely acknowledged as valid in the history of human societies, namely, gain' (Polanyi, [1944] 1957, p. 30). Not only was an autonomous economic sphere being created in the nineteenth century, but this depoliticized sphere, or civil society, *tended* to subordinate the political sphere, the state, to its motive of economic gain.

As Polanyi argues, this wrenching of the independent economic sphere out of its previously integrated and subordinate role in precapitalist societies was not a natural phenomenon.

There was nothing in mercantilism ... to presage such a unique development. The 'freeing' of trade performed by mercantilism merely extended the scope of regulation. The economic system was submerged in general social relations; markets were merely an accessory feature of an institutional setting controlled and regulated more than ever by social authority (Polanyi, [1944] 1957, p. 67)

The movement towards a self-regulating market economy meant not only an autonomous economic sphere based on rights to property ownership but a society in which markets alone determined production and distribution. 'Self-regulation implies that all production is for sale on the market and that all incomes derive from such sales' (Polanyi, [1944] 1957, p. 69). This implies minimal interference in the competitive operation of markets where prices are determined and implies, moreover, that labour and land – the real substance of society – become transformed into factors of production to be privately controlled and sold in markets.

It is only capitalism, which 'liberates' labour as technical activity from this normatively sanctioned direct social regulation and develops its character of 'indifference' more generally, its pure goal rationality, by institutionally separating economic activity from other spheres of social life ... and positing the production of 'wealth' on an ever growing scale as their aim. (Markus, 1979, p. 272)

Thus, 'to allow the market mechanism to be sole director of the fate of human beings and their natural environment, indeed, even of the amount and use of purchasing power, would result in the demolition of society' (Polanyi, [1944] 1957, p. 73). The self-regulating market society would be one where only the blind forces of the market – economic gain and fear of starvation – determined the nature of social priorities and the future course of social development. Market competition, the impersonal forces of supply and demand, would dominate all spheres of social existence, and in such a society the 'economic laws' of classical and Marxian economics could truly be said to govern. Polanyi believed that the demolition of society was immanent in the forces of the self-regulating market because the social fabric itself would be subordinated to market dictates. This movement of social dislocation and upheaval created a profound material and emotional insecurity for the majority of the population.

The political sphere and thus social control would be *completely* subordinated to blind market forces and would appear very much as epiphenomena; thus 'society protected itself against the perils inherent in a self-regulating market economy – this was the one comprehensive feature in the history of the age' (Polanyi, [1944] 1957, p. 76).

The significance of Polanyi's view for the Budapest School's neo-Marxism is his demonstration that

> the situation in England during and after the industrial revolution, which revealed the prevailing laws of the self-regulating market and, at the same time, their catastrophic consequences, was a brief, transitional period in the history of capitalism. The liberal theory thus appears as one of the least realizable (negative) utopias in the history of humanity. If Polanyi's theses are on target, and surely they are, then the historical tendency of capitalist society does not and cannot correspond to that which Marx predicted. (Vajda, 1981, p. 47)

As this statement indicates, both Marx and classical liberal economists 'misread the history of the Industrial Revolution because [they] insisted on judging social events from the economic viewpoint' (Polanyi, [1944] 1957, pp. 33–4). They based their analyses on what was a tendency, a 'brief transitional period in the history of capitalism' in those years approximately between 1750 and 1850. But why cannot the historical tendency of capitalism conform to Marx's analysis? Because 'the dynamics of modern society was governed by a *double* movement: the market expanded continuously but this movement was met by a countermovement checking the expansion in definite directions' (Polanyi, [1944] 1957, p. 130, original emphasis). Thus the unfolding of the market economy did not result in the 'demolition of society'. This countermovement is what Polanyi refers to as society's protective response:

> the principle of social protection aiming at the conservation of man and nature as well as productive organization, relying on

the varying support of those most immediately affected by the deleterious action of the market – primarily, but not exclusively, the working and the landed classes – and using protective legislation, restrictive associations, and other instruments of intervention as its method (Polanyi, [1944] 1957, p. 132).

Polanyi's dialectic, composed of market forces and protective response, is simply a less economistic version of Marx's class dialectic. Marx's dialectic is one-sided in that its capital–labour antinomy is constituted in only one of Polanyi's movements: the self-regulating market. They are both conceptualizations that are antinomous, but Marx reduces the forces of the protective response (which he definitely addresses in the context of 'class' struggle) to developments within the economic sphere.

In the actual constitution of capitalism's social relations, Polanyi's dialectic is broader only in the sense that he rejects making the economic sphere the sole determining element and gives substantial emphasis to the political sphere and to the state. In Polanyi's view the political sphere and its relations are not to be construed as epiphenomena of the economic sphere. Polanyi would agree that the market and property relations of the economic sphere and civil society dominated the political sphere of the protective response once the double movement of the nineteenth century was underway; but this recognition does not oblige him or the Budapest School to view the political sphere as an epiphenomenon, nor does it contradict the idea that Polanyi gives equal weight to both spheres in constituting capitalism's institutional relations. In other words, capitalism became an economic society through a process that was largely political – the disembedding of the economy simultaneous with the protective response.

In the unleashing of self-regulating market forces, a separate economic sphere was being created out of societies in which economic activities had previously been embedded by social norms and customs. The protective response represented society's spontaneous efforts at re-embedding the economy. However, to the extent that the economic sphere has not been re-embedded in the Western mixed economies, one can say, in agreement with Marx, that civil society (the separate economic sphere) has continued to dominate the political sphere. However, this is different from stating that the political sphere is an epiphenomenon of the economic

sphere. The state and political sphere become an epiphenomenon for
Marx because his analytical conception of capitalism begins with a
pre-existent economic sphere already divorced from the political
sphere. Marx begins with a conceptual framework that, as an
abstraction from reality, conceives capitalism as a system in which
the economy has already been disembedded and has already come to
dominate the state. What Marx did was then to fill in this conceptual
framework of class society with historical data. His class-based
conceptual framework is an abstraction from what was one tendency – the disembedding of economy from society. It is a framework based on what capitalism would have become had there been
no protective response. In effect Marx's analysis captures the
essence of a tendency but not the essence of capitalism itself. What is
missing in Marx's framework is the extent to which the political
sphere not only allowed but actually participated in the process of
disembedding the economy from society.

In effect Marx's analysis of capitalism, founded on the principle of
class struggle and an economically determined materialism, would
have been more accurate had there been no protective response but
only a single movement (or tendency) of the market. Marx was, in
effect, looking at the totality of capitalism but within a conceptual
framework that only recognized Polanyi's movement of market
forces.

The State as the Vehicle of the
Protective Response

From the Budapest School's perspective, what is important in Polanyi's thesis is that the protective response of society is just as vital in
determining the evolution of Western capitalism as is the disembedding of the economy and the development of the self-regulating
market. However, not only is the protective response isomorphic
with the self-regulating market, but the process of disembedding itself
passed through the state and political sphere. It was the state that
allowed and facilitated the emergence of the autonomous economic
sphere. In a very literal sense it was the state's action that constituted
the unfolding of the market. This is very clear in Polanyi:

> There was nothing natural about *laissez-faire*; free markets
> could never have come into being merely by allowing things to

take their course. *[L]aissez-faire* itself was enforced by the state. The thirties and forties saw not only an outburst of legislation repealing restrictive regulations, but also an enormous increase in the administrative functions of the state. (Polanyi, [1944] 1957, p. 139)

In general it was the 'state [that] created niches for [the] market' (Hjern and Hull, 1983, p. 310) and thus allowed the free market process to develop. However, the economy never became totally dis-embedded because simultaneously the protective response began to counter this tendency also through state action. 'While *laissez-faire* economy was the product of deliberate state action, subsequent restrictions on *laissez-faire* started in a spontaneous way. *Laissez-faire* was planned; planning was not' (Polanyi, [1944] 1957, p. 141).

Polanyi argues that there was no anti-liberal conspiracy bent on restricting the universalization of the self-regulating market, but on the contrary the protective response was spontaneous. He cites a whole host of legislative acts passed in Britain in the second half of the nineteenth century, all of which attest not only to the diversity of society's reaction to the market, but also to the role that the state played.

[E]ach of these Acts dealt with some problem arising out of modern industrial conditions and was aimed at the safeguard-ing of some public interest against dangers inherent either in such conditions or, at any rate, in the market method of dealing with them. (Polanyi, [1944] 1957, p. 146)

Moreover, as the state created the niches for the market and allowed the disembedding of civil society, it then had a continuous, although not exclusive, role in expressing the protective response. The role of the state in civil society widened and expanded into the twentieth century. As Heller suggests:

Although after Karl Polanyi's analyses even the liberal *laissez-faire* seems to have been nothing but a utopia, while state interventionism in *some* form was as old as capitalist society, nevertheless, the function of the state was far from being of the same importance in the nineteenth century as the twentieth century. (Heller, 1978b, p. 882, original emphasis)

As Polanyi indicated, protection begat protection. As the protective response decreased the automaticity of the market, further social dislocation followed, precipitating further intervention by the state.

Even the term 'interventionism' is somewhat inaccurate because it tends to portray civil society as a sphere that is antecedent to the state and whose origins are somehow unrelated to and independent of the state. It also mistakenly implies the notion of the state as epiphenomenon of civil society. Interventionism creates the impression that civil society stands alone as an entity in which the state then intervenes. Moreover, in the mixed economy literature it is usually assumed that this form of intervention requires justification and legitimation because it is an intrusion into what often appears as a self-legitimated economic sphere. Thus,

> even if, as we know from Polanyi and others, it was not true that the state had no role in economic processes (there has never been a time in modern development in which not only municipal but also state legislation of a kind regarding economic transactions did not exist), the role of the state was, initially, undoubtedly limited. (Feher and Heller, 1982a, p. 31)

The state's role was limited in the nineteenth century, but only enough to allow the creation of a separate sphere of civil society in which at least tendentially there existed a depoliticized market economy whose functioning could meet most needs without direct political control. The protective response as manifested through the state did not subordinate civil society to social or political authority but only checked the growth of the market's worst social effects. It is still the case that the economy became sufficiently disembedded to take on a self-regulating appearance and thus a depoliticized character. The point, as Vajda states, is that

> Neither for liberalism nor for Marx does the political-power structure belong to the essence of society; neither of the two theories attributes a structural importance to the state in the totality of society. The idea that the state is a factor that not only helps preserve the private bourgeois structures but perhaps also modifies them ... is accepted by Marx. But the idea that it also determines them is as alien to Marx as it is to liberalism. (Vajda, 1981, p. 73)

Polanyi's influence on the Budapest School's neo-Marxism is also indicated by Vajda's definition of the state as an 'organ for the self-regulation of society as a whole'. It is neither an epiphenomenon of the self-regulated market economy nor an instrument of the bourgeoisie, but this does not imply that state and civil society are fully democratic either. As Vajda says:

> Just as the capitalist form of production does not exist for the sake of exploitation but for the sake of social production and yet represents the exploitation of the worker, so too the state is not present for the sake of political oppression but for the sake of regulating the social totality, and yet is an organ of political repression. (Vajda, 1981, p. 75)

The fact that the state played a major role in constituting the separate economic sphere and its social relations is a neo-Marxian concept. As Vajda says, it implies that the state is, as it has always been, an agency for regulating the social totality. From an orthodox Marxian perspective one would say that the state played a role in shaping the formation of the capitalist and proletarian classes. On the contrary, from a neo-Marxian perspective the Budapest School is more likely to say that, because of the state's role as the primary but not exclusive vehicle of the protective response, it prevented society from becoming dichotomized between capitalist and proletarian classes. This is the structural importance of the state to which Vajda refers.

The Relation of the Protective Response to Formal Democracy

Given the preceding remarks one can argue that it is Polanyi's thesis of the nineteenth-century double movement that reveals the economism in Marx's method. Following Polanyi, the Budapest School views the double movement of market and protective response as one in which the social relations of capitalism are constituted not in the autonomous economic sphere but through a process of codetermination between both economic and political spheres. In addition it is the continuous interaction between state and civil society – between tendency and countertendency – that characterizes society's attempt to preserve itself from the ravages of the self-regulating market.

Yet if countertendencies of the protective response were manifested through the state, what was the specific nature of the state that accommodated the great transformation? The disembedding of the economic sphere and society's reaction to it took place on the basis of formal democracy (what we frequently refer to as political democracy). It was this specific type of state, in other words, that provided the avenue for society's protection against the market. Yet formal democracy itself was also a product of the disembedding of the economy and was extended through the actions of the protective response.

For Polanyi as well as the Budapest School the problem of Marx's economism is that it 'deduces formal democracy from a mysteriously self-moving and automatically increasing system of capitalist and industrialist activities' (Feher and Heller, 1983a, p. 218). On the contrary, formal democracy itself evolved and became more concrete as a result of the double movement of the nineteenth century. Its materialization is the genuine result of the clash of market and protective response. This view of formal democracy runs counter to both the social democratic idea, which sees formal democracy as independent of civil society, and the Leninist argument that it is an epiphenomenon of civil society. Lukacs himself was Leninist in this sense because, as Feher states, 'Following in Marx's footsteps, Lukacs's writings are full of invective against mere formal democracy'. (Feher, 1983, p. 82).

Yet what is meant by mere formal democracy? For the Budapest School it entails,

> in the first instance, a relative (never complete) separation of state from [civil] society. Its democratic character is constituted by a fundamental document (mostly in the form of constitutions) which formulates the democratic civic liberties (the so-called 'human rights'), pluralism, the system of contract, and the principle of representation. (Heller, 1978b, p. 867)

Thus in general it has three features the Budapest School considers significant: (1) constitutionally recognized political pluralism, (2) formally free citizenry and (3) a trend towards increasing political equality, although this is clearly distinguishable from economic equality (see Feher and Heller, 1983a).

Marxian invectives against formal democracy result from the fact that they reduce the fundamental relations of power to those constituted by property relations in the economic base. Consequentlly, formal democracy becomes a fraud because effective power is derived from the class structure – formal democracy is merely an epiphenomenon.

This contrasts sharply with the Budapest School's neo-Marxism. In other words, 'It was not capitalism that made formal democracy universal, but the struggle against capitalism' (Heller, 1978b, p. 869). The struggle against capitalism is the countertendency, or countermovement, of the protective response, and it is here in the protective response that formal democracy actually developed and became universalized. By contrast orthodox Marxism may tend to reduce the struggle for formal democracy to one of 'class struggle', yet to do so would be an abstraction. The economic classes of the Marxian dichotomy did not in reality exist. It was a struggle carried out by diverse social groups that in no way can be conceptually unified as a proletariat. Certainly the ideas of formal democracy emerged in the eighteenth century and the basic notions of pluralism and protection of individual liberty and property were welcomed and advanced by the rising bourgeoisie. However, for the bourgeoisie such liberties were intended to protect them from encroachments from above – from the monarchy and aristocracy in the absolutist state.

Polanyi discusses the English Chartist movement in the 1930s and concludes that

> The more viciously the labor market contorted the lives of the workers, the more insistently they clamored for the vote. The demand for popular government was the political source of the tension. Under these conditions constitutionalism gained an utterly new meaning. Until then constitutional safeguards against unlawful interference with the rights of property were directed only against arbitrary acts from above. (Polanyi, [1944] 1957, p. 225)

As many have noted, extending formal democracy to the social groups below itself was never part of the bourgeoisie's intention, yet as Polanyi makes clear with his comment about the free labour market, it was the protective response that led to formal democracy's universalization. 'Inside and outside England, from Macaulay to Mises, from Spencer to Sumner, there was not a militant liberal who did not express his conviction that popular democracy was a danger to capitalism' (Polanyi, [1944] 1957, p. 226).

Nevertheless, popular democracy continued towards universalization well into the twentieth century. Feher and Heller comment that although the social democratic parties in Europe were part of a parliamentary system and wanted to remain part of the system

> they achieved spectacular results. Hardly a socialist agitator, Max Weber testified to the fact that the credit of gradually transforming a far from democratic liberal regime into a parliamentary ('formal') democracy could be given solely to the working class parties. (Feher and Heller, 1982b, p. 127)

Thus during the nineteenth century political democracy was a major tool for social change, while at the same time it became more accessible to the voices and needs of those subordinate social groups consistently threatened as well as victimized by the market mechanism (see Boella, 1979). Formal democracy, therefore, was and continues to be 'in the making' (a term the Budapest School has borrowed from E. P. Thompson; see Feher and Heller, 1983a).

The formally democratic state together with civil society's market forces has codetermined the relations of power in capitalism. Consequently, with this we begin to understand the commonalities shared by the Budapest School and Polanyi. As Vajda (1981, p. 7) has said, 'I was forced to understand that one cannot deduce the political power from the economic one'. Clearly Vajda's position here is at least consistent with Polanyi's *Great Transformation* if not derived from his reading of it.

Form and Content in Formal Democracy

There is an additional significance of formal democracy that becomes important for the Budapest School in articulating its model of radical democracy. The word 'formal' does not mean false or vacuous, but only that the specific content of this type of democracy is not specified. Thus 'formal democracy leaves open and undecided the problem of the concrete structure of society' (Heller, 1978b, p. 868). Accordingly formal democracy means that 'in the majority of liberal parliamentary states there is nothing in the constitutions (very much in contrast to a popular belief widely held on the left) that would *prescribe* capitalist organization of society' (Feher and Heller, 1983a, p. 233, original emphasis).

Heller has called attention to the idea that the United States'

Declaration of Independence is a statement of the principles of formal democracy and yet ironically all the principles of democratic socialism are inferred within it. For her this is self-evident, but she acknowledges that most Marxists, at least historically, would disagree. Again the main reason they would disagree is because the formally democratic state is viewed as an epiphenomenon of the real, class-determined power relations in civil society. She argues that the *Declaration* legalizes the principles of formal democracy and leaves open possibilities for substantive economic democracy. It retains the possibility of extending the principles of political democracy into the economic sphere.

> The concrete forms of realization of these possibilities could not be formulated. Moreover, they *should* not be at all. The formality of democracy presupposes that the forms of realization depend on society itself. (Heller, 1979a, p. 109, original emphasis)

What the *Declaration* accomplished was the expression of the liberation of civil society from the feudal state. Thus 'the same democratic principles – since they are formal – can be the fundamental principles of both a capitalist and a socialist society incorporated in a constitution' (Heller, 1978b, p. 868). In a capitalist constitution the protection of property as a civil liberty tends to subordinate other rights. However, in a socialist constitution, since formal civil liberties do not specify any priority directly, other civil liberties can assume precedence over property rights. Ultimately the issue is one situated within the discourse of rights, as Bowles and Gintis (1986) have recently pointed out. The right of property does not have to prevail over the right of employment.

For the Budapest School the historical process through which formal democracy evolved, that is, the protective response, indicates serious problems in Marx's economistic method. However, it also indicates that formal democracy is still 'in the making' and can be the basis for a transformation in its content, a transformation towards a radical democracy in which the right of equal participation in social decision-making is paramount. Consequently, 'Formal democracy is precisely the great invention ensuring continuously the democratic character of a state' (Heller, 1978b, p. 869).

The Protective Response and the Absence of a Proletariat

To this point the Budapest School's neo-Marxism has been negatively developed, stating only that Marx was incorrect in positing the fundamental social relations of power in capitalism solely within the economic sphere. Furthermore, according to Polanyi's thesis of the double movement, the conflictual and antagonistic character of capitalist social relations cannot be reduced to the capitalist–proletariat dichotomy, because this is an economic reduction that excludes the fundamental role of the state and political sphere in constituting capitalist relations. Marx's concept of a dichotomized, class-based society, and thus his concept of the proletariat, is derived from viewing capitalism as the result of a single movement – that of the unfolding of the self-regulating market economy. What remains of his notion of the proletariat once the double movement is considered?

Above all, as Vajda states, the point in going beyond Marx's class structure analysis is

> to understand that Marx himself (not to speak of later shallow Marxism), when he reduced political forms of power to property relations, that is, to class relations, had simplified the actual pluralism of power, the real organization of society. (Vajda, 1981, p. 68)

In other words, the social relations of capitalism once the double movement is understood reveal a greater pluralism of power in these relations, a pluralism that is at least in part obscured by Marx's class analysis and the base–superstructure dichotomy. Vajda admits 'that one must understand property relations in order to explain and understand every society', and this is Marx's 'Copernican discovery'. 'But that a comprehension of property relations provides the only key necessary for an understanding of social phenomena is already more than questionable' (Vajda, 1981, pp. 65–6). Had the self-regulating market been allowed to unfold without a protective response, then property relations would undoubtedly provide the essential key to understanding capitalism. Likewise, if the economy had been completely disembedded from society, Marx's base–superstructure dichotomy would also apply.

However, if capitalism's social relations as constituted by the double movement indicate a greater pluralism of power than in Marx's class analysis, what does this mean for the existence of the proletariat? Does it exist or did it exist at one time? Again the Budapest School argues that Marx's proletariat was premised upon the complete unfolding of the self-regulating market economy, which, because of the protective response, never came about. Had there been no protective response then a homogeneous proletariat with nothing to lose but its chains might have resulted. Both Lukacs and Marx subscribed to the notion that 'the proletariat, which is not at all homogeneous at the beginning of capitalism, would become step by step a homogeneous class' (Vajda, 1981, p. 17). Vajda adds,

> to the extent that the liberal image of capitalism is an accurate description of capitalist reality, Marx's critique is irrefutable. Since the image is not accurate, it does not reflect the reality of society but merely a tendency, the tendency which the bourgeoisie as a conscious class would like to actualize. (Vajda, 1981, p. 72)

Therefore both classical liberals and Marx shared the same predilection for falsely abstracting from reality and economistically over-simplifying the dynamics of capitalism.

> And today at last we have to admit the fact: the homogeneous proletariat – which is alleged to be theoretically existent in spite of its 'apparent' dividedness, in spite of its dissolution into interest-groups, and which came to be theoretically existent because such an entity is *necessary* to transcend the given society – does not exist in reality. (Vajda, 1981, p. 30, original emphasis)

In a general sense the nineteenth-century double movement, rather than homogenizing the proletariat, led to its general dilution as a class. The tendency of the self-regulating market was a 'dichotomizing' tendency in that its uninhibited realization would have created the two polarized classes of proletariat and capitalist. The protective response, which in no way can be simplified or reduced to pre-existent proletarians 'fighting back', checked the dichotomizing tendency and created not only a more pluralistic power system but a more stratified one as well. Therefore 'there is no such historical period, either in modernity or prior to it, when the totality called society could be reasonably exhausted, or accounted for, by the entities called "classes" ' (Feher and Heller, 1983a, p. 214).

Does this mean that the Budapest School has completely rejected the use of the term 'class'? Feher and Heller have tried to redefine 'class' in such a way that although the term retains some useful analytic qualities it is again evident that it cannot capture the essence of capitalist social relations as Marx had intended. They argue that social classes, if they exist, must be dichotomous in character, that is, they are 'mutually constitutive pairs of interconnected social entities none of which can exist ... without the other' (Feher and Heller, 1983a, p. 212). They are antagonistic as well. What is unique in their definition, however, is that 'social classes are human social ensembles which essentially and consciously contribute to social change via purposeful action' (Feher and Heller, 1983a, p. 212).

If classes can enact social change then there is an element of freedom or free space inherent in them. The liberty that is integral to the Budapest School's definition of class thus means, as the writers admit, that the master–slave dichotomy is not a class dichotomy (Feher and Heller, 1983a, p. 213). Consequently, again borrowing E. P. Thompson's term, they say classes are not structural but always 'in the making' (Feher and Heller, 1983a, p. 214). Feher and Heller argue that the classes of proletariat and capitalist do apply to capitalism, but that they are 'open classes' in the sense that one is not born into one's class standing and one's class standing does not have to be permanent in capitalism. There is actual and potential mobility between these classes; individuals can move up or down in this class dichotomy. Therefore there is an element of free social space around them, unlike caste or tribal systems of relations. They accept Weber's distinction between political classes and socioeconomic classes. In capitalism and with the universalization of formal democracy, political classes tend to be eliminated as equal rights are extended to all individuals regardless of property ownership.

However socioeconomic classes continue to exist in relations of dependence or exploitation (Feher and Heller, 1983a, p. 213). That these classes are 'open' in capitalism is due in part to formal democracy's elimination of political classes as well as to the basic separation of the economic sphere of civil society from the political sphere of the state. It is the openness of capitalism's classes, guaranteed through formal democracy, that allows for diversity and heterogeneity in the make-up of the working class. Additionally this openness signifies that the reduction of capitalist social relations to the Marxian dichotomy of capital and labour not only is inaccurate but simplifies and obscures the 'actual pluralism of power' pointed out by Vajda (1981, p. 68). The openness of capitalism's classes, which results from formal democracy and thus indirectly from the double movement of the nineteenth century, makes them 'flawed' classes according to Feher and Heller (1983a, p. 222). To the extent that the term 'class' applies to capitalism, it is as a tendency only. Ultimately it is Polanyi's protective response that accounts for the flawed character of these classes, because had the self-regulating market tendency not met with a countertendency, its dichotomizing effect would have created flawless classes of capitalist and proletariat. Classes are 'open' in capitalism because they exist as a tendency only.

> Therefore the dream (explicitly manifest in practically all socialist doctrines of the nineteenth century except that of Rosa Luxemburg) that modern society as a whole can be reduced to the bipolarity of two classes alone is a utopia. It is a utopia not in the sense of an Ought which is socially productive, but in the sense of *impossibility, unfeasibility*, which is socially counterproductive. It is also a fairly *negative* utopia. (Feher and Heller, 1983a, p. 221, original emphasis)

An additional consequence of the utopian conception of a homogeneous proletariat relates to Marx's theory of revolution. Without a class to achieve class consciousness and thus to become the revolutionary subject of capitalist transformation, Marx's theory of revolution becomes problematic as well. Polanyi's double-movement thesis as interpreted by the Budapest School casts doubt on Marx's conviction that the proletariat would achieve class consciousness because it casts doubt on the proletariat's existence as a class. This also explains the school's difficulty with Lukacs's distinction between imputed and empirical consciousness of the proletariat. Unlike Lukacs, the Budapest School did not attempt to swallow the myth of the proletariat or try to reconcile imputed with empirical consciousness. Polanyi's influence distinctly shifted their thinking away from reliance on class categories.

The fact that there is no homogeneous proletariat to become class conscious does not obviate the problem of the missing revolutionary subject, nor does it obviate the problem of false consciousness and reification. It does help to explain reification and false consciousness; and it does mean that one must look for the emergence of radical needs and consciousness in a much broader context and within a less economistic framework. It cannot be maintained that one's consciousness is solely a function of one's place within the social division of labour. The fact that the social relations of capitalism cannot be reduced or narrowed to class categories translates into an understanding that consciousness is a function of a much broader and more heterogeneous package of ideological influences and elements in which most of these influences have no 'class-belonging' whatsoever. For example, can one really say that religion or sports are 'bourgeois' (see Mouffe, 1979; Laclau, 1979)? Still, in Vajda's terms:

> The major defect of the Marxist analysis of modern bourgeois society closely related to the major defect of historical materialism as an 'objective science' which does not comprehend reality hermeneutically, is that it views organization according to class – which is very important in bourgeois society – as the sole objective factor, independent of other role patterning and even determining them. Thereby it eliminates from theory the subjective, tradition-bound aspects of social organization which have become part of consciousness. (Vajda, 1981, p. 71)

Likewise even as the double movement of self-regulating market and protective response distanced capitalist social relations from the prototype of a dichotomized class society, so too there was a parallel development with respect to consciousness. Had there been no protective response countering the dichotomizing effect of the market, both the proletariat and its consciousness would have been different. Thus the double movement had subjective as well as objective consequences and dimensions. For Vajda the protective response, manifested through the state and formal democracy, not only thwarted the growth of a homogeneous proletariat but also checked some of the dehumanizing and reifying effects that the market tendency has on consciousness.

> The real and practical unmasking of the false consciousness of objectivism must also show that the subject never completely becomes an object, that the reification of human relations and

human consciousness is only a tendency, which though dominant in the bourgeois era, never successfully eliminated
counter-tendencies. (Vajda, 1983, p. 121)

The proletariat as the sole majoritarian, economically determined
class that Marx deified as the revolutionary subject and bearer of
socialism never came to fruition as a class-in-itself and as a consequence neither did it reach fruition as a class-for-itself. This is not
to deny that a majority of the working class have lives with
proletarian features, that is, wage-earner status, unsatisfying work
conditions and an 'us–them' relation on the shop-floor or in the
office (see Feher and Heller, 1983a, p. 222). On the other hand these
features are not sufficient to constitute or forge a group of people
who therefore have a unified and common set of interests derived
from these shared features. Polanyi would call this belief a 'prejudice' of Marxism and liberalism (see Polanyi, [1944] 1957,
p. 154). Moreover these features alone do not necessitate a set of
common interests sufficient to reduce capitalism to 'class' struggle.
As Polanyi also argues,

> class interests offer only a limited explanation of long-run
> movements in society. The fate of classes is much more often
> determined by the needs of society than the fate of society is
> determined by the needs of classes. Given a definite structure of
> society, the class theory works; but what if that structure itself
> undergoes change? (Polanyi, [1944] 1957, p. 152)

It was precisely the countertendency of the protective response,
engaged in a dialectic with market forces, that caused the structure,
that is, the totality of social relations, to undergo change. Marx's
dialectic infers that the actual human struggles that manifest this
change emanate from the economic sphere alone. Polanyi and the
Budapest School are informed by a dialectic that is less economistic
and more inclusive. Marx's analysis presupposes a 'definite structure of society' in which state and civil society have become separate
entities and in which the tendency of the unfolding of the market
economy has reached unhampered fruition. As Polanyi says of both
Marx and the classical liberals:

> They establish a watertight case for the assertion that nine-
> teenth century protectionism was the result of class action, and
> that such action must have primarily served the economic

interests of the members of the classes concerned. Between them they all but completely obstructed an overall view of market society, and of the function of protectionism in such a society. (Polanyi, [1944] 1957, pp. 151–2)

Protectionism was an intuitive and spontaneous response that, rather than being the expression of 'class struggle', was itself antecedent to the formation of the dichotomized class society anticipated by Marx. As a result of the re-embedding effect of protectionism, capitalism did not become a dichotomized class society. Capitalism considered as a 'class' society existed as a tendency only – as a tendency inherent within the disembedding of economy from society.

From Class Structure to Stratification and the Mixed Economy

By viewing the formation and evolution of capitalism's social relations through Polanyi's dialectic of the double movement, the Budapest School writers went beyond Marx's historical materialism. Their neo-Marxian approach to capitalism is derived from this. Although they are now under the umbrella of Polanyi's dialectic rather than Marx's, this does not signify that they are non-Marxists. Neither Polanyi nor the Budapest School would argue that counter-tendencies to the self-regulating market via formal democracy have democratized capitalism's social relations, but they have altered these relations in a way that orthodox Marxism did not envision in its class analysis. Like Marx, Polanyi and the Budapest School view capitalism from a dialectical, materialist and conflictual paradigm. It is an antinomous society, and they, like Marx, operate through a critical theory paradigm. Their neo-Marxian approach, while embracing Marx's cause and vision, is founded primarily on a rejection of Marx's economism, and in this sense it is negatively constituted. This implies, negatively stated, that (1) the state is not an epiphenomenon of the economic base and (2) the essential social relations of capitalism are not those of the capital–labour dichotomy.

What is necessary is to go one step further and draw out those implications of a positive theory of capitalist social relations – a positive understanding of the Budapest School's neo-Marxism. The real essence of Polanyi's influence and the rejection of Marx's class dialectic is that these writers have elaborated at the theoretical (not the empirical) level both the stratification of capitalism's social relations and the origin of the social democratic mixed economy. By arguing what capitalism is not (that is, a dichotomized class society where the state plays no role in constituting the essential relations of power), they theoretically lay the basis for what capitalism is: a mixed economy of stratified power relations – a middle-class society. In other words, rather than becoming a class society capitalism became a stratified society. It became a society in which the distribution of power is more pluralistic and diffuse than that suggested by class dichotomy.

Briefly, the reasoning is that the countertendencies of the protective response operating through the state's formal democracy provided protection to the interests of subordinate business and non-business social groups. Using the formal democratic character of the state, these groups were able to press their needs and demands on the state, and the state responded. Although repressive, the state has been the trustee of the social totality rather than a tool of the ruling class. Society's protective response consequently took diverse forms, as *The Great Transformation* documents. There were not only 'class' interests involved but a whole spectrum of subordinate social groups whose existence cannot be adequately characterized as that of the proletariat. The winning of the franchise for propertyless groups, factory legislation, union recognition, welfare for the poor, income maintenance for the disabled, price support for farmers, loan credits for small businesses, housing loans, free public education and so on, all testify to the diversity of the protective response. All of this legislation and policy by the state thwarted the consolidation and homogenization of a proletarian class. It provided a whole range of opportunities and privileges as well as social and economic advances to numerous different groups. It was not 'the proletariat' that made substantial gains in the late nineteenth century (although of course the standard of living did rise substantially, as people like Eduard Bernstein pointed out at the time).

More accurately, all types of subordinate social groups made gains .with respect to both expanded opportunities and material living standards, and in this process – Polanyi's countertendency – the stratification of social relations emerged. The conflict expressed by these groups was not 'class conflict'. The target of their protest was not a capitalist class but rather their insecurity *vis-à-vis* the market structure. Along with this process of stratification the protective response raised the need for state involvement in the regulation of various markets and in the provision of numerous public goods. Thus the mixed economy itself is a by-product, along with social stratification, of the countertendency of the protective response.

Also the formal democracy of the state, which recognized the separation of state and civil society, constituted capitalism's classes as 'open'. The openness of these classes accommodated movements by individuals between classes, that is, basic upward social mobility, and this contributed to the stratification of social relations as well. When Vajda mentions that there is a 'pluralism of power' in capitalist social relations – a pluralism obscured by Marx's categories – he is inferring that the protective response altered these relations in a stratified direction and away from dichotomized class relations. The gains and advances of subordinate groups that brought about the stratified power configuration attest to the pluralism of power.

Again Polanyi's influence is significant, particularly with respect to the idea that classes in capitalism, to the extent that they tendentially exist, are 'open';

> single groups or classes were [not] the source of the so-called collectivist movement, though the outcome was decisively influenced by the character of the class interests involved. Ultimately, what made things happen were the interests of society as a whole, though their defense fell primarily to one section of the population in preference to another. It appears reasonable to group our account of the protective movement not around class interests but around the social substances imperiled by the market. (Polanyi, [1944] 1957, p. 162)

What remaining implications for stratification and the mixed economy can be drawn from Polanyi's dialectic? Above all, stratification always has an object. Thus stratification is always stratification of income, of property ownership, of political power and the like. For the Budapest School, Polanyi's dialectic led to the stratification of power over social decision-making mechanisms and processes (see the epigraph to this chapter). The two primary social decision-making mechanisms in capitalism are the market and the state. Polanyi's view draws attention to the fact that, contrary to Marx's perspective, one cannot say that political power is distinguishable from economic power and that in capitalism the former is derived from the latter. Polanyi's view de-emphasizes the role of property relations in constituting power. It implies that since power relations in general are constituted coterminously by both the state and civil society, then an exclusive focus on either economic or political power is misguided. It is essentially power over social decision-making that is at issue. To say that the decision-making channelled through these mechanisms is stratified means that it is undemocratic. People at the top of the stratified system of power have greater input into social decisions than those at the bottom. One cannot view it as stratification of economic power or as stratification of political power since both spheres are interrelated and codetermining.

In the double movement of the nineteenth century, the economy did become disembedded, at least enough to consider a separate, autonomous economic sphere as a basic feature of the society. As a result the exercise of power over social decision-making largely reflected the interests of those who owned the most property in civil society and thus commanded the most economic resources. The market as a social decision-making mechanism yields power to those with the most property by (1) giving them relatively greater independence from being a supplier of labour in labour markets and (2) giving them relatively greater access to being a buyer of labour in labour markets. More property ownership generally means a greater degree of both of these features, and this in turn implies greater control over social decision-making via the market. It means 'that the ownership of the productive apparatus of a society confers a form of democratically unaccountable power' (Bowles and Gintis, 1986, p. 93). The unaccountable power, as Bowles and Gintis suggest, is first that business owners and their corporate managers have the power to organize the work process in conformity with their own profit-related goals. Secondly, their control over investment decision-making gives them unaccountable power to shape society's development towards their interests. Additionally, 'owners exercise influence over state economic policy, through which substantive limits are placed upon the range of democratic control over economic life' (Bowles and Gintis, 1986, p. 67). In effect the unaccountable power of business owners allows them to assert their interests disproportionately to those of the propertyless majority and thus to exercise greater control over social decision-making. As in Marx's analysis, the social grouping of business owners, operating through the market, still tends to dominate social decision-making through the market and the state.

The stratifying effect of the double movement did not directly challenge the origin of power over social decision-making. Stratification and the protective response did not unseat the position of dominance held by wealthy business groups. Social decision-making continued to be organized around the profit interests of businesses in the market, and, even though subordinate groups made substantial economic and political gains, the wage-earning social groups remained subordinate to their employers and market vagaries. The general process of capital accumulation and resource allocation remained largely profit led. Although the state responded to the needs of diverse social groups it did not subordinate civil society to social control; it did not exercise public control over the use of markets in general, nor did it subordinate profit-making incentives to other social needs. Capitalism remained a market economy, profit motivated, with propertied groups exercising the greatest degree of control over social decision-making. A hierarchical system of power distribution continued to exist in which the poorest, least propertied groups were at the bottom; the emerging middle classes of professionals, small businesses, skilled trades, and so on, were in the middle; and the wealthiest capitalists were at the top.

The gains of non-business groups, although they were substantial and often at the expense of capitalists, did not fundamentally challenge prerogatives of business and its profit-motivated criterion of social decision-making and resource allocation. These gains and the accompanying stratification were not radical in one sense because they did not seek to fully democratize the system of social decision-making; they did not subvert the principle of profit-led growth or unequal distribution of property and resources; they did not subordinate the principle of self-regulating markets but only ameliorated their worst effects.

The protective response was not in general a conscious effort to democratize capitalism's social relations. It was not a movement to assert collective control over the workplace or social and democratic control over market forces and the allocation of the social and economic surplus. It was society's reaction to the destructive effects of the self-regulating market and was thus *reactive*, not proactive. Although the protective response had socialist and radical democratic elements, it was not a conscious movement aimed at transcending capitalism. Although it helped to check the centralizing effects of power inherent in the movement of the self-regulating market and thus fostered the pluralism of power, the protective response has not been conscious of itself as a democratic movement directed at a fundamental redistribution of power. Therefore the result of the protective response has been some decentralization of power, recognition of the interests of subordinate social groups and a diffusion of power – at least relative to what otherwise would have been the case.

Power over social decision-making mechanisms was neither democratized nor dichotomized by the double movement of the nineteenth century. It was stratified. The fundamental *undemocratic relation*, which defines pure self-regulating market capitalism, is that derived from the concentration of productive property in the hands of one group such that all others exist through *a relation of unequal dependency* on the property owners. This is what Marx considered essential to capitalism and referred to as the 'unmistakable relation of dependence, which the smug political economist can transmogrify into one of free contract between buyer and seller, between equally independent owners of commodities' (Marx, [1867] 1967, p. 769). The relation of unequal dependence allows property owners, that is, businesses, to make social decisions affecting the lives of subordinate groups on the basis of advancing their own interests. This relation subordinates the majority of society to the criterion of profitability and exists as an unequal relation of dependency because those with the least property tend to be more dependent upon property owners than vice versa (the wage-labour condition). The protective response did not eliminate this undemocratic relation of dependency but definitely moderated its effects. The stratification of power that resulted made this relation of dependency less extreme and less devastating. It reduced the degree of dependency; but it is a stratification of power that occurred *within* the context of this fundamental capitalist relation of power. The undemocratic relation of dependency is more stratified now rather than dichotomized. It is more pluralistic. For Marx the class dichotomy meant that capitalists had power and workers did not. If the surplus was produced by workers but appropriated by capitalists then decision-making was the prerogative of capitalists. They decided how the surplus would be disposed.

Stratification means, on the contrary, that decision-making is unevenly distributed. The resulting stratification is due to the fact that the protective response developed as a spontaneous reaction to the self-regulating market. As a countertendency it was not an attempt to overthrow or transcend the market economy and its capital–labour relation of dependence. Thus for the Budapest School, as well as for Polanyi, capitalism, even though the protective response altered its social relations in a stratified manner, is still capitalism; it is still fundamentally undemocratic. Propertied interests in civil society, largely organized through the exercise of corporate power, still assert a disproportionate share of power over social decision-making mechanisms. The unequal distribution of resources, given a system of property rights and market allocation, implies that those with little property depend upon and are subordinate to those who own the most. Decisions that affect the lives of those who own little property are made without full and equal input from these groups. As Vajda says:

> Without a counter-trend, that is, without a trend towards repoliticization of the relations within civil society, the society would not be viable. Nevertheless, as long as these counter-trends, which have existed throughout the history of capitalism, merely limit (without becoming subject to) the basic trends of capitalism, in order to maintain in existence the relations of private ownership, capitalism remains capitalism. This is precisely the situation which exists today in more developed Western societies. The state, i.e., the political sphere, plays an incomparably greater role in the economic sphere than in so-called pure competitive capitalism, but without suppressing the fundamentally private nature of ownership. (Vajda, 1981, pp. 143–4).

Vajda means that although the state 'plays an incomparably greater role in the economic sphere than in so-called competitive capitalism', it does so without subordinating civil society to social control, that is, to democratic control, and without directly threatening the profit-based system of power distribution. Its role has not been to undermine or directly subvert conditions of private capital accumulation or the existence of dominant business interests and social groups. Rather its role has been to respond to those less powerful social groups threatened by the market. The pinnacle of power in capitalism's stratified social relations still lies with those who command the most resources in civil society. The state also was reactive, not proactive, and has consistently accepted dominance by market mechanisms and profit-led growth. In acting as a vehicle of the protective response, as a countertendency, it has generally addressed problems at the level of symptoms rather than causes. It is the *protective* response in its essence, represented by the state, and *not* the *democratic* response (although popular democratic movements have historically been expressed through the state). To the extent that the capitalist state has voiced democratic impulses, it has not done so with the intention of democratizing the economic sphere. It becomes necessary to distinguish between the role of the state *vis-à-vis* the economy and the nature of the state itself. The state to some extent has been a vehicle of democracy, while at the same time this has created a protectionist role for it in the economic sphere. It has tried to respond to various and diverse problems of subordinate groups without sacrificing the interests or power base of dominant groups – those that the market most directly serves. It has functioned to ameliorate market-based problems without violating business interests. This process has led not only to the stratification of power but to the mixed economy itself.

The mixed economy is a product of the protective response. Social democracy is a product of the double movement as well. The state's role, which the mixed economy signifies, has not been to re-embed the economy within the political sphere but to 'protect' a whole range of groups adversely affected by the market. Furthermore its effort to protect was never an effort to sacrifice the market system but simply to ameliorate its most disastrous effects.

Formal democracy was universalized through this process and stratification of power occurred as well. However, power is lodged in civil society, and those with the most power are those who decide the fate of most of the resources through market allocation.

It is the paradox of formal democracy that it does not reveal anything of the economic structure of society, of its relations of contract and correspondingly its power relations. This is why formal democracy can coexist with capitalist society. (Heller, 1978b, p. 877)

There is an openness in the capitalist state in which a diversity of social groups have been able to obtain some protection. It has responded to the most powerful as well as the least powerful. The social democratic mixed economy is the major expression of this openness. As Poulantzas (1978) has argued, it is neither independent of civil society nor a tool of the capitalist class but an arena in which contending groups compete. It has no uniform or consistent political will within it because it is an agent of protection – a counter-tendency. It operates in the context of a system of stratified power relations, and therefore

> [i]t is easy to cite numerous examples of the imperfections of the mixed economy. It is nearly as easy to explain why they exist, or, more to the point, why they persist. The central reason is the political element which is so characteristic of decision-making. (Preston, 1982, p. 31)

The social democratic mixed economy is not a fully democratic society but an 'impure' and 'messy' (see Preston, 1982) system of stratified power over social decision-making. It has always tried to protect and ameliorate without subverting those that most enjoy the benefits of the market process. '[I]t is a useful characteristic of the mixed economy that public policy tries to cope with problems as they arise and, perhaps, even when they are imperfectly understood' (Preston, 1982, p. 21).

In general the neo-Marxian conception of industrial capitalism views the Western mixed economy as a product of social forces largely related to *society's* reaction to the disembedding of the economy from society. Contrary to Marxist orthodoxy, it does not view contemporary capitalism as a product of class struggle. Drawing on Polanyi the Budapest School does not assume a pre-existent capitalism composed of separate spheres of economy and polity in which the conflict of dichotomized economic classes determines the direction of society. It has rejected Marx's econo-mism and in so doing has become aware of a 'pluralism of power' in capitalism. Consequently capitalism, viewed as a product of both the tendency of market forces and the countertendency of the protective response, became a society characterized by a stratified distribution of power over social decision-making mechanisms. It became a mixed economy with stratified power.

[3]

Implications of the Budapest School's View of Capitalism

As long as he is true to his task of creating more abundant freedom for all, he need not fear that either power or planning will turn against him and destroy the freedom he is building by their instrumentality. This is the meaning of freedom in a complex society; it gives us all the certainty that we need.

Karl Polanyi

This chapter examines two implications of the Budapest School's neo-Marxian view of capitalism. The first implication has to do with the nature of fascism. The Budapest School agrees with Marxist analysis that fascism represents a crisis of capitalism. However, the Budapest School's theory casts doubt on the validity of the traditional Marxian class-based analysis of fascism. Vajda's neo-Marxian treatment of fascism is elaborated here in an effort to flesh out some of the remaining implications of stratification in the mixed economy. The second implication concerns Marx's vision of socialism. The Budapest School argues that transcending capitalism does not mean transcending bourgeois society. Bourgeois society has the individual (and its associated freedom) as its unique feature; it has kept alive the notion of the full and free development of the individual. Consequently, these writers believe that if the social inequalities of capitalism are to be overcome without sacrificing individual freedom then a major revision of Marx's socialist vision is necessary. Marx felt that a reconciliation of the 'individual' with equality could be achieved through a condition of absolute abundance. The Budapest School rejects the possibility of this type of abundance, given our present knowledge of non-renewable resources and the limited recuperative powers of the environment. As a result of limited resources any future society based on democratic decision-making, but still recognizing the goal of equal self-determination, will require a role for the state. Unlike Marx, the Budapest School suggests that its model of radical democracy will require constraints on the individual and subjection of the individual to the external authority of the state. In this sense, as Vajda says, bourgeois society cannot be transcended.

Fascism in the Context of the Budapest School's Approach

For Polanyi the process of the nineteenth-century double movement that created stratified mixed economies also led to the crisis of these economies. The crisis that Polanyi wanted to comprehend was fascism. The social democratic state, acting as a countertendency to that of the self-regulating market, did protect society but in a way that retained the basic features of the market economy.

> In the half century 1879–1929, Western societies developed into closely knit units, in which powerful disruptive strains were latent. The more immediate source of this development was the impaired self-regulation of the market economy. Since society was made to conform to the needs of the market mechanism, imperfections in the functioning of the mechanism created cumulative strains in the body social. Impaired self-regulation was an effect of protectionism. (Polanyi, [1944] 1957, p. 201)

The state's role in protecting a diversity of social groups (which by the turn of the century increasingly organized themselves into a protective establishment) while not challenging the logic of the market impaired the self-regulating character of markets; it impaired their overall functioning. Fascism is the result of political stalemate in the context of impaired markets. 'Fascism, like social-

ism, was rooted in a market society that refused to function'
(Polanyi, [1944] 1957, p. 239).

By relying on Polanyi's framework, Vajda has further developed
his thesis on the origin of fascism. Vajda's attempt to understand
fascism also distanced him from Lukacs's thought.

> It was, among other reasons, the fact that I could only trans-
> plant the Lukacsian concept into the concrete historical context
> by means of extremely elaborate theoretical constructions that
> convinced me ... that Lukacs's concept of class-consciousness
> and the underlying simplified class analysis of 'bourgeois'
> society are untenable. (Vajda, 1976, p. 9)

Vajda's analysis of fascism illustrates the Budapest School's neo-
Marxian approach to capitalism and is therefore at odds with
orthodox Marxian explanations of it. Since fascism is a phenomenon of capitalist society and was produced within capitalist social
relations and institutions, the difference between Vajda's and orthodox Marxian explanations of fascism highlights their differing views
of capitalist social relations.

In general the Marxian theories of fascism, particularly those
views held by Marxists in the 1930s, argued that the form of the
bourgeoisie's rule is irrelevant to the proletariat. Accordingly
whether the political form is formal democracy or totalitarian
makes little difference if the basic property relations of capital and
labour (in the economic base) remain unchanged. Additionally
Marxists argued that fascism was a necessary stage of capitalist
development. Thus the economic contradictions of capitalism produced a political crisis in which the bourgeoisie resorted to totalitarianism in order to preserve its position. According to Vajda, the
problem with theories of this nature is that they

> take as their point of departure an essentially static theoretical
> model of capitalism. [They] try to deduce the fascisation of
> politics directly from the transformation of capitalism's
> economic structure. They explain the *functional* disturbances
> of the capitalist system in the twentieth century as the *final*
> intensification of its inner contradictions, the 'general crisis' of
> the system; the bourgeoisie may find a temporary way out of
> these difficulties by resorting to extreme violence against the
> proletariat, which has become increasingly dissatisfied and,

moreover, revolutionary as a result of the intensification of the contradictions. (Vajda, 1976, p. 55, original emphasis)

This understanding of fascism is a result of the economism in Marxist theory. If the state and formal democracy are an epiphenomenon of the base, then *real* power is still held by the bourgeoisie. For example, Karl Korsch and the Comintern held this view of fascism until 1935. They considered fascism 'a kind of anti-democratic capitalism' and made little distinction between democratic and fascist capitalism (Vajda, 1976, p. 54). Of course history itself was later to prove this view absurd as well as disastrous, because fascism relative to capitalism proved to be far more destructive after 1935 and the loss of freedom vastly greater than that which Marxists associate with capitalism. Logically a view of capitalism that considers the capital–labour dialectic the essence of capitalist social relations is likely to produce such an understanding of fascism.

Against these Marxists, Vajda argues that fascism is not political governance by the bourgeoisie, who previous to the crisis had been able to 'rule without governing'. In fact the state had always had enough relative autonomy from civil society to impose some policies against the will of business interests. In the case of fascism the bourgeoisie in both Italy and Germany was relatively weak compared to the British, Dutch and French bourgeoisie. In disputing this economistic view of fascism Vajda says:

> But it is impossible to lay down any kind of general 'formula' by which the fascist threat can be 'calculated' from the data at our disposal. Each concrete case of fascism becoming a mass movement and seizing power can only be explained by the totality of the social situation in that particular country and by the whole complex of economic, social and political evidence. (Vajda, 1976, p. 73)

Vajda follows Polanyi's argument that in the 1920s, in the aftermath of both the Bolshevik Revolution and the economic crisis precipitated by the First World War, a situation resulted in which working-class parties were politically potent enough to bring down a government but unable to govern effectively. Political paralysis resulted, which had further implications for the economies. 'A clash of group interests that resulted in paralyzing the organs of industry or state – either of them, or both – formed an immediate peril to society. Yet precisely this was the case in the twenties' (Polanyi, [1944] 1957, p. 235). Fascism became 'an escape from an institutional deadlock' and moreover 'a reform of market economy achieved at the price of the extirpation of all democratic institutions, both in the industrial and in the political realm' (Polanyi, [1944] 1957, p. 237). Or as Vajda puts it, the fascist movement meant 'the *renunciation* of the specific form of human emancipation that was made ultimately possible by the conditions of the hitherto existing world order (i.e., capitalism)' (Vajda, 1976, p. 23, original emphasis).

What is important in Vajda's analysis of fascism in Italy and Germany is the stratification of capitalist social relations that evolved during the second half of the nineteenth century. It is the middle classes, not the bourgeoisie, that are the key to the mass movement behind fascism. The middle classes were part of the stratification process of the protective response but were left in the 1920s with few specific organizations to advance their interests. They did not have wealth, their own political parties or trade unions to protect their interests. They felt their interests to be forfeited and their economic position tenuous as a result of the transition to capitalism's intensive growth phase. The concentration of capital was squeezing petit-bourgeois groups and they felt threatened and insecure. Consequently their forms of organization ended up being that of the storm-trooper (Vajda, 1976, pp. 44–5).

The protective response did not protect these groups as well as it protected traditional wage-earning groups.

> It is the middle classes who, because of their position in the social structure of production, are not only opposed to the layers below and above them but are also constantly coming into conflict with members of their own layer. The traditional petty bourgeois – the artisan, the smallholder, the retailer – is more affected by competition. (Vajda, 1976, p. 40)

The middle classes 'had no form of organization like the working class's trade unions with which to fight for and achieve the satisfaction of their interests' (Vajda, 1976, p. 29). The protective response was organic and spontaneous and in many respects, compared to the middle classes, it was easier for workers (assembled in factories) and the wealthiest business interests to organize themselves and pursue private collective action against market vagaries. It was these groups that had organized themselves into a protective establishment prior to the First World War, while the middle classes were more diffused politically as well as economically and were thus unable to participate in the protective establishment.

In the 1924–9 period in Germany, the German working class witnessed 'a lot of social reforms ... which in the USA were only carried out under the New Deal' (Vajda, 1976, p. 69). Yet the middle classes resented these programmes, because they felt that they disproportionately bore the burden while receiving little direct benefit. Social democracy was firmly implanted in Germany in the 1920s and in the 1929–32 period of depression the labour movement's strength was sufficient to bring some relief to German workers but again at the expense of the middle classes. In Italy the working class had strong unions and had made substantial gains as well. The Italian industrialists fostered unionization in the hope that they could more easily wrest power from the landed classes. A situation of polarization emerged between the working class and industrialists and, as a result of their marginalization, the middle strata of German and Italian society played a pivotal role in supporting the fascist movement.

> The essence of bourgeois democracy consists (a) in the fact that the various particular groups may dispose freely of the representation of their interests, and (b) in the belief that the struggle of these particular groups and the conflict of the particular interests will produce a social system which best suits the interests of the totality. (Vajda, 1976, p. 28)

Yet if this is true for the top and bottom strata, for the middle classes it appeared otherwise. Fascist ideology relied on the middle classes to support the dismantling of formal democracy as well as the abolishing of working-class organizations – its parties and trade unions. Fascist ideology became important in making fascism a mass movement because it appealed to the threatened middle strata and was able to mobilize their support. For Vajda, it was a 'totallizing' ideology and attempted to subsume 'classes' under the umbrella of nation and race. Rather than being a specific ideology articulating the interests of a specific social stratum, it was general, or totallizing, as it was opposed to any and all parties that appealed to one class or another (Vajda, 1976, p. 19). Fascist ideology 'completely politicized all those spheres of life which had until then been completely free of political influence, or had at least appeared to be so' (Vajda, 1976, p. 68).

Part of the blame for the success of fascist ideology can be placed on the left parties in the 1920s. As Laclau and Mouffe point out, they continued to view all ideological influences and elements, for example, religion and the family, as necessarily having a 'class-belonging' (see Laclau, 1979; Mouffe, 1979). The left parties believed that concerns for stability of the family and religious values were essentially bourgeois or petit-bourgeois influences, and failed to take such concerns seriously enough to try to make them organizing issues. They did not take the elements of fascist ideology seriously because they considered all of its aspects 'bourgeois'. According to such reasoning, all aspects of appeal in ideology could be reduced to being either bourgeois or proletarian, and if such influences were not judged either proletarian or socialist they were effectively ignored. However, it was precisely race and nation that should not have been ignored; they have no real 'class-belonging'. In other words, the interest that working-class and middle-class groups showed in these areas cannot be attributed to the economic status of these groups, nor is it a deductive by-product of the capitalist organization of society.

Fascist ideology based itself on an appeal to the middle classes using racist and nationalist ideological elements that were clearly not bourgeois. Polanyi, the Frankfurt School and Reich recognized that the racism and emotionalism of fascist ideology could not be reduced to epiphenomena of the economic base of capitalist society. The cultural elements and meanings to which fascist ideology appealed have their sources in the historical and cultural backgrounds of European peoples and do not simplify to a class context. Additionally it was Marx that argued that such feudal holdovers would be rendered meaningless by capitalist society. Had the left parties understood what Polanyi, Reich and the Frankfurt School realized, then they could have mobilized anti-fascist opposition around these same ideological elements, incorporating them into a more democratic and reform-oriented ideology. Consequently they could possibly have prevented fascism.

In general, for Vajda, one cannot understand fascism if one reduces capitalist social relations to those of economic classes. It is the interrelationship of state and civil society that determines these relations. Fascism makes this clear. One cannot understand fascism if it is assumed that political power is an epiphenomenon of the economic power held by a capitalist class. It is the stratification of society through the protective response that created the middle classes whose security was threatened as a result of the disembedding of the economy from society. Additionally the role of the middle classes in fascism cannot be reduced to their interests as derived from their place in the economic base of society. As Vajda (1976, p. 33) points out, 'I wish to emphasize once again that in this respect, the status of the middle layers is not solely nor even fundamentally determined by the position they occupy in the organization of production'.

He proceeds to affirm Fromm's and Reich's views that family structure, character structure, community fragmentation and psychological factors of loneliness and isolation all play an important part in explaining the support that the middle strata gave to the fascist movement. Fascism comes about in a stratified society in which tensions regarding the distribution of power over social decision-making mechanisms erupt and dissolve formal democracy. An analysis premised upon the class dichotomy captures neither the role of the middle strata nor that of the political sphere in constituting fascism.

Enormous changes with devastating consequences took place under fascism, yet the basic property relations, those of capital and wage-labour, did not change at all. The nature of social decision-making, as Vajda points out, is the key factor, and this became much more undemocratic under fascism. Yet an economistic approach that views fascism as direct political governance by the bourgeoisie obscures the origins of fascism in the middle strata and fetishizes the bourgeoisie. The bourgeoisie had much less control over the state than orthodox Marxian analysis would suggest, even though the bourgeoisie's interests in the market economy were not threatened. Hitler's and Mussolini's fascism was imposed on an enfeebled bourgeoisie. Fascism did not fundamentally alter the property relations of civil society, but it did destroy the pluralism of power characteristic of social democracy. It was not an effort to transcend the market economy but a response to its impairment. Vajda's analysis shows that property relations and the capital–labour class struggle are less important than the distribution of power over social decision-making mechanisms. Fascism from a neo-Marxian view reveals the degree to which the freedom of formal democracy is not illusory.

Furthermore the issue of freedom is significant in distinguishing the neo-Marxian from the orthodox Marxian and classical liberal views. Both orthodox Marxism and classical liberalism tend to conceive of freedom as absolute and indivisible. According to the Marxian view at the time of the fascist take-overs, capitalism, whether fascist or bourgeois democratic, was a system of unfreedom. Whether the bourgeoisie ruled by governing or not, theirs was a system of domination – a state of unfreedom for the working majority. Similarly for the classical liberals prior to the fascist take-over, Polanyi suggests:

> Planning and control are being attacked as a denial of freedom. Free enterprise and private ownership are declared to be essentials of freedom. No society built on other foundations is said to deserve to be called free. The freedom that regulation creates is denounced as unfreedom; the justice, liberty and welfare it offers are decried as a camouflage of slavery. With the liberal the idea of freedom thus degenerates into a mere advocacy of free enterprise. (Polanyi, [1944] 1957, pp. 256–7)

Thus for the classical liberal, capitalism prior to fascism was a system of freedom. The two views are contradictory, one arguing that the system is unfree; the other arguing the contrary. However, they share a common view that freedom itself is indivisible – it either exists or it does not.

Their common conception of freedom paved the way for fascism. On the one hand, the classical liberals remained intransigent in opposing reforms that would have subordinated profit-making to social policies of equity and freedom. According to Polanyi ([1944] 1957, p. 257), 'the victory of fascism was made practically unavoidable by the liberals' obstruction of any reform involving planning, regulation, or control'. On the other hand, the left parties opposed similar reforms because they viewed them as bourgeois, and additionally they rejected them because they did not remove private property and profit-making altogether. Thus Marxists viewed such reforms as cosmetic, serving only to preserve the basic condition of unfreedom in capitalism. Although the means of escape from the fascist stalemate and crisis could possibly have been provided by a package of radical reforms, both liberals and Marxists rejected such reforms. Both their economism and conception of the indivisibility of freedom prevented them from embracing a system of reforms that would have retained markets, private property and profit-making but subordinated these institutions to broader social needs and rights. While classical liberals argued that such reforms would destroy freedom, Marxian orthodoxy argued that they would not create it.

Polanyi and the Budapest School, on the contrary, argue that freedom is divisible; it is a spectrum in which the freedom of capitalism, demonstrated by the fascist counter-example, can be expanded by specific types of reform. This is what Polanyi means (see the epigraph to this chapter) by stating that 'creating more abundant freedom for all' can be accomplished by using social power and planning to subordinate (rather than eliminate) property and profits (Polanyi, [1944] 1957, pp. 256–7). Orthodox Marxists have maintained that the condition of capitalist unfreedom can be replaced by a future communist (or socialist) condition of absolute freedom. However, the Budapest School, by viewing freedom as divisible, argues that the fascist counter-example not only illustrates the pluralism of power in capitalism but demonstrates that capitalism has an important sphere of individual freedom that must be preserved in any future society. Moreover, a communist society of absolute freedom is unrealistic. By arguing that bourgeois society cannot be transcended, the Budapest School claims not only that the individual freedom advanced by bourgeois society must be preserved, but that it can be expanded by degrees, approaching but not achieving Marx's vision of absolute freedom. Consequently a neo-Marxian view of freedom, as implied in Vajda's study of fascism, argues that the freedoms that accompany capitalism can be expanded but not to such a degree that external authority and state compulsion are obviated. Marx's vision of socialism must be revised, in the light of the divisibility of freedom, to account for a permanent role for the state. Implicitly the Budapest School's statement that bourgeois society cannot be transcended reflects two beliefs: that capitalism is not a state of unfreedom, and that absolute freedom is unobtainable.

Bourgeois Society Cannot Be Transcended

Thus far the neo-Marxian interpretation given to the Budapest School has involved two major revisions of Marx: (1) the state, the

78

political sphere, is not an epiphenomenon of the economic base, and
(2) 'stratification of power over social decision-making processes'
more accurately describes capitalist social relations than the class
dichotomy of bourgeoisie and proletariat. This leads to a third
revision of Marx regarding the extent to which freedom of the
individual can be realized in any future society.

To understand this last revision of Marx's concept of individual
freedom it is first necessary to examine the achievements of bourgeois society, capitalism and formal democracy. Heller, in *A Theory
of History* (1982d), has argued that the modern age is composed of
three interrelated trends: (1) civil society, (2) capitalism and (3)
industrialization. These three forces represent three different logics
of development, yet all have occurred together. Bourgeois society (or
what the Budapest School calls modernity) is the product of the
simultaneous occurrence of all three of these trends. According to
Heller:

> The relative independence and autonomy of civil society is in
> itself a form of existence with *two* internal logics (a double
> dynamis). It ensures the relative independence of the private-
> economic sphere. Accordingly, one of its logics is the universali-
> zation of markets, of the exclusive character of private prop-
> erty, of the growth of inequality and domination. [This is also
> the thrust of the logic of capitalism.] At the same time, it
> establishes the negative but equal freedom of individuals, thus
> its second logic is the unfolding and enforcement of this
> freedom (of human rights) in the process of democratization,
> equalization, decentralization of power. Simultaneously, the
> development and growth of industry implies a third logic to an
> ever increasing extent; the limitation of the market through the
> centralization of the allocation of resources by the state.
> (Heller, 1982d, p. 284, original emphasis)

What bourgeois society therefore created was the idea of the full
and free development of the individual. When the economy was
disembedded from society and the material reproduction of society
became depoliticized, the idea of individual self-development was
forged. The logic of civil society, for the Budapest School, freed the
individual as potential self-development from its embeddedness in
the political societies of feudalism and mercantilism. 'As Marx put
it, bourgeois society completed the severing of the individual from

the community's umbilical cord. The individual became free ... But only in exceptional cases can he realize this freedom' (Vajda, 1976, p. 38). Formal democracy sanctioned the separation of political and economic spheres and legitimized a sphere of individual freedom in civil society and simultaneously developed political equality.

As Vajda suggests above, 'the individual becoming free' in the creation of civil society meant neither material equality nor economic democracy. It did not mean equal control over decision-making. It did not mean equal ability to actualize freedom. The idea of the openness of capitalism's classes simply attests to this concept of individual freedom protected through formal democracy. Thus upward mobility is at least possible. 'The interpretation of freedom and of the absolute autonomy of individuals, as the full and total self-development of the person as a "goal in itself" is a conception which can rightly be described as super-Enlightenment' (Heller, 1982a, p. 350). Thus the value of the 'individual rich in needs', which is so much a part of Marx, is ultimately a product of both the Enlightenment and bourgeois society, and more specifically of the one logic of civil society. On the other hand the logic of the market, as Heller points out, universalizes unequal property ownership and market relations and creates inequality and domination. Bourgeois society is a combination of the extension of individual freedom and material inequality.

However, Marx's value of individual self-development was not his alone.

> John Stuart Mill, Marx's contemporary and the leading figure of liberalism whom Marx despised (and not entirely without justification) came to precisely the same conclusion. Indeed, the formulation: 'the development of all individual abilities and capacities' comes from the tradition of liberalism. Marx transformed liberalism into radicalism in asking the question: under what conditions can all the human abilities and capacities of all individuals freely develop? (Heller, 1982b, p. 360)

Polanyi too recognized that formal democracy and its sanctioning of the disembedded economic sphere went hand in hand with individual freedom.

> Yet these are freedoms the maintenance of which is of paramount importance. They were, like peace, a by-product of

nineteenth-century economy, and we have come to cherish them for their own sake. The institutional separation of politics and economics which proved a deadly danger to the substance of society almost automatically produced freedom at the cost of justice and security. Civic liberties, private enterprise and wage-system fused into a pattern of life which favored moral freedom and independence of mind. Here again, juridical and actual freedoms merged into a common fund, the elements of which cannot be neatly separated. We must try to maintain by all means in our power these high values inherited from the market economy which collapsed. (Polanyi, [1944] 1957, p. 255)

If 'the basic achievement of the bourgeois society – the freedom of the individual' – is a value to be preserved, it is still an individual freedom that, as Polanyi says, sacrifices justice, security and equal control over self-actualization (Vajda, 1981, p. 86). It is still an individual freedom in civil society that allows those who benefit most from the market and profit-led growth to exercise the freedom to restrict others' freedom (Vajda, 1976, pp. 38–9). It is individual freedom characterized by greed and self-interest. It is, in the context of the market, the 'universality of egoism' (Heller, 1974b). It is the 'double dynamis' of capitalism and civil society, for Heller, that accounts for the conjoint appearance of individual freedom along with the 'exclusive character of private property'. There is in bourgeois society both inequality and domination (as they exist in the stratified system of social relations) together with individual freedom, political equality and democratization. In effect, as Bowles and Gintis (1986) have argued, bourgeois society is a system of competing and conflicting rights in which the freedom of property supersedes that of equal participation.

If capitalism is equivalent to bourgeois society then abolishing the inequality and domination of capitalism means abolishing bourgeois society. However, abolishing bourgeois society runs the risk of abolishing its foremost achievement of individual freedom. Destroying capitalism implies destroying the achievements of bourgeois society and, if so, then the 'freedom of the individual is only a dream' (Vajda, 1981, p. 87). From Vajda's perspective Marx did not distinguish between capitalism and bourgeois society, but rather 'he necessarily equated the reality of bourgeois society with the distorted image of it in the minds of its most admiring ideologues, that image of society which Polanyi termed the most unrealizable utopia so far in world history' (Vajda, 1981, p. 87).

Feher and Heller have considered this problem by analysing two values: equality (its opposite being part of capitalism) and freedom (associated with civil society). If capitalism, as one of the three logics composing bourgeois society, cannot be separated and conceptually distinguished from bourgeois society then the demand to abolish capitalism's inequality, to end exploitation and domination by market relations, sacrifices individual freedom (Feher and Heller, 1982a). If the logics of civil society and capitalism cannot be divorced then attacking capitalism's inequality sacrifices the individual freedom achieved through formal democracy and civil society. The danger in a socialist revolution, which becomes apparent in examining soviet societies, is that equality is achieved while individual freedom is destroyed. For Feher and Heller, 'the status of equality in Marx's thought was, to say the least, dubious' (Feher and Heller, 1982a, p. 23). However, as they indicate,

> Marx clearly drew from the 'Babeuf-story' the consequences that all *substantive* conceptions of equality are, in their capacity as the main principle of social regulation and particularly those which aim at a forcible homogenization of needs, by definition tyrannical. This principle had to be overdetermined in his theory by the principle of freedom and 'man-rich-in-needs', the latter figuring as the protagonist of a non-alienated future. (Feher and Heller, 1982a, pp. 25–6)

Babeuf concluded that equality must be achieved at the expense of freedom, and this reasoning ended up legitimating the Jacobin dictatorship and the Reign of Terror in 1793. It is precisely this same logic that the Budapest School sees as evident in the Bolshevik Revolution and operating in soviet societies (see Chapter 4).

The Budapest School argues that capitalism and bourgeois society are not identical. This is a conclusion derived from their non-economistic view of capitalist social relations. Therefore the three logics of modernity (civil society, capitalism and industrialization) can be divorced. The inequality of capitalism can be overcome without sacrificing the individual freedom of civil society, but this means 'bourgeois society cannot be transcended. It is a practical fact of our age' (Vajda, 1981, p. 80). That is, if the value of equality is to be reconciled with individual freedom, then this implies the continuance of a separate sphere of civil society divorced from the state and political sphere; if there is going to be modern and dynamic industrial society (the third logic of bourgeois society), then there are other conclusions as well.

Vajda argues that bourgeois society cannot be transcended for four reasons: (1) 'Modern dynamic expanded production ... is inconceivable if the division of labour is abolished' (Vajda, 1981, p. 85), (2) in an integrated global economy impersonal relationships will always exist, (3) an industrial society of mass production and consumption will require some coercion by law and the state, and (4) some alienation from others will always exist in such a society. In other words, Vajda does believe that many of the problems of inequality, exploitation and domination by market institutions can be overcome, that is, that capitalism's stratified distribution of power over social decision-making can be democratized. It is the inequality in the distribution of this power that can be eliminated, but to do so and retain individual freedom means living within the parameters of bourgeois society, and therefore realistically we must accept the consequences. Along with the division of labour, he says:

> The disintegration of closed communities with no mutual interrelationships ... and the universalization of human contacts ... necessarily excludes the possibility that the majority of people's relational contacts should be relations between persons rather than between functions. (Vajda, 1981, p. 85)

Some dehumanization will therefore always exist. Additionally, 'the conditions of modern production and "world communications" render illusory any notion of eliminating the alienated administration of society and its institutional system' (Vajda, 1981, p. 86). Finally, 'the elimination of alienation in consciousness, on the other hand, is an illusion in every way. Despite being socially determined, the intersubjectivity of existing consciousness is always individual' (Vajda, 1981, p. 86).

In sum, since bourgeois society and capitalism are not isomorphic, preserving the individual's full developmental potential and self-determination while simultaneously equalizing decision-making participation means accepting some dehumanization characteristic of bourgeois society. According to Vajda, the purpose of a critique of bourgeois society is not to transcend it but to alert consciousness to negative trends – which should never become total – in the bourgeois world system, so that we can go to that maximum limit which does not threaten the retention of the basic achievement of bourgeois society – the freedom of the individual. (Vajda, 1981, p. 86)

The democratization of social decision-making that advances the individual freedom of bourgeois society without eliminating all dehumanization is democratization that advances freedom by degrees. Its premiss, as Polanyi and the Budapest School believe, is that freedom is not absolute but divisible.

However, for Marx, as his analysis of the French Revolution indicates, bourgeois society can be transcended and thus freedom of the individual and equality in decision-making can be reconciled. Marx had a concept of human liberation that obviated the problem of equality by overdetermining it with freedom, but Marx's vision did not entail, as Vajda's does, certain dehumanizing trade-offs. It is a vision based on the belief that freedom is indivisible. It is with respect to this issue that the Budapest School writers subject Marx to another revision. They believe, like Marx, that individual freedom (equal self-determination) is the fundamental value and goal. They also believe, like Marx, that this can be reconciled with equality (transcending capitalism's inequality of social decision-making). However, the Budapest School argues that this reconciliation in a future society involves some realistic constraints and sacrifices, as Vajda suggests. Marx, on the other hand, does not accept this, because his notion of freedom is absolute.

Reconciling equality and freedom means obtaining an organization of society in which the unlimitedness of individual self-development, which is the logical corollary of individual freedom, is available to all people equally. Marx believed that the material and social conditions for such a society were conceivable. To the question, 'Under what conditions can all the human abilities and capacities of all individuals freely develop?' Marx answered that 'it is only possible in a society (or in a "realm") free of constraints or necessities of any kind' (Heller, 1982b, p. 360). *Abundance provided Marx with the means to transcend bourgeois society and overdetermine equality by freedom.* In a society of abundance the self-development of each does not sacrifice the potentiality of self-development of others. Thus the problem of inequality is rendered moot by a context of freedom-through-abundance. It is this idea that the Budapest School disputes.

By sanctifying the individual and giving birth to the individual rich in needs, the Enlightenment simultaneously raised the issue of unlimitedness. Other than death and finiteness of material means, there is no limit to self-development, to the full and free development of the individual's capacities. This creates the modern paradox of the 'dissatisfied society' (Heller, 1983a). There is never too much development for the individual rich in needs. There is an unlimitedness to needs in this circumstance. For Marx, technology would create abundance sufficient to obviate the problem of unlimitedness once it was extended to all people (that is, once equality and freedom were reconciled). Satisfied society was possible through abundance. This is Marx's material condition for human liberation, one in which there is freedom from any external constraints. However, Heller disagrees:

> Marx's dreams cannot come true. We cannot conceive of the continuously expanding individual need structure and the simultaneous satisfaction of all human needs in the same breath, for several reasons. We cannot believe any longer what it was reasonable to believe in the nineteenth century, that the natural resources of our planet are unlimited, nor can we believe that even in case of a continuously expanding demand for material goods a state of complete abundance can ever come about. The objection to such a reservation, that, namely, it is only spiritual, not material, needs that will unlimitedly expand, is irrelevant. This is so, firstly, because even the satisfaction of the so-called spiritual needs presupposes a certain amount of material investment (it is not less expensive to produce books, pianos, and especially equipment for scientific research than cars or foodprocessors). Thus complete abundance, on the one hand, and unlimited need expansion, on the other hand, cannot be conceived of together. (Heller, 1983a, p. 369)

Marx's notion of the freedom that overdetermines equality, according to Heller, is the realization of the liberal ideal. It is a type of indivisible freedom — an absolute freedom achieved through material abundance. Yet this is truly unrealistic. Like Marx, Lukacs also accepted this notion of an individual who has 'internalized norms to such an extent that there is no need for independently existing, external, alien moral demands' (Feher, 1983a, p. 85). On the other hand, Polanyi is in agreement with the Budapest School: 'No society is possible in which power and compulsion are absent, nor a world in which force has no function' (Polanyi, [1944] 1957, p. 257).

For Polanyi and the Budapest School Marx's vision of a totally unalienated society with no dehumanization is a utopia. One option – the Babeuf option – is to eliminate the inequality of capitalism by sacrificing individual freedom. Soviet society represents the historical embodiment of this option. Marx's preference was to transcend bourgeois society and to reconcile freedom and equality through abundance, but given the 'unlimitedness' of individual self-development along with the 'finiteness' of resources, this is not a viable option either.

As Heller indicates, what is utopian is 'complete abundance' and 'unlimited need expansion conceived of together'. Abundance is conceivable together with limited needs, as is essentially the case in many precapitalist societies. Here social norms circumscribe the individual's structure of needs, and furthermore the individual as an individual remains embedded in the political and social structure of the society. On the other hand, what the Budapest School suggests is a model in which need expansion is not restricted, where the unlimitedness of the individual rich in needs is acknowledged. However, abundance is 'relative', not absolute or complete. In such a situation ethical norms and external authority constrain the individual. Freedom is advanced by degrees but is not absolute. As Heller states,

> I am fully aware of the fact that the moment we start looking for any regulative principles for action, we engage in an endeavor which was specifically rejected by Marx, as we suggest thereby the acceptance of certain *external authorities* in order to regulate human life. (Heller, 1982a, p. 362, original emphasis)

Marx's notion of freedom is insufficient without complete abundance. Yet this conception of human liberation cannot be realized. Consequently the Budapest School proposes a 'democratic notion of freedom'. This involves moral authority and the acceptance of norms that people adopt 'consensually'. Authority external to the individual will then exist, but each individual will also have equal input in the decisions that affect his or her life. Democratic freedom is not freedom from constraint but freedom to participate equally in the society's social decision-making mechanisms. This is the practical significance of the value-standard of 'equal self-determination'.

A person is free insofar as he or she has an equal right and equal possibility to participate in any decision-making process which concerns and affects his or her city, state, nation, or community. In public decision-making processes, individuals have to observe the norms-and-rules of the community. These norms-and-rules can be tested or queried and can be replaced with new ones. The democratic concept of freedom does not contradict the existence and acceptance of external moral authorities. (Heller, 1982b, p. 367)

Heller's concept of democratic freedom is a divisible freedom and corresponds to what Polanyi called the 'task of creating more abundant freedom for all' (see the epigraph to this chapter). Thus the Budapest School's neo-Marxian approach to capitalism adopted from Polanyi is fundamentally a non-economistic and non-reductionist interpretation. As a result, it distinguishes between three tendencies of bourgeois society: civil society, capitalism and industrialism. By viewing each of these as tendencies, this interpretation suggests that in the absence of Marx's abundance, equality of decision-making can be reconciled with the unlimitedness of self-development only by accepting the necessity of external authority, and thus a permanent role for the state. In other words, there will never be enough resources to allow each person to pursue his or her own self-development without fear of sacrificing such opportunities for others. The state's role through superior authority (the monopoly on the use of force) will be necessary in mediating conflicts.

The Budapest School writers reject Marx's idea of absolute abundance, yet they also reject the neoclassical postulate of relative scarcity. However, if they adhere to a belief in unlimited needs and accept the limitedness of resources, what is the difference between their concept of relative abundance and the neoclassical idea of relative scarcity? It seems logical to conclude that people experience capitalism as relative scarcity for two interrelated reasons: (1) the existence of capitalism's disembedded economy, in which the economic motives of gain and fear of starvation are the essential incentives for production, and in which the fulfilment of basic needs is dependent upon exchange in markets, and (2) the unequal distribution of productive resources, such that the security of many is determined by their ability to sell their labour-power. On the other hand, relative abundance still contends with unlimited wants and limited resources but through a system of democratic social decision-making in which markets are subordinated to social control and security is not solely a function of the sale of labour. Contrary to Marx's belief, bourgeois society cannot be transcended, but it can be democratized. Without absolute abundance the realization of freedom and equality, when conceptually fused as the value of equal self-determination, requires a society in which the state not only exists but does so independently of civil society.

Capitalism and Equal Self-Determination

The Budapest School's neo-Marxian view suggests a different interpretation of social democratic mixed economies from that offered by orthodox Marxism. In this context how do the Western social democracies measure up to the standard of equal self-determination? Above all, we recognize there is a direct correlation between the principle of equal self-determination and the articulation and fulfilment of human needs. The process of human needing is the fundamental object of self-determination. In other words, to what human process does equal self-determination refer? The answer: the process of need articulation and fulfilment. Thus equal self-determination means equal control over the social processes of need expression and fulfilment. People determine themselves by determining both their needs and the means for satisfying these needs. Equal self-determination can mean no less than equal self-determination of needs (both quantitatively and qualitatively). In essence it is on the basis of needs that people are constituted as a 'becoming' species, that is, as transcendent beings. Needs are the medium through which people determine themselves. Equal self-determination does not imply equality of needs but rather equality of control over needs.

Consequently, in adopting the value-standard of equal self-determination we are more specifically interested in the extent to which capitalism both fosters and is compatible with equal control over the social processes of need articulation and fulfilment. Moreover, the value of equal self-determination is violated if needs are arbitrarily or authoritatively restricted. What can be said of the process of need articulation and fulfilment in capitalism, given this standard?

Generally, in the neo-Marxian view, the disembedded market economy, along with the Enlightenment, has created both a niche for the individual and the idea of the unlimitedness of self-development. As Heller indicates:

> The beautiful and plastic idea according to which all we need is for man to develop his essential forces, and all he needs for this purpose is to bring about a human society which will make this possible for everyone is something I myself accept, with one qualification: that 'all he needs' is indeed everything. (Heller, 1979d, pp. 3–4).

In other words the standard of equal self-determination is itself a product of the modern age, but its realization for everyone has been thwarted in capitalism by the stratification of power over social decision-making. Self-development through the expanded articulation of needs becomes more a privilege of those occupying the upper strata. This notwithstanding, the idea of individual freedom is a major accomplishment. 'The bourgeois world has not depraved or completed man; it has simply made him an individual, whose needs are not given or determined by birth' (Vajda, 1981, p. 13). If what the individual is to become is not given at birth then neither are his or her needs. Precapitalist societies were such that the 'value-hierarchy of needs evolved within the community' and what the individual was to become was, to a much greater extent, given at birth (Heller, 1976a, p. 68). Thus 'freedom as the only and absolute value can shape our need-structures in only one way: by making them unlimited' (Heller, 1982b, p. 365). Hence, equal self-determination requires that the range of needs not be arbitrarily restricted.

By allowing the formally free individual with potentially unlimited needs to emerge out of society, and simultaneously by allowing the emergence of a self-regulating market economy based upon consumer demand, capitalist society organized itself around commodity-oriented need fulfilment. Relative to precapitalist societies, the concept of the self and its determination were given greater recognition as values, but the undemocratic character of capitalist relations biased the process of self-determination towards the commodity form. Capitalism, based on the double motives of economic gain and fear of starvation, seizes the unlimitedness of individual self-development and channels it into the commodity form of fulfilment. In other words, for the Budapest School as for most Marxists, both orthodox and neo-Marxian, the manner in which needs are fulfilled and the way in which they are articulated is socially determined. A widely overlooked fact, most especially so in neoclassical economics, is that tastes and preferences are not exogenously given in the economic system, but are molded and shaped by the culture and social relations of capitalism itself. As Heller writes:

> If we state that the structure of need as a whole can only be interpreted in its correlation with the totality of social relations ... then it follows that only socially produced needs exist, and 'natural needs' ... also have this 'socially produced' character. (Heller, 1974b, p. 31)

More specifically, the form or manner in which needs are fulfilled is a process of objectification. Needs have a material component or dimension that is itself socially determined. 'Human need therefore comes about in the process of objectification; the objects of need "guide" and "steer" man, who is born in human society, in the formation of his needs' (Heller, 1974b, p. 41).

Thus the social determination of need articulation, situated in a market setting, does not attempt to restrict needs in general. The market economy responds positively to the unlimitedness of needing inherent in the self-development of the individual. What the stratified power system of social decision-making effects is not a generalized restriction of needs but (1) their expansion channelled through the commodity form of fulfilment and (2) unequal access to the means for self-development. The hierarchy of social decision-making, dominated by profit criteria and those strata that most benefit from the market, implies a socially shaped structure of needs whose fulfilment is unequally distributed and primarily organized around buying commodities in markets. Capitalism recognizes the unlimitedness of individual needing, which is a major change from preceding social formations, but it is an unlimitedness itself narrowed to a specific form: consumerism. Thus modern consumerism is the product of two forces: the commodity bias of a market economy in which there is incentive to fulfil needs by commodities, and the unlimitedness of needs inherent in the Enlightenment idea of the free, self-determining individual.

According to the Budapest School,

> capitalism is the first essentially dynamic society, in which not only the sum total of available consumer goods increases, by means of an incredible acceleration of the rhythm of production, but also new goods and new kinds of goods are continually invented, and in consequence the needs for them as well. (Heller, 1976a, p. 68)

Corresponding to capitalism's stratified power relations, its need structure is dynamic but also market and profit oriented; it is profit biased. 'Capitalism creates needs that are "rich and many-sided"' but simultaneously moulded and shaped by the criterion of profit and, more generally, by the pecuniary values of the market economy (Heller, 1974b, p. 47). Heller has made this point with respect to consumerism since the Second World War:

> The new stage of industrial development made it appear as if the social forces which had till then been thought of as revolutionary ... had been integrated into capitalist development, and had taken up the alienated way of living which this society offered it, along with the rise in their living standards and the increased satisfaction of their needs. The relative and temporary success of the manipulation of needs and the manipulation of public opinion has lent a central importance to the critique of everyday life and thinking. (Heller, 1976b, pp. 42–3)

Consumerism simply transforms Marx's concept of the individual rich in needs into the individual rich in commodities. Industrial capitalism of the twentieth century, constituted by corporate-dominated mass production and mass consumption, has as its aim the equation of the good life with the goods life. The prejudice of the market economy, reflecting the interests of the upper strata of the hierarchical power system, is to steer need fulfilment down the avenue of commodities. Thus self-determination becomes commodity oriented. It is the form in which self-determination appears that is compromised. In the market setting human needing is not subject to democratic social control but is subordinated to impersonal market forces and the competition of personal pecuniary enrichment derived from others' need. The majority whose livelihood is dependent upon the sale of their labour-power are denied the social decision-making processes that offer the choice between meaningful, participatory employment and fulfilment solely through increased goods. That the good life should be the goods life is a social decision made privately and by the *de facto* means of market power. It is not compatible with the value of equal self-determination because it is not an expression of equal control over the social processes of needing. It is a social decision not subject to democratic accountability.

Consumerism for the Budapest School is only part of the problem. Not only is there the undemocratic distortion of commodity-biased need fulfilment, but the needs of those who lack sufficient employment and property are largely unrecognized. They lack the means necessary to actualize equally their self-determination. There are additionally a host of other needs, such as those for various kinds of public goods or for love, belonging, community, participation, and so on, that simply are not profitable.

> In general, one can say that *no profit-regulated* society recognizes human needs in their totality for the perfectly simple reason that a great variety of eminently human and non-alienated needs are not profitable. (Feher and Heller, 1982a, p. 37, original emphasis)

However, given the unlimitedness of the capitalist need structure, Heller also suggests that consumerism may be less destructive than alternative avenues of manifesting insatiability. She cites Kant's observation that there are three insatiable drives of the modern individual: lust for having, lust for fame and lust for power. Consumerism – the lust for having – often provides a sublimated means to satisfy the other two more pernicious forms of lust. If one is not famous or powerful one can, through consumerism, imitate the dress and appearance of those who are (Heller, 1983a, p. 364).

In general, the Budapest School writers argue that the potentiality for need articulation and self-determination must be extended to all people. They do not propose to restrict the unlimitedness of self-development; consequently they do not suggest the restriction of need articulation, as this would violate the value-standard of equal self-determination. They argue for the reconciliation of equality and individual freedom but not as a result of absolute abundance. Even though the democratization of social decision-making mechanisms implies a redirection of need articulation away from the commodity form, absolute abundance is unrealizable.

However, the system of need articulation in capitalism is itself characterized by relative scarcity. The unlimitedness of needs relative to available material resources always creates a situation of relative scarcity. Feher and Heller acknowledge the condition of relative scarcity in capitalism:

> Relative scarcity means a social condition in which there are more socially articulated needs than commodities to satisfy them with *and* (this is a proviso most important for us) this situation appears as an unbridgeable gap in the sense that there are no existing social mechanisms to mediate between unsatisfied needs and the production of commodities. (Feher and Heller, 1982a, p. 37, original emphasis)

The problem of relative scarcity is due to the fact that in capitalism there are no 'existing social mechanisms to mediate between unsatisfied needs and the production of commodities'. The Budapest School suggests that the precondition of extending to all people the equal ability and means for individual self-development is not absolute abundance but the creation of social mechanisms that mediate between the unrestricted recognition of needs and the limited resources available for their articulation. If absolute abundance is utopian and the restriction of needs violates the fundamental value of equal self-determination, then effective democratic mechanisms to bridge the gap between unlimited wants and limited resources are the only rational alternative. The Budapest School refers to the conditions of such an alternative as relative abundance. However, as they have said, relative abundance does not mean transcending bourgeois society but rather making its decision-making mechanisms fully democratic. It does not imply freedom from external authority but a notion of 'democratic freedom' in which freedom is expanded by degrees. It necessitates the democratizing of the stratified system of power in the social democratic mixed economies.

As they currently exist these economies do not provide equal self-determination because the processes of need fulfilment and articulation are not fully democratized. Clearly the market economies provide a wide range of self-expression and a pluralistic system of needs without simultaneously subordinating the *system* of these expressions to democratic, equal control. Although capitalism fosters a notion of the independent self subject to its own determination, it is a social process of self-determination that is not fully democratized because equal control over the determination of needs has yet to exist.

Summary

First, with respect to Western capitalism, the Budapest School's approach is considered neo-Marxian because it rejects Marx's economistic logic, which states that the capitalist system can be best understood through the dialectic of wage-labour and capital. Secondly, it is neo-Marxian because it refuses to view the activities of the capitalist state as an epiphenomenon of the class-constituted property relations in Marx's base–superstructure dichotomy. Drawing on Karl Polanyi's ideas, Chapter 2 argues that what Marx devoted his life to analysing (in the reduction of capitalism to the capital–labour antinomy) was merely one tendency within the total process of disembedding the economy from society.

From the very beginnings of capitalism in the sixteenth century there were countertendencies that checked the unfolding of the self-regulating market economy. Most of these countertendencies were the reactions of various social groups that were victimized by the vagaries of self-regulating market tendencies. What Marx referred to as struggles between classes, Polanyi describes as diffuse reactions against the vagaries of the market. At the point that Marx describes these nineteenth-century events as class struggle, the classes in Marx's sense of the term had not yet developed, nor did they ever develop as Marx envisioned them. The social conflict of the nineteenth century is market constituted rather than class constituted, but it is this conflict itself that protected society and kept capitalism from becoming what Marx thought it was all along.

As most of these countertendencies were manifested through the state, often by relying on the rights and liberties formally recognized by constitutional democracies, the state, rather than being an epiphenomenon of capitalist property relations, was in fact constitutive of capitalism's social relations. The state's actions on behalf of disaffected social groups prevented capitalism from becoming a 'pure' class society composed of one homogeneous proletariat struggling against a capitalist class. This suggests that capitalism is better understood as a stratified society than as a class society. Thus formal democracy and the state provided diverse social groups with a vehicle to protect and advance their interests. Therefore the social democratic mixed economy of Western Europe and the welfare-state mixed economy of the United States are the result of the interaction between conflicting social groups (tendency and countertendency) within a stratified structure of power over social decision-making.

For the Budapest School these mixed economies, because of their stratification, are still fundamentally undemocratic with respect to the processes and mechanisms of social decision-making. However, from a neo-Marxian perspective their evolution demonstrates that formal, constitutional democracy has contributed significantly to the advance of subordinate groups, and furthermore that the capitalist system has kept alive a notion of individual freedom and the sanctity of the individual that is vital to the achievement of a more democratic society.

The individual freedom preserved in bourgeois society (because of the disembedded economic sphere) was obscured when Marxists at the time of the Bolshevik Revolution equated capitalism with bourgeois society. The Bolsheviks, like Babeuf, put equality before freedom, and their revolution subsequently transcended bourgeois society and sacrificed much of its individual freedom. The analysis of existing socialism in the following chapter demonstrates the role played by the separate sphere of civil society in preserving bourgeois society's freedom. Moreover it reveals also that freedom is divisible. Existing socialism, like capitalism, is not a society of absolute unfreedom. However, by the same token, the neo-Marxian view suggests that in degrees of freedom it does not measure up to capitalism.

[4]

A Neo-Marxian Conception of Existing Socialism

> To give a critical account of these societies demands significant revisions and modifications of the very conceptual framework of Marxist theory. And for this reason the problem of Eastern European societies has a vital importance for the theoretical fate of Marxism itself.
>
> Ferenc Feher, Agnes Heller, Georg Markus

The purpose of this chapter is to develop and elaborate a neo-Marxian conception of existing socialism based upon the Budapest School's critical analysis of Eastern Europe. The interpretation given here is that the Budapest School has implicitly a neo-Marxian view of soviet societies. I have identified four essential features of their conceptualization of Eastern European societies, which they call 'dictatorship over needs'. Taken together these features of the dictatorship-over-needs model emphasize not only the absence of the need-articulating function of markets in soviet societies but also their totalitarian character, in which the ruling apparatus is able to administer politically the manner in which needs are fulfilled.

There are two factors that account for the neo-Marxian character of the Budapest School's analysis of soviet societies. First, the revolutions that established these societies were explicitly anti-capitalist, but the ideas that inspired them and legitimated what came to be the basic structure of soviet societies were founded on

96

Marxist orthodoxy's misguided economism. Soviet societies and their domination are not so much a result of a distorted view of Marx as they are a result of Marxist orthodoxy's distorted view of capitalism, in which it mistook a tendency of the nineteenth century for capitalism's essence. They are founded on the notion that capitalism is fundamentally a class society in which the state is an epiphenomenon of the economic base.

Secondly, the Budapest School's conception is neo-Marxian because it maintains that these societies are post-capitalist but remain inexplicable by Marx's basic class-based categories. Therefore to understand these societies fully one must go beyond Marx's economistic approach and view them as new social formations requiring a fresh approach. They are fundamentally 'political societies', which means in Polanyi's terms that the economy has been re-embedded in society. A 'political society', for the Budapest School, is one where there is no separate economic sphere that is independent of the state. In this sense precapitalist societies were also political societies. In both soviet societies and traditional societies strictly economic motives do not govern priorities. Their economic activities are subordinated to noneconomic norms, customs, or political decisions. In soviet societies the economy has been assimilated by the state, that is, it has been completely politicized. Additionally, the soviet state is totalitarian in character because of the absence of political pluralism. The soviet state absorbed civil society and simultaneously eliminated formal democracy and political pluralism. The final result has been the abolition in soviet societies of capitalism's greatest achievement: its nurture of individual freedom and liberty (see Chapter 3). This makes soviet societies a 'product of a de-enlightenment process, in contrast to which even mere liberalism appears as an embodiment of human freedom' (Feher, Heller and Markus, 1983, p. 203).

A neo-Marxian view of capitalism emphasizes the role it has played in laying the ground for the individual rich in needs and consequently for equal self-determination. By contrast a neo-Marxian view of existing socialism indicates the degree to which these societies have retarded, if not reversed, the conditions for both the individual rich in needs and equal self-determination. In assessing the prospects for social change in Eastern Europe the analysis of the Budapest School leaves one with the inescapable conclusion that struggles for marketizing reforms similar to those in Hungary and

China and advocated by Polish Solidarity should not be discounted and are generally progressive.

The Need for a New View of Existing Socialism

A neo-Marxian approach to existing socialism begins with the notion that it represents a social system that has proved itself to be viable but not clearly explained by Marx's categories. Additionally, soviet society owes its inspiration as well as its form of domination to Marx's economistic view of capitalism. However, as neo-Marxists the Budapest School writers have retained Marx's critical theory paradigm. In this respect Markus (1982, p. 308) states that 'the task of the critical theory of these societies is to discover the specific rationality of the system and thereby the tendencies, strains, and contradictions of its development'.

The idea that a new, historically determined social formation has emerged in Eastern Europe is itself neo-Marxian. The Budapest School argues that there is no real historical precedent for such a formation. 'It is a self-reproducing social order in which many elements declared to be "transitory" (for reasons of camouflage) are constitutive of, and indispensable for, the functioning of the system' (Feher, Heller and Markus, 1983, p. 121). Markus (1982) has argued that it is a social system that Marx did not predict, nor would he have been able to predict such an outcome from movements inspired by his critique of capitalism. 'Soviet absolutism, however, is an outcome of a revolution which has destroyed all forms of traditional organization so that an entirely new one has had to be created' (Feher, Heller and Markus, 1983, p. 160). In fact as Vajda (1981, p. 66) has said, Marx's 'property relations cannot illuminate this social structure'. Marx's method suggests that economic property relations determine political power. However in soviet society political power relations exercised by the state have constituted the actual property–economic relations. In other words, soviet society is difficult to explain with Marx's categories mainly because of his economism. Along with its neo-Marxian view of capitalism, the Budapest School also views soviet society as one where political power cannot be deduced from economic power. In fact, this is what the term 'political society' is meant to convey.

However, as Markus concludes, Marx's critical theory paradigm is still applicable:

> My own conviction is that the Marxist tradition in its historical totality does retain its critical potential with reference to the societies of Eastern Europe, and, that it offers both a theoretically deeper and practically more radical-critical understanding of these societies than the simplistic alternative, namely, the liberal theory of authoritarian political systems. (Markus, 1982, p. 295)

As Markus suggests, giving up Marx's economism does not necessitate acceptance of the liberal view. According to Vajda:

> If I give up this reductionism, the class division of society ceases to be the only important and decisive factor in the constitution of social groups, and, moreover, I have to take into consideration the fact that even in a society where classes simply play no role at all, where they do not even exist, nevertheless this particular society may have a definitely hierarchical structure. (Vajda, 1981, p. 6)

The implication of Vajda's remark is that soviet society is not a class society in Marx's sense but is a post-capitalist society that is better described as a stratified or hierarchical society. Vajda's point is that soviet society proves 'that the abolition of class differences does not automatically create a kind of homogeneous society in which the social status of all individuals would be equal' (Vajda, 1981, p. 6).

For the Budapest School writers, it is not enough to say that soviet society is a stratified society and is therefore neither democratic nor socialist. They insist that the problem of freedom in soviet society is related to Marx's ideas and the socialist movement at the turn of the century. 'These societies, however tragic this may be, do belong to the international history of that social and intellectual movement which bears the name of socialism' (Feher, Heller and Markus, 1983, p. 43). One cannot dismiss the domination apparent in soviet society by simply stating that although it is not capitalist, neither is it the ideal of socialism. Consequently the neo-Marxian view of existing socialism shows that the particular type of hierarchical relations and domination characteristic of soviet society cannot be understood without realizing that it is a by-product of both Marx and the socialist movement at the time of the Bolshevik Revolution.

Marx's economism meant that the problem of capitalist society was its class structure in which capitalists were able to exploit the labour-power of the proletariat. This understanding of capitalism had specific implications for the theory of socialism subscribed to by Marx's Bolshevik followers. The socialism they created, although it is not socialism as the ideal form of democracy and equality, is still socialist as many understood it from Marx's analysis. However, it is a socialism based upon Marxist orthodoxy's false understanding of capitalism. According to Vajda:

> If I hold that objectively the political theory of socialism ultimately points in the direction which has been historically realized, then this simply proves to me the fact that Marxist socialism was a real, although in many respects false conscious-ness of history. (Vajda, 1981, p. 64)

Thus neither Marx nor the socialist movement can extricate them-selves from responsibility for a type of society that calls itself socialist but manifests both economic exploitation and political domination.

For the Budapest School the invasion of Czechoslovakia in 1968 was a major turning point in their thinking. At that time they began to realize that the social systems of the Soviet Union and Eastern Europe were not transitory societies or simply deviations from the ideal of socialism. They were, instead, new social formations capable of self-reproduction even in the face of political collapse, as in Hungary and Poland in 1956, and again in the invasion of Czechoslovakia in 1968. The dictatorship-over-needs framework developed in this chapter is a conceptual model created by the Budapest School writers to distinguish Eastern European societies as unique social formations and furthermore to emphasize their belief that these societies cannot adequately be understood by the prevail-ing perspectives of the Western left (see Feher, Heller and Markus, 1983; Feher, 1978).

The Budapest School writers reject the major left theories of existing socialism. They have specifically discussed the inadequacies of what they consider to be the three dominant explanations of these social systems: the state capitalism theory, the transitional society theory and Asiatic mode theories. None of these, they believe, comes to terms with the real essence of existing socialism.

The first theory with which they take issue is the state capitalism theory. This theory argues that soviet societies can still be understood with Marx's categories used to describe capitalism. The Soviet Union is then a system where the state has become the monopoly capitalist in general, and in particular the party comprises the capitalist class (see, for example, Andreff, 1983). The majority of people are wage-workers who sell their labour to the state and thus are the counterpart to the capitalist system's proletariat. The state exploits the labour of the workers and the party members appropriate the economic surplus produced by the working class. With respect to the class issue there is at best a loosely analogous relationship. Marx understood capitalism as a system where capitalists control all the means of production and buy the labour-power of propertyless workers. The similarity with soviet society is that the state controls all the means of production and buys the labour-power of its propertyless workers.

However, for the Budapest School, the motive of production is entirely different in these two systems. As Markus (1982, p. 308) says, 'the logic of the system is not that of capital'. The most important reason for this is that soviet societies have 'set themselves up ... as anti-capitalist regimes' by totally absorbing capitalism's autonomous economic sphere within the state (Feher, Heller and Markus, 1983, p. 23). They are fundamentally 'political societies', which means there is no separate sphere of civil society. Consequently there is the conspicuous absence of self-regulating markets, profit-motivated decision-making, market-based resource allocation and private property. There are few price-determining markets and little scarcity pricing or market-based competition between enterprises. Decisions about investment spending, growth and resource allocation are essentially political decisions, not economic ones, and this is primarily because there is no separate economic sphere.

In capitalism economic activities are not subordinated to centralized political control by the state. The nature of growth and the course of social development are largely determined by economic decisions made by private-sector corporations in search of profits or power. On the contrary, in soviet society economic activities are governed by the state's overarching goal of maintaining social control. Although this is elaborated under the dictatorship-over-needs model in the following pages, the Budapest School's point is that the political logic of maintaining social control in soviet society gives it a much different character from capitalism, despite any class-related similarities. In Polanyi's terms, the economy has been re-embedded in society, and it is this fact that accounts for the basic difference in the two systems.

Additionally, if the state were behaving (in markets based on scarcity pricing) as the maximizing capitalist, whether it be profit maximization, sales maximization, or output maximization, there would be signs of greater economic rationality and efficiency than what is presently visible (Feher, Heller and Markus, 1983, pp. 26–7). However, the Budapest School argues that the primary motive of soviet society is the ruling elite's desire to maintain social control. Therefore since economic decisions must conform to this desire, production is ultimately for the state rather than the consumer. This type of direct political control results in a variety of economic inefficiencies that are absent in market economies governed by the maximizing behaviour of consumers and producers (see Kornai, 1986; Nove, 1983, for examples). Thus state capitalism theories 'work with a concept of capitalism which, applied to Eastern societies, makes them out to be "irrational" economies' (Markus, 1982, p. 305). 'Theories of state capitalism can do no better in this respect than to declare all these phenomena signs of an "inherent irrationality" ' (Feher, Heller and Markus, 1983, p. 30).

The only reason soviet society appears irrational is because the principle of market rationality does not apply to the functioning of soviet society. Therefore all of the economic dysfunction and enormous resource waste of the soviet system must be explicable only within the alternative principle of rationality: the state's goal of maintaining social control. The key to describing this different rationality of soviet society is the fact that it is a politicized society lacking an autonomous economic sphere. The apparent waste and inefficiency in soviet resource allocation can only be explained by viewing soviet society as a post-capitalist but entirely new social formation, operating with its own peculiar principle of state control. The dictatorship-over-needs framework is then the Budapest School's attempt to address the questions left unanswered in theories of state capitalism.

The second theory the Budapest School writers dispute is the transitional society theory. They generally attribute the origins of this theory and its contemporary variants to Trotsky (Markus, 1982, p. 296). The major inadequacy of this theory is that it is based upon an over-simplification derived from Marx. According to this view, based on Marx's understanding of how the dialectic would determine the course of history, the future offers two choices: either capitalism or socialism. If soviet society is neither one then it must be something between these two social formations. Consequently the socialist revolutions of Eastern Europe have been diverted off course and distorted by bureaucratic elites who have justified their domination by appeal to Marx's ideas. This sort of thinking, according to the Budapest School, is founded on an over-simplified dichotomy of capitalism versus socialism.

Markus has also stated that since most transitional theories are founded on the belief in a bureaucratic elite that has seized control, these theories fail to comprehend the real structure of power in soviet society. It is not simply a situation where a small elite has class-based control and power while others are totally deprived of power. According to Markus, this sort of theory

> refuses to acknowledge the necessary connection that exists between the paternalism of the state *restricting* the power of management within the enterprise and the enormously *enhanced* (in comparison with a capitalist system) administrative power the bureaucratic apparatus as a *whole* (the 'state') has over the 'sale' of labour-power (the wages) throughout the whole economy. (Markus, 1982, p. 300, original emphasis)

In effect soviet societies are bureaucratic, but power is distributed in a stratified manner rather than residing with one elite only. It is largely for this reason that soviet society is stable and capable of self-reproduction. Consequently there is little reason to believe that it is transitory or that it is currently evolving towards a more democratic form. The Budapest School argues that the post-Stalinist period, although it has witnessed some reforms and reduction in terror, shows no evidence of substantive or qualitative changes in the essential structure of the system. From this point of view, soviet society is not in a period of transition towards either democratic socialism or capitalism.

Moreover, the Budapest School states that transitionalists tend to identify capitalist elements in soviet societies with the various market-related reforms. Since transitionalists oppose capitalism they view such reforms and existing mechanisms as regressive. On the other hand they see socialism in command planning, which they then continue to defend (see Feher, Heller and Markus, 1983, p. 14). The Budapest School rejects the 'planning versus markets' dichotomy. From its neo-Marxian view it is the marketizing reforms that are progressive, while the reliance on command planning is regressive (a view it also shares with Alec Nove; see Nove, 1983). The point is to transcend the false dichotomy. Planning and markets should not be viewed as diametrically opposed such that the only alternative is one or the other rather than a mix of both.

Additionally, the transitional theory continues to argue that capitalism is a class society as Marx said it was, and thus the solution to capitalism is to get the revolution back on course and again headed towards socialism. The neo-Marxian view rejects this type of economistic reasoning. Soviet society is a unique post-capitalist society that is not transitory.

The third category of theories the Budapest School has criticized is that of the various Asiatic mode theories. These are explanations of Eastern European societies that emphasize their precapitalist features, and argue that soviet society, although it may be post-capitalist, has enough similarity to either the feudal mode or Marx's Asiatic mode of production that it can be modelled along these lines. The Budapest School has in mind Bahro's theory in *The Alternative in Eastern Europe* and Konrad and Szelenyi's *The Intellectuals on the Road to Class Power* (see Markus, 1982). The similarities between soviet societies and precapitalist societies include (1) the use of forced labour in the Gulags and agriculture, (2) semi-bondage to the land and restricted freedom of migration and (3) the use of non-monetarized privileges for some of the upper strata (Markus, 1982, p. 314).

However, given these similarities the Budapest School argues that soviet societies are integrated social systems and that although they may share some of these features with precapitalist societies they are qualitatively different. The Budapest School considers the Asiatic mode a 'loose analogy' only, primarily because these theories disregard the different elements determining precapitalist and soviet societies. In this respect, because the Asiatic mode of production did not have a political centre from which all decisions about resource allocation were made, it is considerably different from soviet societies (Feher, Heller and Markus, 1983, p. 42).

The most important similarity that does exist between soviet societies and virtually all precapitalist societies is that they are politicized societies lacking a disembedded economic sphere. They are all non-market economies. Like precapitalist societies, soviet societies' 'fundamental characteristic is that state and society are not separated from one another' (Feher, Heller and Markus, 1983, p. 257). It is this distinction between precapitalist and soviet societies on the one hand and capitalism on the other that is obscured by Marx's schema. The real property relations that exist in soviet societies are considered as 'institutional' property relations by the Budapest School, and in this respect they are similar to the church's property in feudal Europe (Feher, Heller and Markus, 1983, p. 69).

Szelenyi and Konrad refer to soviet societies as systems of 'rational redistribution', arguing that because they use a political system of redistribution rather than the market to allocate resources, they are similar to precapitalist societies. Much of Szelenyi's and Konrad's analysis in *The Intellectuals on the Road to Class Power* is drawn from Polanyi's work in economic anthropology. Polanyi maintained that all social systems have methods of integrating economic functioning within society so that they reproduce themselves. He distinguished between precapitalist and capitalist societies on the basis of these integrative mechanisms. In precapitalist societies 'reciprocity' and 'redistribution' were the major mechanisms, because these were politicized social formations in which economic activities were embedded in the societies by both political decision and custom. However in capitalism 'market exchange' developed as the major mechanism to organize social reproduction because the economy had become disembedded from society. Konrad and Szelenyi go on to argue that soviet societies, because the economy has been re-embedded, are best described as 'rational redistribution' systems. They call precapitalist societies 'traditional redistribution' systems and state that the difference is primarily the fact that soviet societies are technologically based and growth oriented while precapitalist systems were not.

The Konrad and Szelenyi thesis argues that intellectuals in Eastern Europe are in the process of consolidating power as a class. Even though the Budapest School disputes this, they agree that soviet societies share important similarities with precapitalist societies since all are non-market economies. Therefore, Konrad and Szelenyi and the Budapest School are all influenced by Polanyi. As a result, they emphasize the re-embeddedness of the soviet economy, making it, at least in this one respect, similar to precapitalist societies.

Excluding the overarching political character that makes soviet and precapitalist societies similar, the Budapest School says, 'The specifically "precapitalist" features of these societies are subordinated to mechanisms of social-economic reproduction *which have no analogies in history and ought to be regarded as sui generis*' (Markus, 1982, p. 315, original emphasis).

The major point the Budapest School has tried to make is that a new approach to soviet societies is necessary. According to Markus:

> East European societies cannot be described through a potpourri of pre-capitalist, capitalist and post-capitalist characteristics; they represent an integral social system. That is, they are capable of reproducing themselves in all their strains and contradictions. (Markus, 1982, p. 315)

Left explanations of Eastern European societies, in the Budapest School's view, have not fully explained the oppression and social domination in these 'self-reproducing systems of unfree paternalism' (Feher, 1978, p. 42). These writers' analysis is addressed to the Western left but with the intent of salvaging the vitality, critical acumen and respectability of the socialist movement and heritage.

> Movements with an original socialist intent, largely transformed and degenerated theories with an initial socialist thrust, met real social demands and trends inherent in failed attempts at modernization and in ossified social structures, and in the underlying operative tendencies to industrialization. They produced regimes which are, in fact, anti-capitalist but which are not socialist but rather an abominable caricature of everything socialists have lived and fought for. Thus every militant with a will to genuine socialism is confronted with a situation which is far more complex than the first day of the outbreak of the First World War, when socialists whose moral integrity was still intact felt that the idea and the movement had already become hopelessly compromised. (Feher, Heller and Markus, 1983, pp. 235–6)

Both from their experiences and their analysis they conclude that there is nothing socialist about soviet societies. It is an 'historical dead end despite its self-reproductive capacity' (Feher, Heller and Markus, 1983, p. 121). Furthermore, 'socialism as a whole, if it is ever to transcend its present miserable state, needs radical self-criticism of what has happened in the last 60 years' (Feher, Heller and Markus 1983, p. 222).

The Budapest School believes that Western Eurocommunist parties and theoreticians have avoided a serious study of Eastern Europe. According to Markus,

> the emergence of a leftist opposition in Eastern Europe by its very existence and perhaps, to a lesser degree, through its writings, has compelled some segments of the Western left to face the reality of what socialism is *not* – thus helping to develop a better consciousness of what socialism may be, must be. (Markus, 1982, p. 293)

The Western left has avoided moreover any suggestion that there might be a definite connection between the obvious denial of human freedom in these countries and Marx's approach. Yet a neo-Marxian view suggests that such a connection exists. In the next section the relationship between Marx's economistic view of capitalism and the domination characteristic of existing socialism is elaborated. Following that, the Budapest School's new approach to soviet societies – the dictatorship over needs – is developed, and it is through this framework that one can also appreciate the group's neo-Marxian view of existing socialism.

The Marxian Heritage of Existing Socialism

To understand what existing socialism means with respect to the value of equal self-determination and also to make comparisons between it and capitalism, it is necessary to recognize that soviet society is at least partially the fulfilment of Marx's dialectic. For the Budapest School it is a negative realization of the Hegelian dialectic to which Marx had given a materialist rather than an idealist foundation. Its partial fulfilment in soviet society was not the realization of human freedom but the negation of bourgeois freedom. Soviet society considered as dictatorship over needs is the negation of bourgeois freedom.

The historical basis for this development in Eastern Europe involves the interrelationship of three factors: (1) a radical, intellectual elite, (2) its desire to overcome class-based exploitation and (3) its desire to overcome the irrationality of market-based allocation (see Feher, 1978; Boella, 1979). The first factor relates to Leninist vanguardism. The second and third factors are a function of the acceptance of Marx's economism by Lenin and Second International socialists. The conclusion is that existing socialism must 'be recognized as a type of response to capitalism and its contradictions' (Feher, Heller and Markus, 1983, p. 121). They are 'consciously created social formations, deduced from allegedly scientific principles' (Feher, 1978, p. 33).

The Budapest School's major criticism of Leninist vanguardism is its Jacobin character, and consequently they refer to the Bolsheviks as the 'Jacobin legacy' (Feher, Heller and Markus, 1983, p. 225). In many respects it is a criticism similar to Rosa Luxemburg's view that party vanguardism involved an alienated ethics that justified coercion and terror if the masses did not immediately embrace the party's policies. The Budapest School argues that the Bolsheviks had a pessimistic view of human nature because they believed, like Bentham and classical liberals, that people are basically lazy. In addition, the Bolsheviks subscribed to a moralism that 'one group knows best'. Ultimately, when politically applied it meant 'the state as the great teacher to the masses'. They also had a 'technocratic-statist spirit' adopted from Saint Simon, which meant that all values should be subsumed under that of the growth of material wealth (Feher, Heller and Markus, 1983, pp. 225–7).

The Bolsheviks devised an ideology based on scientific knowledge of socialist transformation. They claimed that their goals embodied the interests of the working class and that their policies would eliminate the anarchy of capitalist production and create a truly 'rational' system of economic organization. If such policies met with resistance or hesitation from the working classes, the Bolsheviks, adopting Lenin's vanguardism, were in a position to argue that the people simply did not understand. According to the Budapest School the party was actually in the process of consolidating its own power, and thus the interests of the party were substituted for the interests of the working class. Feher (1978, p. 31) emphasizes that by the late nineteenth century radical intellectuals began to take over the socialist movement in Europe, and thus the 'movement prefigured what was to come in the future: a growing passivity of workers in whose name intellectuals tend to become increasingly the only historical actors'. This was apparent to many 'left communists' at the time, including Luxemburg, Korsch, Pannekoek and Lukacs, all of whom protested Lenin's authoritarian political strategy. The Budapest School emphasizes that Lenin's vanguardism was justified during this time by an appeal to the correctness of the Bolsheviks' Marxist view of history. Since Marx had a correct judgement about the domination and exploitation in capitalism, and because the drift of history would be towards socialism, then the Bolsheviks' authoritarian politics based on this knowledge was justified, whether the masses understood or not.

Of course the party's interest was not the maximization of its own material wealth but rather the maximization of the power to direct the course of the revolution and the organization of the new society. Furthermore this meant that Lenin's vanguardism 'or at least its *inherent dynamic* was heading for an elimination of political pluralism in general, towards a monolithic society' (Feher and Heller, 1982b, p. 131, original emphasis). If the party was certain of the correctness of its views then it sensed that any protest or resistance, whether it came from propertied classes or working classes, could result in political stalemate and thwart the revolution. Political pluralism was considered a bourgeois ploy that could jeopardize the revolution and therefore could justifiably be abolished.

The Budapest School maintains that after Marx, Lenin and other Marxian socialists *interpreted* Marx's ethics as class based. Hence not only is good behaviour that which is in accord with the interest of the proletariat, but self-sacrifice for one's class is virtuous as well. This implied that if the party embodied the proletariat's long-run interests then one should submit to the party's decisions. Lenin also believed that workers would consistently act according to their immediate interests in higher wages, making their long-run interests recognizable only to the party. Heller argues that this was a misinterpretation of Marx's ethics. She feels that Marx would not have sanctioned such submission to external authority. However, with Leninism 'one owes *blind self-sacrifice* to the Party, this repository of class interest' (Heller, 1982a, p. 356). Accordingly individual workers should no longer think for themselves but let the party do the thinking. 'The Marxian philosophy of super-Enlightenment thus turns into an ideology of "de-enlightenment" ' (ibid., p. 356, original emphasis).

The acceptance of this form of distorted Marxian ethics merely fuelled the trend towards a monolithic society directed by a planning elite whose power was legitimated by appeals to scientific and expert knowledge. More specifically it was a power legitimated by a knowledge of how science could be harnessed for the interests of the working class. It was an appeal based on knowledge of how to rationalize scientifically Marx's 'forces of production' in the service of the majority of working people. However, as the Budapest School suggests, this type of legitimacy is ultimately derived from Marx's economistic contradiction between forces and relations of production in capitalism.

> But when, in keeping with the exigencies of a philosophy of history, Marx remained with the paradigm of production and constructed the basic contradiction of capitalism as the collusion between the forces and relations of production, he, too, opened the way to substitute the consciousness of one specific (the second) logic of civil society. The consciousness of the forces of production is the *technocratic consciousness*, the consciousness of a planning elite already propounded as such by Saint-Simon. Marx would have never accepted a new technocratic elite as the bearer of the socialist transformation. All the same, if the basic contradiction in modern society can be located between the forces and the relations of production, then only a planning elite could become the bearer of this transformation. (Heller, 1982d, p. 287, original emphasis)

In other words, from an orthodox Marxian perspective based on Marx's economic reduction of capitalism to the contradiction of forces and relations of production, the problem presented by capitalism is how to use capitalist forces of production to serve the general interest. It was the answer to this question that the Bolsheviks sought to monopolize through Jacobin politics. Thus the Budapest School says that

> according to our firm conviction, it was not the proletariat that created the new social order (which was created only in the name of the proletariat) and it was not the realm of any bourgeoisie that came about but rather the elitist dictatorship over needs. (Feher, Heller and Markus, 1983, p. 224)

In other words the new anti-capitalist social order was not the result of a majoritarian movement for popular democracy. Soviet society was the product of a radical elite whose creation is neither state capitalism nor socialism but a dictatorship over needs.

The second historical factor that led to the dictatorship over needs is the desire by the radical intellectual elite to overcome class-based exploitation. Marx's economistic analysis of capitalism deduced all political power from that of the capitalist class, which monopolized ownership of the means of production in civil society. Therefore as an epiphenomenon of the economic base the state was considered to be an instrument of the capitalist class whose power rested on the right of private property. The exploitation of labour – which Marx considered to be a major feature of capitalist domination – was premised on the unequal ownership of the means of production sanctioned by formal democracy. Since formal democracy was a sham and the state only a tool for the bourgeoisie, then the solution to exploitation was to smash the capitalist state, replace it with a workers' state, and eliminate private property altogether. According to Vajda:

> If power, if the political, if the state, is nothing more than the superstructure of production, that is, property relations; if political power only has instrumental reality; if political power cannot determine property relations because the latter unam- biguously determine the former, then one only has to abolish private property to deprive all political power of its footing. (Vajda, 1981, p. 65)

The practical outcome of such a view was the assimilation of civil society by a 'workers' state' in which all of the decision-making was exercised by the radical elite. In the process of abolishing private property, that is, in an effort to go to the root of capitalist power, the state absorbed civil society. 'Capitalist private property does not exclude the right of everyone to property ... but as a result of the practice of that right it excludes *de facto* the majority of population from that property' (Heller, 1978b, p. 878). Thus the political sphere swallowed civil society by both appropriating all private property and eliminating the formal democracy that guaranteed private ownership.

Eliminating private property as a means to eliminating labour exploitation (and the capital-labour dialectic of class struggle) resulted in the 'negative abolition of private property' (Heller, 1978b). If the practical effect of capitalism is to prevent a majority from owning property then, according to this understanding of Marx, the Bolsheviks created a society in which no one would own

property. The 'positive abolition of private property' would theoretically have extended property ownership to everyone, but the
state's appropriation of property in soviet society implied that such
ownership would be extended to no one but the state. It was Marx's
economism that obscured the pluralism of power in capitalist
society and overlooked the substantive aspects of individual
freedom constituted by formal democracy. It portrayed the state as
an epiphenomenon of the economic power wielded by capitalists.
Yet the Bolsheviks who embraced this view destroyed the embryonic
bourgeois state evolving in Tsarist Russia, and in its place substituted a more totalitarian state rather than a more democratic state.
As Vajda says:

> The abolition of private ownership of the means of production
> and conditions of labour does not mean the elimination of every
> kind of oppression. Furthermore, when this abolition is accom-
> panied by the destruction of the state apparatus the new
> situation which suddenly comes about is not a community free
> of oppression but a vacuum, where the old, tradition-bound
> political forms of power in all probability are almost auto-
> matically restored. (Vajda, 1981, p. 77)

If under a capitalist regime there was no likelihood that all would
own property, then the Bolshevik solution was to deny it to all
through state collectivism – a negative abolition of private property.

The third historical factor leading to the dictatorship over needs is
the radical elite's desire to abolish the anarchic effects of market-
based allocation, the major symptom of which was the capitalist
business cycle. The Bolsheviks claimed that capitalism's separate
economic sphere, where human needs were met (or not met) on the
basis of markets and profit-motivated decisions, involved a type of
irrationality that resulted in unemployment, inflation, bankruptcies
and the perpetuation of inequality. The solution to these problems
involved the elimination of decentralized, market-based decision-
making and its replacement by a system of centralized planning in
which the state politically directs the allocation of economic
resources. Western scholars generally refer to soviet resource allocation as command planning. However, the Budapest School argues
that planning of any type connotes a process in which there is a
consensus reached by a variety of groups or individuals about how
resources will be allocated. On the contrary, the soviet system is 'an

112

integrated system of binding orders which aims to determine the essential characteristics of the economic behavior of all subordinate units' (Feher, Heller and Markus, 1983, p. 77). Therefore, the soviet economy is a directed economy rather than a planned economy. Also,

> Lenin's preparations were aimed as 'confiscating the revolution' on behalf of a dedicated political elite which would allegedly bring rationality into an irrational world, a rationality by definition superior both to the capitalist order and to the masses' mere 'spontaneity'. (Feher and Heller, 1982b, p. 131)

In general by the turn of the century the Jacobin elements in the socialist movement had adopted Marx's economistic view of capitalism and carried out specifically anti-capitalist revolutions that sought scientifically to rationalize capitalism's anarchic production. Unquestionably there was strong appeal for any approach that could overcome depressions and recessions.

> Jacobin–Bolshevik efforts at establishing a political society have one serious advantage over all their weaker predecessors: they claim to embody, precisely through dictatorship over needs, an all-embracing economic justification (based on substantive rationality) as against the blind type of capitalist economy which causes catastrophes. (Feher, Heller and Markus, 1983, p. 253)

Consequently the radical elite equated capitalism with civil society itself. This meant that for the elimination of capitalist exploitation and its market anarchy resource allocation had to be centrally commanded by a state that owned all the means of production. To overcome capitalism civil society must also be abolished. For the radical elite,

> Civil rights are *bourgeois* rights, civil society is the realm of bourgeoisie. If we want to transcend capitalist society, we have to destroy civil society as well, replacing it by an omnipotent state which plans in harmony with science, puts an end to the relative independence of the private sphere and which can only disappear, if at all, when the whole population – or perhaps whole humankind – develops a kind of collectivistic ethical attitude capable of reproducing society in the same way without the constraints of the state. (Heller, 1979a, p. 110)

This form of 'radical negation of bourgeois society' resulted in the dictatorship over needs (Vajda, 1981, p. 80). In the neo-Marxian view, the destruction of capitalism's civil society meant that the individual freedom it had nurtured and preserved was also destroyed. Thus by equating capitalism with civil society and by abolishing both, these revolutions transcended bourgeois society. Yet individual freedom was sacrificed.

The ability of the new 'political society' to command all resource allocation and administer all property gave it the ability to dictate the manner in which the needs of the population would be fulfilled. The Budapest School argues that this was a radical act because needs are at the root of all human freedom – the freedom to determine oneself is the freedom to determine the articulation and fulfilment of one's needs. Thus by addressing needs this act went to the root of the problem. However, this is a perverted radicalism because it is the antithesis of Marx's 'individual rich in needs'. It is the antithesis of the concept of equal self-determination, because if needs are dictated then one's ability to determine oneself is negated. The individual rich in needs is a product of bourgeois society and is kept alive, at least as a value and idea, by capitalism's civil society. The neo-Marxian view reveals and emphasizes this historical fact through its critique and analysis of soviet society and through its characterization of soviet society as a dictatorship over needs.

The Budapest School's view illustrates a distinction between the Marxian radicalism that created soviet society and what Heller calls 'left radicalism'. Left radicalism is what emerges from the Budapest School's neo-Marxian view.

> One can be called radical if one wishes to transcend capitalism with all its implications, but one should be called a left radical only if one conceives of that task within the framework of formal democracy. A left radical is one who not merely fulfills the role of the enlightener ... but who acknowledges the reality of all human needs ... who knows that the knowledge of the intellectual is expertise and that in the selection of values all human beings are equally competent, who admits that in deciding the problem 'what is to be done' no elite can play a crucial role. (Heller, 1978b, p. 872)

Thus the anti-capitalist nature of the Eastern European revolutions created the ideological principles that effectively constituted these new social formations, even to the extent of being present in their national constitutions. Founded on anti-capitalist ideology with the abolition of markets for allocating resources, coupled with the collectivization of productive resources by the state and the formalized hierarchical organization of power, the material conditions emerged for a new social formation – the dictatorship over needs.

Existing Socialism as the Dictatorship over Needs

The dictatorship over needs is a conceptual framework developed by the Budapest School not only to characterize soviet society but to emphasize the essential distinctions between it and capitalism. Capitalism is not a dictatorship over needs in this neo-Marxian perspective.

Dictatorship over needs is a metaphor used primarily to emphasize the element of social control exercised through direct political power. It is the form in which human needs are fulfilled that is the object of social control in soviet societies, and it is the control over this process that makes soviet society a radical departure from capitalism. We can identify four essential features of the dictatorship-over-needs model. It consists, first, in production by alienated labour. Secondly, it is a system characterized by a form of state paternalism. Thirdly, production is motivated by the political directive to maximize material output subject to the constraint that this also maintains or increases social control. Finally, it is a 'political society' with a hierarchical power structure that, in the absence of political pluralism, is also totalitarian.

With respect to the first feature, production by alienated labour results from the condition that 'all of society is transformed into a conglomerate of wage-labourers' (Feher, 1978, p. 34). 'We are all wage-earners of the state' (Feher, Heller and Markus, 1983, p. 251). Markus maintains that in soviet society there is no 'free labour'; one does not have rights to bargain over the wage (Markus, 1982, p. 312). The Budapest School refers to the allocation of labour in soviet societies as a 'socialist non-market trade of labour' (Tökés, 1979, pp. 197–8). In this trade, workers are guaranteed some form of employment by the state and *cannot easily be fired by the*

115

enterprise. The 'sale of labour-power on the "pseudo-market" of labour [is] where prices (wages) are basically administratively set and politically enforced, but the competition among workers is also severely reduced' (Feher, Heller and Markus, 1983, p. 72). Thus although wage-labour exists, it does so within the context of administratively controlled markets.

Alienated labour in soviet production is a 'social form of wage-labour within a system of paternalistically operating, but essentially impersonal, relations of dependence' (Feher, Heller and Markus, 1983, p. 72). There are no forms of public assistance or unemployment compensation, so not only does this reduce 'casual labour' (temporary and part-time employment conducive to non-career life-styles) but it forces the working majority into a relation of dependency upon the state. Once on the job the soviet worker has little say in the basic conditions of the work process (see Haraszti, 1978, for an excellent sociological account of the work process in a typical Hungarian tractor factory). 'The working majority of the population in Eastern European societies has no control over the conditions, process or results of its own labour' (Feher, Heller and Markus, 1983, p. 45). It is alienated labour in the sense that the state has the power 'to establish all the conditions of the contract of labour for almost all categories of jobs' (Feher, Heller and Markus, 1983, pp. 71–2).

Alienated labour forms the basis for an 'us versus them' dichotomy. The 'us versus them' feeling of most workers reflects a dichotomy between 'those who can and do decide upon the lives of others and those who merely implement such social decisions' (Feher, Heller and Markus, 1983, p. 125). However, the Budapest School cautions against over-simplifying the 'us versus them' dichotomy; for example there are enormous conflicts among the 'us', such as those between urban and rural workers and those between intellectuals and industrial workers. At the same time the Budapest School maintains that in the dictatorship over needs there is a tendency towards levelling all needs (and thus all individuals) to the least common denominator. It is a 'hierarchically articulated, etatistic homogenization', and even though it operates to reduce all people to a common life-style it does not overcome the basic division between the decision-makers and the decided-upon (Feher, Heller and Markus, 1983, p. 125).

The most significant effect of alienated labour is the following:

The reduction of everyone to the level of wage-labourers is a result of the planning elite's effort to approach people at their very core: at the level of working activity, at the cross-roads of work time and free time and of the needs originating from and related to both. Only in this way can the overall regulation of a universal system of needs be achieved or, in the terminology of the planning elite, can that society be protected from the dysfunctions typical of capitalism. (Feher, 1978, p. 34)

The reason for this is that 'once human needs are granted *some* freedom of articulation, conflicts and dysfunctions cannot in principle be averted' (Feher, 1978, p. 33, original emphasis). In effect the imperatives of social control dictate that the system of needs for the society as a whole be brought under central control, and this then requires that the labour process, which determines the manner in which needs are fulfilled, be controlled. Thus wage-labour, as a relation of dependency to the state, is a necessary precondition for the regulation of the system of needs.

The second feature of the dictatorship-over-needs model is that, unlike mixed economy capitalism, there is a very marked form of state paternalism.

Paternalism of the state constitutes an essential characteristic of the whole process of social reproduction in these societies and it imposes definite limits over the available means of economic compulsion and therefore over the real power of management within the enterprise – limits unknown in capitalism. (Feher, Heller and Markus, 1983, p. 16)

Thus

Everything that a subject may get (consumer goods, a flat, heating, clothes, theatre tickets, etc.) is 'due to the state'; it is not granted as a right or given in exchange for something else, but provided as an amenity that can be revoked. (Feher, Heller and Markus, 1983, p. 180)

This kind of paternalism does have an important legitimating function, particularly with respect to job security (Feher, Heller and Markus, 1983, p. 76). In order to maintain functional legitimacy in the eyes of its working population, there is little ability to allow the aggregate unemployment characteristic of the West. Thus, paternalistic, employment security is essential to compensate soviet workers for the relative lack of individual freedom they experience *vis-à-vis* capitalist nations, and it provides the state with one demonstrable benefit with which to ideologically assert soviet society's superiority over capitalism. The state does allow some occupational choice and workplace choice but only because it controls labour demand and wage rates, and through its control of education it also controls the long-run supply of labour.

From the Budapest School's perspective soviet paternalism also has a coercive side to it. Rather than simply giving the right to a job, paternalism imposes the legal obligation to work in 'administratively recognized jobs'. Not only does this reduce the independence one could achieve through temporary and part-time employment, but it helps prevent the emergence of alternative life-styles and thus enhances the state's ability to dictate the manner of need fulfilment (Feher, Heller and Markus, 1983, p. 73). Also,

> The more restricted the practical job-opportunities for a definite kind of work … the more this impersonal dependence of the labour force upon the apparatus as monopolistic employer tends to become a personal subjection of the employees to the managers of their concrete workplace. (Feher, Heller and Markus, 1983, p. 73)

Workers in Eastern European societies cannot easily be laid off or fired; however, their appreciation of this is duly captured by their quip that 'everything allowed is compulsory' (Feher, Heller and Markus, 1983, p. 181). Thus everyone is allowed the right to a job because full employment is compulsory and administratively governed. The Budapest School refers to this form of compulsory paternalism as the 'guaranteed society'. It means that 'in exchange for minimum amount of goods ensuring his physical and cultural self-reproduction at a low level, the individual renounces the possibility of social alternatives' (Feher, Heller and Markus, 1983, p. 248).

Thus what the dictatorship over needs has to offer in exchange for needs regulation is a form of minimal material security.

> This is a security of unfree life, or a life without political objectives and activities, a life without genuine culture, a life without the burden of having an opinion of one's own, but

118

undeniably a life not exposed, except at the top, to the risks of competition of losing one's prestige because of incompetence or sheer bad luck in a dynamic and egoistic society, a life which does not demand the unpleasant business of self-governing one's own fate. Therefore, everything people like and dislike in this world, has hardly anything to do with insecurity, and can only be expressed in and through another overriding category: lack of freedom. (Feher and Heller, 1983c, pp. 151–2)

To the extent that the abolition of exploitation and the irrationality of the market are the two major goals sought by the radical elite and used by it to legitimate Jacobinism, they translate into a guarantee by the state that all members will be provided access to employment and minimal consumer goods.

The third feature represents a combination of two related maximization principles that together provide the dynamic element in Eastern European societies. The first maximization principle is the political goal of the ruling elite to maximize social control over the course and direction of soviet social development. It is this goal that makes existing socialism qualitatively different from capitalism. It means that as a 'political society' existing socialism is governed not by an economic logic but by a political logic. The second maximization principle is the maximization of output. Although this is an economic dynamic it is governed ultimately by the first principle of social control. The Budapest School refers to this counterpart of the capitalist profit motive, that is, the 'goal function' of soviet economies, as 'the maximization of the volume of the material means (as use values) under the global disposition of the apparatus of power' (Feher, Heller and Markus, 1983, p. 65). Thus the goal-function is the political goal of maintaining social control, and it is this that is 'governing the economic activities of the state', that is, the output maximization goal.

Although the goal-function implies the attempt by the apparatus of power to maximize the material means for social control, it also seeks to maximize production subject to this principle of social control. Therefore the goal-function

constantly recreates, under conditions of an economic dynamism, the material foundations upon which the monopoly of the apparatus rests in establishing and controlling all relations of social interaction and cooperation within the whole society.

The total system of social domination is not directed here at securing an expanded appropriation of surplus by one class of society, but this appropriation constitutes the only material basis for the expropriation and monopolization (in principle) of all means of socialization and social organization by a single apparatus of power. (Feher, Heller and Markus, 1983, p. 70)

Control over the disposition of the economic surplus becomes a means to the directly political end of maximizing social control in general. In so far as the maximization of social wealth is an energizing principle in the dictatorship-over-needs model, it is therefore subject to the constraint that it must also advance the 'power of disposition of the apparatus over this material wealth' (Feher, Heller and Markus, 1983, p. 243). For the Budapest School, it is not an economic but a political logic that governs soviet society.

The major problem that arises from this type of motive is the lack of incentives to increase productivity. Alienated labour is needed for social control and guaranteed employment is needed for legitimation. Either greater workplace democracy or fear of being fired would provide the necessary incentive, but neither of these is a desirable option for the ruling elite. The state faces the problem of how to increase work effort in the post-Stalinist period of intensive growth when neither the carrot nor the stick is usable. Disciplining workers is difficult because state paternalism assures job security. On the other hand the carrot approach of giving workers (or enterprises) greater autonomy would threaten social control. Ultimately, 'the preferences of the economic policy are dictated not by considerations of profitability, but by the criterion of how far the apparatus of power retains a direct control over the means invested' (Feher, Heller and Markus, 1983, p. 67).

The fourth and final feature states that in the dictatorship-over-needs model what is directly a 'political society' – as a consequence of the elimination of civil society by the state and the abolition of an autonomous economic sphere – becomes, in the absence of political pluralism, a totalitarian society. 'Political society means the identity of the private and public sectors, the identity of man and *citoyen* (or subject), a society where there are no life manifestations outside the state' (Feher, Heller and Markus, 1983, p. 162). Not only is the economic sphere assimilated by the state, but because of the absence of the reifying effects of the autonomous market, the directly political character of these societies requires that the dominant class exercise a much greater degree of ideological control. In other words, unlike the business stratum in capitalist society, the planning elite in the dictatorship-over-needs model cannot rule without governing. Consequently since the economy is directly controlled by political decisions, the 'state can authoritatively define what human needs in general may be and what structure they may assume in order to fulfil the system's goals', and thus 'production is allowed only in order to satisfy those needs that are sanctioned by the state' (Feher, 1978, p. 35). 'Such an economy does not really satisfy needs but confines itself to dominating and guiding them' (Boella, 1979, p. 66).

The Budapest School also argues that soviet societies are totalitarian as well as political in character. In adopting Mussolini's definition of totalitarianism, they suggest that soviet societies are totalitarian in the sense that 'all values are homogenized by the state' (Feher, Heller and Markus, 1983, p. 194), and that 'there is only one system of norms which is recognized as valid' (Feher, Heller and Markus, 1983, p. 205). Thus the ability to totalize social control in the dictatorship-over-needs model is premised upon the state's imposed monopoly on the representation of the interests of any and all social groups.

> Its social domination over the whole society rests upon the fact that no social group outside it [apparatus of power] has either the opportunity or the right to articulate and to attempt to realize its own particular interests either *vis-à-vis* the apparatus itself or in relation to other social groups. (Feher, Heller and Markus, 1983, p. 131)

The state's monopoly on representation is an expression of a 'form of social domination that is not restricted to the sphere of economy proper, but has a universal character and embraces all forms of social interaction' (Feher, Heller and Markus, 1983, p. 70; Markus, 1981, p. 246).

The most blatant manifestation of soviet society's totalitarianism lies in the absence of political pluralism. Vajda has argued that even this travesty of Marx's ethics was inherent in his economistic view of capitalism, which informed the Bolshevik Revolution. If capitalism is essentially private ownership and the plurality of interests that goes with it, and if, additionally, the capitalist state is what balances these interests, then socialism, as the negation of capitalism, really must eliminate political pluralism, in addition to destroying private ownership of the means of production. If the aim of socialism is a society where production does not create any form of social differentiation nor therefore any form of difference of interests between individuals, then under socialism political plurality really must disappear. (Vajda, 1981, p. 100)

What Vajda is referring to is the link between differing economic interests in the economic sphere and political pluralism in the political sphere. Differing economic interests are what necessitate political pluralism. If the Bolsheviks understood that the major differing economic interests in capitalism are those between capitalists and proletarians, and if the political sphere is simply an epiphenomenon of the economic sphere, then by abolishing the primary 'social differentiation' in the economic sphere a plurality of interests would no longer exist in the political sphere. Thus political pluralism, as a by-product of economic differentiation, is no longer necessary in soviet society because there is no longer any 'social differentiation' – economic classes are abolished.

By denying individuals the right to organize themselves into different interest groups and by denying any such groups the opportunity to have their interests heard by the state or present in the process of social decision-making, the ruling elite can dictate the manner of need fulfilment. This is due then to the fact that there is a 'complete lack of a public political arena within these societies' (Feher, Heller and Markus, 1983, p. 111); or as Vajda says, 'In the process, the plan does not recognize existing needs, but rather dictates consumption through authoritarian decisions' (Vajda, 1981, p. 135).

Distribution of Power in the Dictatorship over Needs

According to the Budapest School, the political and totalitarian nature of Eastern European societies creates a pyramidal structure of power. As Heller argues, the negative abolition of private property in the dictatorship over needs does not abolish property itself. Rather it creates a hierarchical or stratified system of social decision-making that has an inherently political basis. Disposition over the allocation of resources and property is hierarchically controlled.

> The abolition of the right to property does not at all mean the abolition of property. Disposition of that sort is, however, attributed now exclusively to political power. It follows that political power will be the only organ of disposition, as a result of which it decides who and to what extent will participate in the enjoyment of property. By this very act the state deprives not only the former private proprietors of their properties, but the whole society of the bare possibility of ownership as well. (Heller, 1978b, p. 879)

On the other hand, the collectivization of property by the state does not mean that the ruling elite owns all the property either. It is a 'bureaucratic structure of domination' (Vajda, 1981, p. 134). In effect, 'society corresponds structurally to an all-encompassing pyramid with stratified, socially indistinguishable layers which represent different levels of political power, depending on the proximity to the peak' (Vajda, 1981, p. 136).

The 'us versus them' aspect of wage-labour, although it is a dichotomy, occurs within the overarching hierarchy of power. At the higher levels of the state bureaucracy, the 'them' refers to the 'self-appointed representatives of the best and real interests of direct producers' (Feher, Heller and Markus, p. 126). At the bottom of the hierarchy, the 'us' refers to those 'who not only have no real chance but also no formal possibility and no right to articulate their own interests ... themselves' (Feher, Heller and Markus, 1983, p. 126). The denial of these rights to the soviet working class suggests that it cannot be considered a Marxian proletariat who, as Polanyi's protective response indicates, exercised these rights through formal democracy. The proletarian in capitalist society has the right to quit a job, to seek employment in different occupations and to struggle for advances and better working conditions. With the universalization of formal democracy the proletarian gained the right to organize and articulate his or her interests. However the soviet wage worker does not have these rights.

Not only is production centralized under state control but all of society becomes subordinated to a single administrative hierarchy in which appeals to scientific rationalization and efficient production serve to legitimate the claims of the planning elite to hierarchical power and status (see Boella, 1979). There has been general confusion and debate in soviet studies regarding the exact nature of the ruling elite, and the Budapest School has addressed this in *Dictatorship over Needs* (Feher, Heller and Markus, 1983). The writers argue that the bureaucracy is not a bureaucracy in the strict Weberian sense because there is no distinction between members who are appointed and those who are elected, yet all members do receive their power from holding office. The ruling elite that the Budapest School considers to be the uppermost strata of the bureaucratic hierarchy does not have the kind of total power that it could exercise if it were the substantive class proprietor of state property, for if so it would be difficult to explain the ruling elite's tolerance for the economic dysfunctions that now exist. There is a 'disproportionality between the economic power exercised by the ruling elite and its capability of actual private appropriation' (Feher, Heller and Markus, 1983, p. 58). Unlike the capitalist, no one as an individual at any level has the actual power to appropriate the economic surplus, which again distinguishes soviet society from capitalism and makes Marx's economic categories analytically ineffective.

However, the ruling elite is the 'only independent decision-making body in this society' and yet it 'exercises its power as a fiduciary of the whole apparatus' (Feher, Heller and Markus, 1983, pp. 59–60). Moreover the activity of bureaucrats is both commanded and commanding simultaneously as a result of the fact that power is unified into one enormous hierarchy (Feher, Heller and Markus, 1983, p. 121).

Top party bureaucrats are the ruling elite, but they are dependent upon the intelligentsia for technical know-how (Tökés, 1979, pp. 166–7). Often, of course, these groups clash over the direction and effectiveness of economic reforms. In general all bureaucrats are presumed to subordinate their goals to the general interests and goals of the state. Loyalty is then a key requisite for office. 'The primacy of the interests of state against all individual interests is the basic requirement which the apparatus makes of all its members, at whatever level of the hierarchy' (Feher, Heller and Markus, 1983, p. 54). At the same time membership is based upon individual achievement. The Budapest School maintains that the bureaucracy is a social group with no real historical counterpart (Feher, Heller and Markus, 1983, p. 118). Its closest analogue might be the ruling groups of traditional societies.

Within this single, all-encompassing hierarchy bureaucrats are aware of themselves as a distinct social group, but generally they do not consider themselves to be in an antagonistic relationship to the working class. They view themselves as representatives of the general interests of the working class – a role that, from their perspective, the working majority may too often fail to appreciate. Likewise in this pyramidal power structure the bureaucracy cannot be considered from a Marxian view as the counterpart of the Western capitalist class because, unlike the soviet bureaucrat, the individual capitalist can act as a capitalist and exercise property rights regardless of his or her relationship to other capitalists. In general 'the whole apparatus of power is unified into one enormous hierarchy' in which the bureaucracy acts as a 'corporate ruling group' with its 'pinnacle' the ruling elite (Feher, Heller and Markus, 1983, pp. 118, 121).

In summary, with no political pluralism, no freedom of contract, no right of representation and few if any civil liberties, the state and ruling apparatus seal their control over the articulation and manner in which needs are fulfilled, and thus their control over the society. In this sense the dictatorship over needs is simply a means to assure control over the direction of society in the absence of autonomous markets. No alternative forms for need articulation can be entertained, no independent forms of interest and need representation can exist, and thus in effect no authentic public sphere exists.

Thus 'the only modes of everyday life tolerated are those that "reflect" the state's prevalent ideological outlook' (Feher, 1978, p. 35). This means that life-styles are administered in order to assure the efficient administration of needs in general. Planning 'amounts to grasping social rationality at the level of the needs of people, to declaring despotically that these needs are non-existent, and to substituting for them the theoretical prescriptions of the planning elite' (Feher, 1978, p. 35). The important point is that with all four features combined, the state is then in an authoritative position to plan and thus dictate needs.

Unlike the situation in capitalist societies, where the autonomous market is an efficient mechanism for articulating at least some needs, in Eastern European states the abolition of the market has meant that the state, in order to ensure social control, has substituted itself for the whole process of need articulation. This is quite evident from the fact that in what Feher refers to as 'authentic' market economies businesses must pay at least minimal attention to consumer preferences, whereas in the dictatorship over needs this is generally not the case.

> The system can function in its undiluted form only so long as it imposes a most drastic dictatorship over needs of the absolute majority of the population: an enforced (through chronic shortages) homogenization of demand at the level of bare subsistence necessities and dire poverty. (Markus, 1981b, p. 252; Feher, Heller and Markus, 1983, p. 98)

What makes soviet society different from capitalism is that the state and ruling apparatus, by claiming all property for the state and utilizing command planning, are in a position to determine which needs will be met or recognized and which ones will be ignored. In capitalism markets act as a mediator between producers and consumers, and although producers may attempt to manipulate consumer demand, they cannot dictate needs in the same way that the soviet state can. In the soviet system production conforms to planners' preferences, not consumers' preferences.

Existing Socialism and Equal Self-Determination

Equal self-determination is the standard of value by which we can measure and compare the capitalist mixed economies of the West with the existing socialism of the East. Measuring against this value-standard, the Budapest School's neo-Marxian view of both societies definitely finds soviet society inferior to capitalism. The basis for this assessment lies in the Budapest School's rejection of Marx's economism, and this itself is fundamental to its neo-Marxism. As Polanyi's analysis concludes, the relationship between the state and civil society in capitalism is not the deterministic one suggested by Marx, but rather one that reveals a pluralism of power obscured by Marx's approach. Moreover the relation of state to civil society is one that contributes to the objective conditions for real individuality and individual freedom. A vital sphere of individual freedom was created by the emergence of a separate, autonomous economic sphere, and it was given legal sanction and protection by formal democracy.

The importance of this sphere of individual freedom in capitalism is also brought to light by the counter-example of soviet societies. The dictatorship over needs, which signifies the neo-Marxian assessment of existing socialism, is the negation of the capitalism that existed in the minds of Marx's Bolshevik disciples. From their perspective Marx's analysis was correct. However, the society they created, by destroying civil society, destroyed the sphere of individual freedom that their Marxian economism failed to reveal. Thus existing socialism as a dictatorship over needs is founded on Marx's misguided notion of capitalism. The basis of individual freedom, necessary for the universalization of Marx's individual rich in needs and perpetuated by capitalism, was abolished by the anti-capitalist revolutions in Eastern Europe. This makes soviet society a 'historical dead-end despite its self-reproductive capacity' (Feher, Heller and Markus, 1983, p. 121). In a zealous effort to end capitalism's market anarchy and its inequality of living standards, these revolutions eclipsed its greatest achievement – the social sanction for the pursuit of individuality. Yet it is the recognition and universalization of individuality that is the foundation for a society compatible with the value of equal self-determination.

Another way to compare the situation of the individual in the East and the West is by examining Polanyi's protective response. As a reaction to the disembedding of the economy from society, the protective response signified the spontaneous reactions of disaffected social groups. In Western Europe in the nineteenth century this process passed through the bourgeois state. These reactions to the destructive tendencies of the self-regulating market economy took place through the state and in the context of formal democracy. Consequently although they did not lead to the reunification of state and civil society or to a fully democratic system of decision-making, they did ameliorate the worst effects of the market while preserving the freedom of the individual. By passing through the state, at the expense of not subordinating profit-making to social needs and democratic control, the protective response also protected the sphere of individual freedom.

Nevertheless, the anti-capitalist revolutions in Eastern Europe were also a type of reaction to the destructive tendencies of the self-regulating market economy. However, they were not spontaneous but consciously designed and informed by Marx's critique of capitalism. To the extent that they can be considered a protective response, they are a protective response that did not pass through the bourgeois state. On the contrary, they are a protective response that both abolished the bourgeois state and re-embedded civil society under a new totalitarian state. Thus the social democratic mixed economy of the West and soviet society of the East are the products of two different forms of the protective response. The protective response in both cases could be considered a 'trend towards repoliticization' of the economy. Accordingly, the self-regulating market tendency and its creation of a separate sphere of civil society depoliticized economic functioning by removing it from political control. The protective response in the West did not completely repoliticize the economy because it did not re-embed the economy. By relying on the formal democracy of the bourgeois state it preserved civil society, individual freedom and capitalism as well. It created a stratified, mixed economy instead. However, according to Vajda (1981, pp. 193–4), 'If the trend towards repoliticization were to emerge as victorious, then capitalism would in fact be abolished. In my opinion that is precisely what has happened in the so-called socialist countries.' In other words, the protective response in the Eastern European nations totally repoliticized the economy and negated not only capitalism but its achievement of individual liberty as well.

What does this imply for the prospect of attaining the realization of equal self-determination and Marx's individual rich in needs? Certainly the protective response in the West, as Polanyi documents, did not go to the root of the problem. It was not radical in this sense because it did not directly address the issue of control over the process of how needs are fulfilled and thus how the self is determined. The effects of the protective response did not eliminate the profit-motivated, market-based need fulfilment that biased the process of need articulation towards the commodity form. It did not prevent the creation of a market economy for the fulfilment of basic needs. It perpetuated a sphere for the individual but did not democratize the decision-making process of need fulfilment, which is itself essential for equal self-determination. However, by retaining a separate economic sphere it prevented need fulfilment from being dictated by the state or by business owners. Businesses can try to influence consumers and their workers; they can subordinate consumers' and workers' needs to those of profit; but with markets as mediators they cannot unilaterally dictate the allocation of resources for specific goods and services. They must still respond to market forces. There is a conspicuous plurality of needs in market economies, indicated by the diversity of life-styles. Thus the plurality of needs broadens the material means for self-determination without, however, necessarily equalizing it.

Nevertheless the revolutions that created existing socialism were radical in the sense that they struck at the root of the problem – the process of need fulfilment. Need articulation and fulfilment are likewise at the root of self-determination. These were revolutions that, in abolishing formal democracy and civil society, placed the state in a position to dictate resource allocation and need articulation. By prohibiting free association and representation of interests, by denying civil liberties, by hierarchically subordinating all economic activity to centralized political authority, the dictatorship over needs neutralizes the individual's ability to express needs other than those sanctioned by the state.

By dictating needs, such a system drastically reduces the medium through which people determine themselves. Self-determination is not only unequal but its range of expression is diminished. Dictatorship over needs destroys the consumer choice and plurality of needs evident in the Western mixed economies. To control the process of need articulation it was necessary to control the individual and the expressions of individualism. According to the Budapest School, the individual within free associations and communities is the 'ultimate instance of need articulation'; for the dictatorship over needs, establishing control here is more important than abolishing markets (Feher, Heller and Markus, 1983, p. 254). Loyalty and obedience are the two supreme and 'all embracing virtues' (Feher, Heller and Markus, 1983, p. 210). Thus the issue is one of control over the individual by the ruling elite.

If needs in capitalism are commodified and conform to profit-oriented criteria, in soviet society needs conform to the 'maximal extension of the material basis of the domination of the apparatus over society' (Feher, Heller and Markus, 1983, p. 89). The dictatorship over needs is more than hostile to the diversity of needs, it is hostile to the idea of individualism itself. It is a 'value degradation, a demolition of the potentially free individual whose voluntary association would form an emancipated society' (Feher, Heller and

Markus, 1983, p. 121). Stated differently, the ruling apparatus of soviet society, in its radical negation of capitalism, has understood that if its overall goal is to retain control over the course of society's development, then it must control the process of human needing that is the source of social development and self-determination (see Feher, Heller and Markus, 1983, pp. 227–8). Ultimately it is unfulfilled needs and desires that determine the path of development of any society, and so for the ruling elite to dictate the direction of social development it must dictate the process of need articulation. By doing so it falls far short of the value-standard of equal self-determination.

The dictatorship over needs 'primarily takes the form not of channelling needs into socio-economically prefigured forms of demand, but rather that of the restriction of the supply itself' (Feher, Heller and Markus, 1983, p. 89). Although the post-Stalinist period has seen some 'relaxation' of this restriction in the extending range of consumer goods, such reforms have not subverted the basic system of needs control. As the Budapest School says of Marx's individual rich in needs: 'It is precisely this man that is being oppressed in Dictatorship Over Needs in a total way. This oppression is, therefore, a radical act and as such, a perverted radicalism for us' (Feher, Heller and Markus, 1983, p. 258). It is radical because dictatorship over needs goes to the root of the problem. It is perverted because individuals are not being enriched and the process itself is undemocratic. The Budapest School suggests that radical transformation of either soviet society or the Western mixed economy must involve democratic control over the process of need articulation itself, because equal self-determination requires equal control over this essential process.

Soviet society in the neo-Marxian view is not only the negative abolition of private property through a perverted radicalism but is ultimately hostile to the whole idea of equal self-determination. Its recognition of equality reduces to the equality of needs themselves, yet equal self-determination requires equal control over the needing process and implies a broadened diversity and plurality of needs. Furthermore,

> since to achieve the reduction of needs the model requires an authoritarian state, over-centralization of redistribution, and the degradation of symmetrical mechanisms, a new inequality

comes to permeate all of social life: i.e., that between those who distribute and those who are distributed. (Feher and Heller, 1977, p. 12)

This is a process that destroys individuality; it is a process of 'totalization' whereby everyone becomes a wage-worker for the state. Their private lives are severely restricted, according to the Budapest School, and their work life is directed by the state. As Heller suggests, it is a system of political despotism (Heller, 1979a, p. 111).

Summary

From a neo-Marxian view, the dictatorship over needs is a result of tossing out the baby with the bath-water. For the Budapest School, the separation of economy from society in capitalism substantially increased the degrees of freedom over previous societies. It created a sphere of civil society that advanced individual freedom. However, soviet society, in its effort to eliminate the inequalities of capitalism, sacrificed much of the freedom of capitalism. The anti-capitalist revolutions in Eastern Europe were premised on the notion that capitalism and bourgeois society were inseparable. Thus eliminating capitalism meant eliminating its civil society. This is a notion derived directly from Marx's economism. In the Bolsheviks' effort to eliminate the material inequalities between capitalists and workers, equality, as the 'main principle of social regulation', created a 'forcible homogenization of needs', and in its tyranny it sacrificed the individual freedom preserved in bourgeois society. The principle of the unlimitedness of the individual, itself a part of bourgeois society, was eliminated along with the inequalities of capitalist living standards.

By arguing that capitalism, civil society and industrialism together compose three *separable* logics of bourgeois society, the Budapest School implicitly makes soviet society into a counter-example illustrating the consequences of a failure to distinguish these three logics. The 'Babeuf option' equates capitalism with civil society, and therefore transcending capitalism's inequality takes precedence over civil society's freedom (which in this view is only bourgeois freedom). This is precisely the option taken in Eastern Europe.

Marx's solution was to put freedom before equality and to obviate the problem of inequalities by technological advance and absolute abundance. The Budapest School argues that absolute abundance with the unlimitedness of equal self-determination is inconceivable; by counter-example the dictatorship over needs indicates the historical degradation of free and equal self-determination. The objective precondition for the universalization of self-determination is that freedom should take precedence over equality and thus a separate sphere of civil society should exist to preserve individual freedom. The equalization of this freedom, moreover, requires that social decision-making should be made as democratic as possible within this context. This is what the Budapest School refers to as radical democracy. It is a context in which 'democratic freedom' is the decision-making principle in allocating finite resources for unlimited individual needs, and one in which relative abundance replaces both relative scarcity and Marx's absolute abundance.

Neither capitalism nor existing socialism are compatible with the value-standard of equal self-determination. Yet the plurality of needs fostered within capitalism's economic sphere has generated a broader range of self-expression and a healthier respect for the 'self'. In neither system is the social process of needing subject to democratic decision-making, and therefore the process of self-determination cannot be said to be equal in either case.

Radical Democracy: The Alternative

Neither freedom nor peace could be institutionalized under that economy, since its purpose was to create profits and welfare, not peace and freedom. They must become chosen aims of the societies towards which we are moving. As to personal liberty, it will exist to the degree in which we will deliberately create new safeguards for its maintenance and, indeed, extension. In an established society, the right to non-conformity must be institutionally protected.

Karl Polanyi

The neo-Marxian analysis of industrial capitalism and existing socialism suggests an alternative model of the social conditions necessary for equal self-determination. The Budapest School's neo-Marxian view of both the social democratic mixed economy and soviet society indicates that neither type of society provides the optimum conditions for the universalization of Marx's individual rich in needs. Both types of society have a stratified system of power over social decision-making processes that prevents equal control by every individual over his or her self-development. Neither society can claim realization of the goal of equal self-determination, and thus, stated differently, neither one has reconciled freedom and democracy. What emerges from the Budapest School's critique of the two societies is that the social democratic mixed economies have far surpassed existing socialism with respect to freedom and democracy, and this is a result primarily of formal democracy and the protection of a separate sphere of civil society. The absorption of civil society by the soviet state and its accompanying totalitarianism represents by counter-example what is not progressive. Soviet society did much to destroy capitalism's individual freedom. The dictatorship-over-needs model substantiates and reinforces the Budapest School's neo-Marxian conclusion that formal democracy and the separation of state and civil society have done more to advance individual freedom than anything prior to or succeeding the Western mixed economies.

Radical democracy, considered here as a model of democratic socialism, is the Budapest School's alternative to soviet society and industrial capitalism. There are limits to what can be achieved by a democratic society, and the radical democracy model acknowledges these limits. It is a realistic alternative because it does not require that all alienation be overcome or that all social conflicts be resolved. It is premised upon the acceptance of material and individual incentives to produce, the significance of religious values in people's lives, the role of the state as a socially necessary coercive force and the fact that individuals' personal and social lives will not always be reconciled.

Radical democracy, in terms of its theoretical derivation, is the radicalization of formal democracy and the mixed economy. It suggests taking formal democracy one step further by democratizing the stratified system of power in the social democratic mixed economy. The most fundamental feature of the radical democracy model is the equal right of participation in social decision-making; it is this right that is essential for equal self-determination. Radical democracy is a neo-Marxian theoretical conception of what a society should consist of if it is to advance individual freedom beyond its present state. Because it is a theoretical derivation, the radical democracy model is schematic and abstract. Following the discussion of the need for a radical democracy, the model is elaborated with respect to four different aspects: the completion of formal democracy, the positive abolition of private property, self-management and the equal recognition of all needs. Additionally, the radical democracy model requires the acceptance by society of some fundamental ethical principles. The ethical principles of a radical democracy are developed in this chapter along with its relationship to democratic socialism.

134

The Need for a Radical Democracy

The Budapest School's analysis of capitalism and soviet society leads to the generalization that both types of society share a similar undemocratic character. Both societies have a stratified system of power and control over social decision-making processes. On the other hand, although they share this similarity there is a fundamental distinction. Capitalism has a separate sphere of civil society guaranteed by its constitutional democracy. It has also a pluralistic state and basic civil liberties that have survived despite their brief eclipse by fascism. The stratified system of power in soviet society is not accompanied by these constituents of individual freedom and a plurality of interests. The Budapest School emphasizes that the ruling elite's direct control over economic activity in soviet society, along with the absence of political pluralism, gives it a totalitarian character unlike the Western mixed economies.

With respect to Marx's concept of the individual rich in needs this comparison implies that capitalism may 'deform' and 'manipulate' need structures, but it has no qualm with enriching needs and may profit from the increased commodification of them. However, soviet society 'delimits and impoverishes' need structures (Feher, Heller and Markus, 1983, pp., 260–1). Consequently, with the existence of civil society in capitalism and its absence in existing socialism, people experience the two systems differently:

> The first and overriding factor is that while the average Western citizen's life is determined by *insecurity* (particularly heightened during the last decade in the face of an ever deepening capitalist depression), the life of the subject of soviet societies is determined by a *total lack of freedom*. (Feher and Heller, 1983c, p. 150, original emphasis)

The disembedded economic sphere in the Western mixed economies has not been subordinated to political control. Although most markets in these economies are not completely self-regulating, the overall functioning is unplanned and undirected. They are subject to the effects of decentralized investment decisions and the business cycle. It is the unplanned nature of the Western macro-economy along with profit-motivated employment that makes insecurity a pervasive experience for much of the population. On the contrary, the centralized regulation of soviet economies and the relative

135

absence of individual freedom makes unfreedom a more widespread experience than insecurity. The purpose of a radical democracy is to provide both security and freedom.

Feher and Heller have also suggested that the two systems can be contrasted with respect to the issue of equality. Because of the unequal distribution of wealth in capitalism, equality is only a 'partial principle' within a 'prevailing inequality' (Feher and Heller, 1977, p. 8). Equality before the law and formalized equal opportunity exist, but the inequality of wealth prevails. By contrast, in existing socialism the state 'confiscates all property' in an effort to eliminate capitalist wealth inequality (Feher and Heller, 1977, p. 10). Equality becomes the 'main principle of social regulation', but it is an equality not of decision-making rights but of material needs (Feher and Heller, 1982a, pp. 25–6). In other words the principle of equality in soviet societies is not one of equal control over the social process of needing but rather the equality of needs themselves. It limits the expression of needs and therefore self-determination as well. The Bolsheviks believed that unequal wealth created the unequal ability to express needs. Those with great wealth could express more needs and express them differently from those without. Therefore the Bolsheviks believed that by dictating needs to such an extent that they would be expressed in much the same manner by most of the population, the problem of wealth inequality would be solved. The soviet system became one that emphasized the equality of needs expression.

The capitalist model of equality allows for a 'plurality of needs' and interests (highly differentiated needs), but the 'despotic model', which tries to equalize needs, then reduces needs to a homogenized and dictated manner of fulfilment. Although there is unequal wealth in capitalism, there is simultaneously a substantial diversity in the expression of needs. The radical intelligentsia that carried out the Bolshevik Revolution and established soviet society in Russia viewed the private nature of capitalist property ownership as the major cause of inequality and therefore abolished private ownership through absorption by the state. This is the negative abolition of private property because it attempts to overcome capitalist wealth inequality by completely eliminating ownership. Thus the principle of equality in soviet society becomes 'despotic' because in its attempt to make everyone the same it destroys differentiation in interests and needs. Unlike capitalism, it is an equality directed at 'sameness'.

Other than the soviet approach, another alternative to the inequality of wealth in capitalism is to retain private property but equalize its distribution such that everyone owns some means of production. Such an alternative, which could be considered a society of shopkeepers, the Budapest School considers unrealistic. The third model suggested by the Budapest School is the positive abolition of private property, or what they refer to as radical democracy. Here the focus on equality shifts to equality of rights in social decision-making. This is the nature of equality as it is suggested in the value-standard of equal self-determination.

The inequality of wealth becomes less significant once the right to participate in social decision-making is made available to everyone. The Budapest School's approach to equality suggests that inequality of wealth in the mixed economies continues to be a serious problem because it means that the richest social groups have greater and more varied opportunities to express their needs. However, the solution is not to equalize the way in which needs are fulfilled but to equalize decision-making power in the social process of need fulfilment. Accordingly some equalization of wealth would facilitate democratic decision-making, but simultaneously reforms that democratized decision-making would undoubtedly lead to more equalization of wealth.

As the Budapest School says of capitalism and existing socialism, with their similar stratified character, 'The majority of individuals do not participate in real decision-making processes in either model' (Feher and Heller, 1977, p. 13). The essence of radical democracy is then to establish the means by which social decision-making is democratized so that each individual has the equal ability and opportunity to develop his or her needs. It is this that is the fundamental parameter for equal self-determination, for in this case the form and manner in which needs are fulfilled would not be 'deformed' or 'delimited' but democratically controlled.

The mixed economies of the West perpetuate both inequality of wealth and inequality of social decision-making ability. However, they also have a high tolerance for diversity and differentiation of needs. Soviet societies attacked the inequality of wealth in capitalism not by equalizing social decision-making but by equalizing needs expression. By doing so it destroyed the mixed economies' tolerance for diversity and differentiation of needs.

A radical democracy, because it is founded on the principle of equal self-determination and richness of needs, tries to preserve the mixed economies' differentiation of needs by democratizing social decision-making opportunities. Radical democracy is equal or democratic decision-making coupled with Polanyi's 'right to non-conformity' (see the epigraph to this chapter). It seeks to preserve the differentiation of needs expression in the Western mixed economies while extending control over this process to everyone on an equal basis. In industrial capitalism self-determination is not equal and is shaped by profit-related criteria, yet the 'self', that is, the individual, obtains a realm of freedom resulting from the separation of economy and polity. Likewise, in existing socialism self-determination is not equalized. However, the 'self' is repressed and the realm of freedom diminished by the dictatorship-over-needs structure. A radical democracy must equalize the ability of individuals to determine themselves without equalizing the individuals – without undemocratically restricting the realm of self-expression and needs.

Four Aspects of Radical Democracy

In the Budapest School's analysis and critique of industrial capitalism and existing socialism it has referred to the alternative of radical democracy in a number of different ways. The four aspects of radical democracy discussed in this section are not components of a radical democracy model; they cannot be considered explicit features of the Budapest School's model. Each of the four aspects represents a different way to conceive of radical democracy. The purpose of examining them as a group, however, is to identify better the meaning of a radical democracy and how it compares with the Western mixed economies and soviet societies. Ultimately an accurate understanding of the radical democracy alternative allows one to develop the necessary and logically consistent reform measures for transforming the Western mixed economies into radical democracies. The final chapter of this study elaborates the necessary and consistent reforms for this purpose.

Democratic decision-making is the unifying theme and common feature of the four aspects of a radical democracy. All four of these interpretations of radical democracy are equivalent ways to explain that a radical democracy creates the right of everyone to participate equally in the processes of social decision-making. The fundamental generalization of the Budapest School's neo-Marxian view of both industrial capitalism and existing socialism is that these societies do not have an equal distribution of power over social decision-making mechanisms. Although they are not the same with respect to the degrees of freedom and democracy they create, neither is fully democratic in social decision-making processes. With respect to decision-making, each of the four aspects of a radical democracy presents a slightly different way to explain how a radical democracy diverges from the Western mixed economies and soviet societies.

The four conceptions of radical democracy discussed by the Budapest School are the completion of formal democracy, the positive abolition of private property, the self-managed society and the equal recognition of all needs. In general the group would argue that no society at this stage of historical development has achieved these aspects. However, this does not mean that their actualization is impossible or must be postponed to an unknown future date. The realizability of these aspects of radical democracy rests on the accuracy of the Budapest School's assessment of industrial capitalism and existing socialism. To the extent that their neo-Marxian view is correct, a radical democracy is achievable and not utopian.

The first way the Budapest School writers have conceived of radical democracy is by stating that it is the completion of formal democracy. They argue that the constitutional democracies of the Western mixed economies are formal in the sense that they do not specify the exact make-up of freedom. Constitutional democracies guarantee certain freedoms, such as freedom of speech and religious preference and the right to own and dispose of one's property. At the same time they do not rule out or prohibit the sanctioning of other possible freedoms, such as the right to participate in decision-making at the workplace or the right to employment. Formal democracy by its nature does not preclude certain reforms that would democratize social decision-making and modify property rights so that more people might participate in decisions about the allocation of society's economic surplus. As Bowles and Gintis (1986) have persuasively suggested, the proper context in which to view formal democracy is that of the discourse of rights. Formal democracy creates a discourse whereby rights can be both extended and reordered by popular will and consensus.

Formal democracy generally means political democracy because it provides all members of society with the freedom to participate in the political sphere of society. Citizens have the right to participate in political decision-making processes, but they do not have the comparable right (beyond voting with their money and their feet) to participate in decision-making processes in the economic sphere. In the economic sphere it is the extent of property ownership that determines whether and how much one can participate in these decisions. Vajda has referred to radical democracy as the 'completing of political democracy', suggesting that the freedom to participate in the political sphere should be extended to the economic sphere. This is generally what is meant by 'industrial democracy' and the extension of this freedom to participate is not precluded by formal democracy. Formal democracy as a legal system provides the foundation for a radical democracy, and is malleable enough that it could not only accommodate but sanction the creation of democratic decision-making in the economic sphere.

Radical democracy gives new content to formal democracy. Feher and Heller (1983b) argue that formal democracy's constitutions are considered 'sound' if they do not specify how the separate economic sphere is to be organized, but merely guarantee constitutional freedoms and political pluralism. Generally constitutions do guarantee the right of property ownership but do not preclude differing forms of property ownership or diverse forms of control and decision-making over the property.

Heller (1979a, p. 110) states that because of the formal character of political democracy a 'socialist realization of the principles of the *Declaration of Independence*' is possible. She goes on to argue that such a realization would have to address the issue of property and what it means to be a 'proprietor' of property. Formal democracies do not rule out the possibility of everyone's becoming proprietors through a process of democratic decision-making in the economic sphere. Essentially being a proprietor means having control over the disposition of property. Thus if sufficient self-management reforms were legislated then one could say that a socialist realization of formal democracy had taken place. In this case formal democracy would have a new content but its basic structure would not have been altered. In effect the right of workers, consumers and communities to decide on economic activities would be given priority over the right of property owners to decide exclusively how their property is disposed.

The right of owners to decide exclusively on the disposal of their property allows them to make decisions that affect the lives of those without property, for example, corporate investment decisions resulting in capital flight. As Vajda (1981, p. 104) says, when property ownership is very unequally distributed this right means that some groups realize their interests 'in such a way that other groups cannot realize their own interests'. This is, as Bowles and Gintis suggest, the exercise of democratically unaccountable power. In the context of formal democracy this means that there is economic power sanctioned by formal democracy that has undemocratic consequences (see Heller, 1978b). Vajda contends that it is not a question of eliminating any particular social group or its interests but only one of eliminating the undemocratic consequences. This can be done by completing formal democracy with reforms that democratize social decision-making. For Heller this simply puts radical democracy 'in the spirit of a democratic *tradition*' (Heller, 1981a, p. 43). The realization of the *Declaration of Independence*, that is, extending democratic decision-making into the economic sphere of the Western mixed economy, is a radical democracy.

The Budapest School's conception of radical democracy shows it to be the positive abolition of private property. Heller (1978b) considers the completion of formal democracy to be consistent with what she means by the positive abolition of private property. By contrast, the dictatorship-over-needs model is the negative abolition of private property because private property was confiscated by the state such that none could exercise proprietary rights. If no one could be a proprietor then all people would be denied 'disposition and enjoyment' of property (Heller, 1979a, p. 111).

The mixed economies of the West have a distribution of private property that allows some to be proprietors at the expense of many who are not. Property has an exclusive character so that one group can pursue its interests while denying this opportunity to others. As the neo-Marxian view of capitalism concludes, the stratified distribution of power over social decision-making results from the unequal distribution of property and the rights it confers.

The Bolsheviks had an economistic view of capitalism, concluding that unequal power was solely the result of unequal property ownership. Therefore they had the state appropriate private property with the understanding that this would obviate its exclusive character in capitalism. However, the negative abolition of private property did not in itself make social decision-making any more democratic. It simply removed the benefits of property proprietorship from the population without giving them a greater say in the disposition of property. Rather than extending proprietorship to everyone by democratizing control over property's use, it nationalized all properties and centralized control in the state bureaucracy.

The positive abolition of private property implies granting proprietorship to everyone not by eliminating private property but by democratizing control over its use. Thus a radical democracy eliminates the 'exclusive character' of property in capitalism without allowing its 'general confiscation' by the state. Private property would no longer be the 'prime civic liberty' because the right to participate in decisions regarding the use of the nation's capital would supersede property rights.

Additionally in capitalism ownership of capital confers the rights to appropriate its return. The Budapest School argues that the positive abolition of private property means that ownership and appropriation would become two separate activities; it implies 'the gradual "emancipation" of appropriation from the domination of ownership' (Feher and Heller, 1977, p. 16). By democratizing social decision-making, especially through forms of worker self-management, collective ownership and co-operative production, ownership and appropriation would become divorced. Thus workers and communities would not need to own capital to make decisions regarding how profits would be produced and allocated.

Ultimately the purpose of a positive abolition of private property is to eliminate the inequalities of decision-making made possible by the unequal distribution of property while simultaneously avoiding the dictatorship over needs that results from state confiscation. For the Budapest School this constitutes 'self-managed society in the sense of the producers' ownership' (Feher and Heller, 1982a, p. 36). Consequently, like the conceptualization of radical democracy as both the completion of formal democracy and the positive abolition of private property, it is also a 'self-managed society'.

Thus the third aspect of radical democracy is that it can be conceived as a self-managed society. Democratizing social decision-making mechanisms would not only extend democracy into the economic sphere and give everyone the right of equal participation in determining the disposition of the society's capital, but it would create a self-managed society. Self-managed society is understood here as a broadened form of the concept of self-management that is usually applied to the workplace.

Self-managed society is essentially another theme used to emphasize the fact that extending property ownership to everyone can only be effectively done by 'universalizing' property through self-management and democratic social decision-making. Since giving every individual equal means of production (on an exclusive basis) is unrealistic for a modern society, every individual can have an equal say in the disposition of the means of production only by creating forms of self-management (see Heller, 1978b and 1981a; Feher and Heller, 1983a). As Heller says,

> Insofar as all members of institutions may equally participate in the determination of the way of functioning, the objectives, and the means of every social institution, then everyone disposes and at the same time takes part in the determination of what (and in what amount) should be turned into direct enjoyment and to what kind of enjoyment. (Heller, 1978b, p. 880)

Thus democratizing social decision-making processes is identical to the creation of a self-managed society. 'This alone would mean a new type of democracy: a combination of the representative system with direct democracy' (Feher and Heller, 1982b, p. 157). The social decision-making processes that would be democratized in a self-managed society would therefore apply to both the political and the economic spheres, to both the state and the market mechanism.

Since a radical democracy is a self-managed society, then both economic and political spheres must be democratic. Therefore political pluralism in the state sphere is very important. Vajda argues that a radical democracy will not transcend 'social differentiation' resulting from the division of labour in production. 'Political pluralism must be present ... because the dynamism of production continually recreates new social differences and social tensions' (Vajda, 1981, p. 101). Conflicts of interest will not be eliminated in a radical democracy, and self-management exclusively in the economic sphere would be insufficient to resolve these conflicts without political pluralism in the political sphere.

The fourth aspect of the radical democracy model is the equal recognition of all needs. A radical democracy is different from both the Western mixed economies and soviet societies because, although it does not claim to 'satisfy' all needs, it does 'recognize' all needs (except those that use other people as a 'means', and these are referred to as 'alienated needs'). In general industrial capitalism is a profit-regulated society in which many needs are ignored and unrecognized because they do not generate profits. Likewise, existing socialism is a dictatorship over needs in which the only needs not ignored or repressed are those sanctioned by the ruling elite. However, to actualize the conditions for Marx's individual rich in needs as well as to be consistent with the standard of equal self-determination, all needs should be equally recognized even if not satisfied. Moreover equal self-determination requires the broadest available expression of needs, as it is needs that constitute the medium in which self-determination occurs.

The Budapest School admits that only with Marx's notion of absolute abundance could all needs be satisfied. Since it rejects this condition as a consequence of the finiteness of non-renewable resources and the recuperative powers of the environment, the Budapest School accepts at least partially the neoclassical economic view that individuals must contend with limited resources and unlimited needs. Therefore 'the promise to *satisfy* all human needs is a false promise' (Heller, 1982d, p. 319, original emphasis). In other words, a radical democracy cannot promise enough abundance to satisfy all needs, as diverse and differentiated as they are, for all people. On the other hand the Budapest School does not unconditionally embrace the concept of relative scarcity either. It would argue that there is a middle ground between relative scarcity and absolute abundance, and this is referred to as relative abundance. A radical democracy can produce relative abundance by creating a sphere of human activity in which all non-alienated needs (needs that do not use others as a 'means') are recognized even though they are not satisfied.

In a radical democracy the democratization of social decision-making processes would allow various groups and individuals to express their desires for production in conformity to their differing needs. In capitalist society the processes of social decision-making are not fully democratic so that the needs of many social groups go unnoticed. The needs for meaningful employment, a sense of participation on the job, retirement security, adequate housing, public goods and numerous other needs are not recognized by profit-led production. Feher and Heller argue that the equal recognition of all needs is a 'radical socialist principle *incompatible* with the liberal tradition' (Feher and Heller, 1982a, p. 39, original emphasis). In a radical democracy democratic decision-making would have the subsequent effect of bringing many new needs to light, and profit-making would have to be subordinated to the priorities established for satisfying these needs.

Democratizing social decision-making processes in the mixed economy would recognize more needs, but a new sphere would have to be created in which public debate would help to clarify diverse needs and prioritize them in the absence of their immediate satisfaction. In both industrial capitalism and existing socialism such a sphere or forum is unnecessary because either the market or command planning acts as a rationing device that recognizes some needs and ignores others.

Feher and Heller maintain that the new public sphere for equal recognition of needs would consist of three features: a public debate about priorities in need satisfaction, a 'collective social conscience' where individuals would no longer accept the satisfaction of their needs if they realized it came at the expense of others' rights, and 'solidly-based individual hopes' for the future satisfiability of unsatisfied needs (Feher and Heller, 1982a, p. 38). Likewise, Vajda argues that such a sphere would emerge from the process of democratizing social decision-making. Democratic decision-making itself will expand opportunities to have needs recognized. What is necessary in this new sphere is a type of 'power structure' that not only 'provides for the articulation of needs for all social groups' but accommodates processes vital for compromise solutions (Vajda, 1981, p. 12). The 'power structure' must be democratic so that no group feels maltreated if it must sacrifice the fulfilment of its needs for the sake of another group.

In summary the four aspects of radical democracy are interrelated. Each one provides a conceptual framework in which radical democracy can be contrasted to the Western mixed economies and soviet societies. The purpose of these themes for the Budapest School is to show how a radical democracy would be an improvement over industrial capitalism and existing socialism. As the completion of formal democracy, radical democracy brings democratic decision-making into the economic sphere of the mixed economies, and this is also the implication of the self-managed society. As the positive abolition of private property, a radical democracy would transcend the 'exclusive character' of capitalist property not by eliminating the private nature of property altogether but by democratizing control over it. As the equal recognition of needs, a radical democracy would nurture the differentiation of needs while simultaneously giving everyone equal rights to express their needs. In general a radical democracy has more in common with the Western mixed economies than with the soviet societies. The Budapest School's neo-Marxism suggests that industrial capitalism is sufficiently consistent with the value of equal self-determination that as a social formation it should not be replaced but democratized.

Ethics in a Radical Democracy

A radical democracy would necessitate the democratization of the Western mixed economies' stratified power structure. Democratizing the stratified distribution of power over social decision-making processes, however, would not put an end to the division of labour, to all forms of alienation, or to all social conflicts. A radical democracy is not the realization of Marx's absolute abundance because it accepts the fact that the potential for richness of needs exceeds the resources available to fulfil them. Thus given the conditions of the right to equal participation in social decision-making and the limitedness of resources, conflicts between competing interests and needs will continue to exist. For the Budapest School social stability can only be achieved in this context if there is public awareness and consensus regarding ethical behaviour.

The demand for equal recognition of needs together with the limited availability of resources therefore creates a major constraint on human freedom. The freedom of a radical democracy is not unlimited, and a population committed to this type of 'democratic freedom' must reach agreement about standards of ethical behaviour. According to Heller:

> The 'liberation of humankind' cannot possibly mean liberation from all kinds of constraints, only from specific kinds of constraints ... it cannot mean liberation from all kinds of authorities, norms and duties, only from specific kinds of external authorities, norms and duties. (Heller, 1982b, p. 369)

She suggests that humankind can be liberated from the political and economic organization of society that 'distributes unequal possibilities for participating in decision-making processes' (Heller, 1982b, p. 369). A radical democracy is a limited form of liberation that, because of the existence of conflicts of interest, requires an ethical foundation.

If there could be the 'simultaneous satisfaction of all human needs' then the 'tensions' of human life would be ended (Heller, 1983a, p. 368). On the other hand, if human needs were arbitrarily dictated or homogenized then the tensions of human life would also be diminished; but such an alternative is a violation of the value of equal self-determination. Thus although 'tensions' or human conflicts would not be eliminated in a radical democracy, 'everyone could equally participate in the process of conflict-solving' (Heller, 1983a, p. 368).

With everyone participating in conflict-solving, the Budapest School argues, there must be a publicly recognized set of 'moral maxims'. The 'moral maxims' provide an ethical foundation for political practice in a radical democracy. 'If there are not commonly held ultimate values accepted as self-evident with a gesture, no value dispute can be settled at all' (Heller, 1981c, p. 255). The three moral maxims of a radical democracy that must be recognized by the population are freedom, justice and an end to suffering. The Budapest School believes that the acceptance of these maxims is not too much to expect from a society. These are values that have been created historically in the evolution of humankind and can be upheld by it (Heller, 1982d, p. 311). They are the basis for an ethics of a radical democracy that Heller admits are Aristotelian (Heller, 1981c, p. 248). A functioning radical democracy must be composed of Aristotle's 'good citizens'. In effect, these moral maxims imply an acceptance of the value-standard of equal self-determination. Freedom and justice together comprise equal self-determination; moreover this value must become a norm for everyday life.

The acceptance of the three moral maxims for ethical behaviour would not eliminate conflict in a radical democracy but would provide social stability. Additionally a strong consensus on the value of freedom, justice and an end to suffering would prescribe specific ethical behaviours that the Budapest School refers to as 'democratic politics'. For example, 'democratic politics' applied to the public sphere of equal need recognition and conflict resolution would necessitate that each individual must act according to rules in which compliance is expected of all people. 'Democratic politics' requires that one assume that all people are capable of making political decisions. One must therefore act so that all people can freely discuss their individual plans. Heller (1981a, p. 45) also suggests that a radical democracy's commitment to ending all human suffering requires that each person support those who suffer most – as long as this does not violate other maxims.

The spirit of radical democracy's ethics is captured by Heller's concept of 'planetarian responsibility'. She maintains that ethical behaviour need not be altruistic. A radical democracy does not require complete selflessness, nor should its ethics demand that self-interest be consistently sacrificed for the general interests of society. It does expect its members to take a broad view of self-interest relative to the classical liberal notion. People must be less myopic and demonstrate a greater willingness to understand how their actions are connected both to the lives of others in remote parts of the world and to the unborn generations of the future. 'Planetarian responsibility' means that people behave responsibly by considering the effect of their actions on others. It also assumes that people are capable of deriving pleasure and meaning from contributing to causes and objectives whose scope exceeds their own personal lives (Heller, 1982d, p. 35). 'Planetarian responsibility' presupposes that people can find satisfaction and reward in helping others, particularly with the knowledge that they do so within a just and democratic system.

The emphasis that the Budapest School writers give to ethical behaviour in a radical democracy results from their judgement that such a society will not obviate constraints on human freedom. They consciously avoid vain hopes and utopian conjectures and choose to be realistic about the forms that human liberation can take. Consequently what they feel can be realized is a system that is more democratic, more just and more free than what currently exists in the Eastern and Western blocs. They regard justice, freedom and democracy as divisible, not absolute, and although these values can be increased by degree in a radical democracy, the need for a social consensus on ethical behaviour will not be eliminated. They suggest that modern societies tackle the problem of ethical consensus directly rather than languish in utopian pipe-dreams about human liberation.

Radical Democracy and Democratic Socialism

Radical democracy owes its inspiration to Marx and should be considered a model of democratic socialism. Heller maintains that Marx never answered the question of *how* everyone would participate in social decision-making processes in a socialist society. 'Marx did not answer this question, because for him it did not arise. For us, however, in our times, it has become perhaps the most decisive question of all' (Heller, 1974b, p. 124). Thus the Budapest School's radical democracy is a theoretical contribution towards answering the question of *how* everyone can make social decisions.

For Marx, if everyone participated equally in social decision-making processes, then such a society would constitute socialism. In the hundred years since Marx's death the word 'socialism' in popular usage has increasingly become identified with soviet societies. Consequently for the most part socialism does not connote equal decision-making and democracy but rather domination and repression. Clearly part of the reason the Budapest School refers to its alternative to industrial capitalism and existing socialism as radical democracy is that the word 'socialism' has been largely discredited in both the East and the West. However, another reason the Budapest School prefers radical democracy as a label for its model is because its theory is rooted in the democratic traditions of capitalism. It shares a greater commonality with capitalism than with existing socialism.

Socialism has come to have many different meanings since Marx's death. This should not be surprising, however, because it had a variety of meanings during Marx's lifetime as well. There are two meanings of the word 'socialism' that are important for understanding the Budapest School's radical democracy. The first is that of equal decision-making; socialism is a democratic society in which all people can participate equally in the decisions that affect their lives. The second meaning is that socialism is the negation of capitalism. Thus, in the Hegelian discourse, *if* capitalism is the negation of humanism, then socialism is the negation of that negation. This is the essential meaning of socialism embraced by the Bolsheviks and orthodox Marxists of the Second International.

According to the Budapest School, subscribing to the first definition of socialism implies that there is nothing socialist about soviet society. However, by the second definition there is.

> As far as we conceive socialism as the negation of capitalism, the socialist character of that conception cannot be denied. However, it is a kind of interpretation of socialism which does not grant either more freedom or more equality; moreover, it deprives people even of formal freedom and equality. (Heller, 1978b, p. 879)

Soviet society, if considered a dictatorship over needs, is a radical step beyond capitalism. By abolishing civil society, by abolishing political democracy, by abolishing private property, soviet society is the negation of capitalism. At the same time it is antithetical to the spirit of the first definition of socialism. It is not more humane, nor is it more democratic than industrial capitalism. Additionally, only by conceiving freedom as indivisible and absolute can one judge capitalism as the negation of humanism. Clearly the preceding analysis suggests that it is not.

Radical democracy is a model of democratic socialism if one adopts the first definition, which states that socialism is equal decision-making. For the Budapest School such a generalization would undoubtedly be acceptable. However, radical democracy cannot be considered as the negation of capitalism. Radical democracy is not socialism by the second definition.

Radical democracy does not negate mixed economy capitalism but democratizes it; it 'completes' or 'realizes' the democratic aspects that capitalism creates. In this respect Polanyi and the Budapest School are again very similar. Polanyi said that socialism

> is merely the continuation of that endeavor to make society a distinctively human relationship of persons which in Western Europe was always associated with Christian traditions. From the point of view of the economic system, it is, on the contrary, a radical departure from the immediate past, insofar as it breaks with the attempt to make private money gains the general incentive to productive activities. (Polanyi, [1944] 1957, p. 234)

Polanyi's view of socialism clearly rejects the idea that it should be the negation of capitalism. Socialism should be a 'continuation' of all past efforts at humanizing society, many of which have occurred within capitalism. Radical democracy should preserve and continue the humanization of capitalism that has evolved in the past century rather than negate capitalism altogether. This is a fundamental conclusion to be drawn from the Budapest School's neo-Marxism. By going beyond Marx it has an appreciation for what has been achieved within industrial capitalism. By going beyond Marxian economism we gain a keener appreciation for the freedom that industrial capitalism has engendered without losing sight of the social injustices it perpetuates.

However, if socialism is equal decision-making then the transformation from mixed economy capitalism to radical democracy not only is marked by 'continuation' but is radical as well. The transition is both radical and reformist. It is radical in that it will redistribute power and democratize the social democratic mixed economy. It is reformist because it bases its democratizing efforts on the democracy that has already been achieved within industrial capitalism. As a model of democratic socialism, radical democracy is not the negation of capitalism but the democratization of its stratified structure of social decision-making.

Radical Democracy and Equal Self-Determination

The purpose of a radical democracy is to provide both the objective preconditions and institutional arrangements consistent with equal self-determination as well as the universalization of Marx's individual rich in needs. The major lesson to be learned from the neo-Marxian analysis of capitalism and existing socialism is that in capitalism there is a pluralism of power and needs largely suppressed in existing socialism. However, the social process that today underlies the self-development of individuals is not completely democratic.

Today's man is 'created' by a certain environment, by a world bent on competition because of the very nature of its economic and social structure in a way varying from culture to culture, by a world in which the striving for minimal investment and maximum 'results' is part of the very essence of the 'functioning' of economy and society, but a world in which a group of

151

men, once again as a consequence of the substance of its economic and social structure, constitutes a means for another group, by a world which is constituted in the clash of particularist interests, and in which 'instrumental aggression' provides the norm even if not always in its most extreme form. (Heller, 1979d, pp. 93–4)

Thus, as Heller describes, capitalism is not characterized by democratic control over social decision-making processes, and therefore it violates the value of equal rights of participation in the social processes that shape individual self-development.

A radical democracy is not the absolute liberation of humankind, but it is realizable. The process of self-development of the individual is a social process, and radical democracy is a theoretical prescription; although it does not end all alienation, all impersonal relations, all conflicts, it does lay the groundwork for democratizing the stratified power relations of both industrial capitalism and existing socialism.

It recognizes no cure-all in the form of ideal institutional configurations and takes into account recurrent inequalities and the constant process of equalizing them in the gradual (and practically infinite) task of achieving equality in decision-making. (Feher and Heller, 1977, p. 26)

A radical democracy liberates humankind from institutional arrangements that constitute one social group to be used as a means for another (for example, the use of labour as a means for the augmenting of profit). By doing so it does not eliminate all conflict but operates to equalize the means by which people determine themselves.

In a radical democracy needs articulation is not politically dictated as in the dictatorship over needs, nor is it subordinated to profit-making where it is commodity based and manipulated as in industrial capitalism. For equal self-determination as well as Marx's individual rich in needs, radical democracy means that all human beings decide as equally free persons the *priorities* of their need satisfaction. Additionally it acknowledges that the equal recognition of needs will exceed the society's ability to satisfy them simultaneously. Therefore it presupposes that priorities of need satisfaction can be established on the basis of a common set of ethical beliefs as well as through open and non-coerced communication between competing social groups (Heller, 1982d, p. 318).

Given that all needs cannot be simultaneously satisfied, then with limited resources only their priorities can be democratically determined. By contrast, prior to capitalism 'need structures were satiable because they were shaped by various particular sets of norms' (Heller, 1983a, p. 369). Needs were limited by custom and tradition. However, the Budapest School chooses to reconcile the limitedness of resources available to fulfil needs with the unlimited character of self-development. Their argument for a new public sphere to debate needs and prioritize them is one effort at reconciliation. Heller also suggests that

> the need for having could become the need for having *something*, the need for power for *something* (to execute a particular assignment), the need for being famous in *something* in harmony with the consensus regarding the quality of the good life. If this were so, limitedness and unlimitedness could be conceived of together since the consensus regarding 'the good life' defines the limits, but the individuals are free to choose and rechoose the forms of living, thereby to opt for unlimitedness. (Heller, 1983a, p. 370, original emphasis)

So long as people understand that resources must be shared among competing uses, and so long as they believe that the system of rationing resources is just and democratic, they will be more likely to give careful consideration to the origin and nature of their needs. By doing so they will be better able to specify the object of their needs and choose the appropriate manner in which they can be fulfilled. Inevitably, the Budapest School's position on limited resources and unlimited needs reduces to its dissatisfaction with the capitalist market model and the soviet planning model as methods of rationing scarce resources. Its neo-Marxian approach suggests that neither are as democratic in the rationing process as a radical democracy.

In summary, the radical democracy alternative is neo-Marxian. It is premised on the knowledge that 'bourgeois society' cannot be completely 'transcended'. It is derived theoretically from the knowledge that formal democracy and capitalism's separate economic sphere have been more valuable in preserving individual freedom than orthodox Marxists have recognized. Its major theme is that capitalism suffers primarily from a lack of democratic decision-making.

This theme is reinforced by the Budapest School's analysis of existing socialism as a dictatorship over needs. The subthemes of the completion of formal democracy, the positive abolition of private property, the recognition of all needs, and self-managed society are simply theoretical means to describe a radical democracy. They are summarized as the liberation of humankind in the following statement by Heller:

> 'The liberation of humankind' can then be interpreted under the guidance of a democratic concept of freedom. 'Free humankind' could simply mean the generalization and radicalization of democracy if freedom were so understood. Humankind would be 'liberated' if freedom were so understood. Humankind would be 'liberated' if every human person had the right and the equal possibility of participating in the decision-making processes affecting the present and the future humankind, under the guidance of certain commonly held norms. (Heller, 1982b, p. 367)

Radical democracy is a theoretical model that is consistent with Polanyi's value of institutionally protecting the right to nonconformity, a right that is violated by soviet society (see the epigraph to this chapter). A radical democracy should not only institutionally protect the right to nonconformity – which to a large extent is already protected in the Western mixed economies – but it should provide everyone with an equal ability to decide on the social conditions that make it possible. Marx's individual rich in needs has needs that are diverse and differentiated, and thus the right to nonconformity is this individual's foundation. Equal self-determination as a value-standard also requires the right to nonconformity in lifestyle, yet simultaneously it requires conformity to itself as an ethical norm. Radical democracy is the institutionalized form that universalization of this norm would create. It is the theoretical reconciliation of equality with freedom. Heller (1984) suggests that philosophy must not only give a norm to the world but must also give a world to the norm – it must make the world a home for humanity. The radical reform of the Western mixed economies explained in the next chapter should be considered as an efort of praxis guided by the principle of making the world a home for humanity.

[6]

Defence of the Mixed Economy

> Socialism is, essentially, the tendency inherent in an industrial civilization to transcend the self-regulating market by consciously subordinating it to a democratic society.
>
> Karl Polanyi

This chapter argues that the neo-Marxian views of industrial capitalism and existing socialism not only lead to the alternative model of radical democracy but, more specifically, demonstrate theoretically the necessity of a mixed economy. The major conclusion to be drawn from the Budapest School's analysis of both Western mixed economies and soviet societies is that to universalize the conditions for equal self-determination radical democracy must take the form of a mixed economy. It must consist of a separate sphere of civil society independent of the state, and it must rely on the use of markets as convenient and efficient means for articulating needs. Thus the defence of the mixed economy derived from the Budapest School's neo-Marxism is premised upon two arguments: (1) the most important feature of the radical democracy model is the separation of state and civil society (that is, a separate economic sphere), and (2) the use of markets is important and efficient for the recognition of all needs in a radical democracy. Radical democracy is a mixed economy.

The radical democracy model is the theoretical alternative to industrial capitalism and existing socialism, but it is an abstract model. The purpose of this chapter is to make the model more concrete by showing that it necessitates a mixed economy in which there is both public and private ownership and planning as well as markets. In other words the constituents of a radical democracy, such as self-management, political pluralism and the recognition of all needs, would take the form of a mixed economy.

Also, with respect to social democratic mixed economies, the neo-Marxian view focuses on the need to democratize their stratified relations of power over social decision-making. Since a radical democracy must take the form of a mixed economy, then the difference between it and the existing Western economies is primarily a matter of extending democratic decision-making, or what Vajda refers to as the completion of political democracy and thus the realization of formal democracy. This implies then the need to transform them from social democratic mixed economies to radical democratic mixed economies. This chapter argues that such a change alters the political framework of the Western mixed economies through a series of radical reforms.

The Budapest School's major contribution is a logically consistent theoretical foundation for a set of reforms. These would be radical in the sense that they would redistribute power by democratizing the social decision-making processes of Western mixed economies. They would be reforms because as policy prescriptions they would be implemented within the existing economic and political context of the mixed economy. The reform character of the policy prescriptions is due to the fact that they occur within formal democracy and within societies in which a separate economic sphere already exists.

The Necessity of Civil Society

An important implication of the neo-Marxian view of industrial capitalism is that 'bourgeois society cannot be transcended' (see Chapter 3). The purpose of this chapter is to develop the Budapest School's theme that there are several distinguishable, yet historical, trends comprising bourgeois society. This model of radical democracy transcends the undemocratic character of capitalist property relations, but it intentionally avoids eliminating other aspects of bourgeois society. Careful consideration of this model suggests that a radical democracy consistent with the value of equal self-determination requires a separate sphere of civil society independent of the state but not subordinating it. Radical democracy is still a form of bourgeois society, in other words, because it retains what the Budapest School considers to be a fundamental aspect of bourgeois society – a separate sphere of civil society. Ultimately the purpose of such a configuration is

> to create such conditions under which individuals (*all* individuals) can equally and effectively participate in decisions determining how to shape the social-institutional framework of their life to live *better*, according to their *own* values and needs. (Markus, 1980a, p. 16, original emphasis)

According to Marx this historical objective of democracy and individual freedom could not be realized as long as a separate sphere of civil society existed outside the state. Thus although

> serious doubts can be raised about the viability of the model of marketless society [the absence of a separate sphere of civil society, that is, a separate economic sphere] one cannot have doubts regarding Marx's desire to foretell the disappearance of market together with the abolition of the state. (Heller, 1982d, p. 287)

Marx envisioned the transcendence of capitalism and civil society and then at some future point the abolition of the state as well. The Budapest School disagrees.

The separate sphere of civil society is a fundamental defining feature of a mixed economy. A mixed economy has both a strong private and a strong public sector, and it is the separate sphere of civil society, that is, the separate economic sphere based on private property and freedom of contract, that provides the foundation for the mixed economy's strong private sector. However, the argument for a separate sphere of civil society is based upon a specific interpretation of the Budapest School's theme that 'bourgeois society cannot be transcended'.

The Budapest School writers argue that bourgeois society, or modernity, is a composite of three simultaneously occurring trends: (1) civil society, (2) capitalism and (3) industrialization. In their view bourgeois society must be considered as an amalgam of all three of these developments. For them it is not simply a society dominated by the bourgeoisie, nor is it simply a society composed of capitalist property relations. Such a reduction of bourgeois society is considered economistic. They do argue that capitalist property relations can and should be transcended, because it is primarily these relations that ground the unequal control over social decision-making in the mixed economies of the West. However, since they maintain that a separate sphere of civil society must be retained in a radical democracy, then one of the key features in their definition of bourgeois society is not transcended. From their perspective, if civil society and capitalism are not *both* transcended, then one cannot say that bourgeois society *in its totality* is transcended.

Marx and the Bolsheviks following his lead did not distinguish between civil society and capitalism, although they did distinguish industrialization from the other two. For them bourgeois society consisted of civil society together with capitalism. Civil society as a sphere of human activity was the foundation of capitalist power and could only exist in its capitalist form. Likewise capitalism could not exist without civil society to ground it. By contrast, they regarded industrialism as separable from both civil society and capitalism and thus able to take other forms, in their case specifically a socialist form. Yet since civil society and capitalism were isomorphic then a civil society that was not capitalist was unimaginable.

The Budapest School maintains that all three trends of bourgeois society are separable; they are distinguishable and thus one can exist without the other. Additionally civil society consists of two dynamics: that of individual freedom and that which preserves and extends the inequalities founded by private property and market relations (Heller, 1982d, p. 284; see also Chapter 3). Given the Budapest School's perspective on bourgeois society one can conclude that there are two ways in which bourgeois society can be transcended. The first is the Bolshevik approach, which resulted in soviet society and the dictatorship over needs. The Bolsheviks, like Marx, equated bourgeois society with capitalism and civil society. In effect they made no practical distinction between bourgeois society, capitalism and civil society. Thus by transcending any one of these they transcended them all. In an effort to abolish the inequalities of capitalism they abolished civil society, and thus in one sense they did transcend bourgeois society. From this point of view it can be said to be a radical act. However, in doing so they destroyed the sphere of individual freedom preserved within a separate civil society. Bouregeois society was transcended at the expense of individual freedom and a totalitarian, politicized society was the result.

The second way to transcend bourgeois society is through Marx's notion of absolute abundance. Marx argued that civil society would have to be abolished to eliminate the inequalities of capitalism; hence individual freedom would not be sacrificed if technology created more than enough goods, services and free time. In the case of the Bolsheviks, bourgeois society was transcended at the cost of individual freedom. In Marx's view, however, bourgeois society could be transcended while retaining individual freedom, but the requisite for doing so would have to be the social condition of absolute abundance.

For the Budapest School the first approach is unacceptable because it violates the conditions for equal self-determination. It sacrifices individual freedom. The second approach would be acceptable, but it is not realizable. This leaves one other alternative: an industrial but non-capitalist civil society separate from the state, which itself continues to have a permanent role in a radical democracy. Thus in order to preserve individual freedom a separate sphere of civil society is necessary while simultaneously eliminating the inequalities of capitalism. Given the value of equal self-determination and the inability to create absolute abundance, the alternative of a radical democracy must include a separate sphere of civil society. Consequently, retaining civil society means that bourgeois society is not completely transcended.

Creating a radical democracy does not mean abolishing civil society but rather democratizing it as much as possible. This is another way to approach the Budapest School's concept of democratic freedom. It is the freedom made possible by providing equal opportunity for participation in social decision-making. It is a more restricted freedom than what Marx's absolute abundance would make possible. On the other hand, measured by degrees, it provides more freedom than both industrial capitalism and existing socialism. Conceptualizing radical democracy in this framework suggests that it is still a type of bourgeois society. However, the three logics of bourgeois society – civil society, industrialism and capitalism – are separable. Therefore radical democracy is an industrial society also composed of a civil society independent of the state. However, it is not a capitalist society. It is bourgeois society without capitalism.

What does it mean to say that capitalism, and thus its inequalities, would be abolished without civil society being abolished, without abolishing capitalism's separate economic sphere? First, most mainstream definitions of capitalism consider it to be an economic system that includes the following features: it is a market economy; the means of production are mostly privately owned; and production is profit motivated. By stating that capitalism is a market economy the definition generally means that most needs are met through the process of exchange. The exchange process therefore includes factor markets whereby labour and capital are exchanged. Those who own no means of production can exchange their labour-power for wages and salaries. It was this relation of wage-labour (between the propertyless proletariat and the capitalists who owned all the means of production) that Marx considered to be the defining feature of capitalism. Additionally most definitions of capitalism consider the use of markets to be such that there is freedom of contract between buyers and sellers. Markets are therefore used to make most of the basic decisions about resource allocation.

Secondly, both Marx and Polanyi realized that the most significant aspect of capitalism is the existence of a labour market in which the livelihood of the majority of the population is dependent upon the sale of its labour-power. Businesses buy labour as a factor of production on the condition that it is profitable. For orthodox Marxists and neo-Marxists like the Budapest School, the condition of wage-labour is one that subordinates the material security of the working population to the profit interests of businesses. It is fundamentally a relation of unequal dependency since those who sell their labour tend to be more dependent on firms than vice versa. (A relation of dependency is not in itself necessarily a relation of undemocratic power or subordination; the labour-market relation is, however, an essentially unequal relation of dependency – a relation of subordination.) A non-capitalist civil society is one where the factor market for labour does not create relations of unequal dependency between employees and the firms' owners and managers. A non-capitalist civil society does not subordinate the material security of the working population to the firms' profit interests, because it democratizes relations between owners, managers and workers. Factor markets will continue to exist in a non-capitalist civil society, but as a result of self-management initiatives and public employment programs they will not create an undemocratic relation of dependency.

On the other hand, the idea of a non-capitalist civil society does not necessitate the elimination of goods markets, the profit-motive, or private property because capitalism can only be said to exist when these features become the generalized, exclusive (primary) principles for allocating resources. These are essentially integrative mechanisms, according to Polany'is terminology; that is, they are mechanisms used to integrate economic functioning with the society. When private property is the primary means for allocating resources, as it is for the most part in the Western mixed economies, then it has an exclusive character and generates inequality (see Heller, 1982d, p. 284). Likewise, when the profit motive is not subordinated to other social purposes or public goals, and when goods and factor markets are not supervised or subjected to social constraints, then under these circumstances unequal distribution of property results in the inequalities of capitalism protested by Marx and the Bolsheviks.

Thus a radical democracy is one where there is a non-capitalist civil society divorced from the state, but where the features of the capitalist system are no longer the primary resource-allocating principles. They have been subordinated to social goals but not eliminated. Although it would retain features of capitalism one could not say that a radical democracy is capitalism. A radical democracy uses reforms to make decision-making more democratic without the complete elimination of the profit motive, factor markets and private property.

For example, Vajda argues that even in a radical democracy aspects of wage-labour will continue to exist. However, wage-labour and capitalist become 'roles' played by the same individual and thus lose their character of exclusiveness. According to him, self-management

> transforms the production unit into the group property of a real collective of producers. But this does not affect the basic capital-labour relationship either. The producing collective confronts each individual member of the collective as a group property-owner confronts wage labour. 'Being a capitalist' and 'being a wage-labourer' are roles that the same individual can 'play' and which, by this token, do not necessarily divide society into opposing groups. (Vajda, 1981, p. 90)

In other words, in the non-capitalist civil society of a radical democracy, factor markets for labour will continue to exist, but workers will have a greater voice in the firm's operation and will

161

democratically decide issues of hiring and firing and work organization. To the extent that they participate in the decision-making processes they play the role of capitalist, but to the extent that they abide by and conform to these decisions they behave as wage-workers.

A non-capitalist civil society is one where markets, the profit-motive and private property continue to be used as economic mechanisms, but they no longer act as the exclusive means for decision-making, because as such these mechanisms perpetuate a stratified system of power. Democratizing the stratified power structure of the Western mixed economies involves a series of reforms that do not eliminate these mechanisms but subordinate them to democratic control.

When the Budapest School writers make the claim that bourgeois society cannot be completely transcended, they establish a defence of the mixed economy. A separate sphere of civil society (a separate economic sphere) would be the most conspicuous feature of a radical democracy together with a state that facilitates the democratization of civil society (the state as an agency of redistribution). Thus a radical democracy is a mixed economy with democratized social decision-making.

Another way to view the difference between a capitalist civil society and that of a radical democracy is that in the former there is a 'primacy of the economic' that in a radical democracy has been subordinated. According to Vajda:

> The question – and it is one of the greatest problems of our age – is whether a society which does not submit to the primacy of the economic, or which at least does not allow the economy to function according to its self-reliant laws, would be capable of guaranteeing the dynamism of the production on the one hand, and the freedom of the individual (at least to the degree that capitalism does) on the other. (Vajda, 1981, p. 34)

For the Budapest School a radical democracy is the answer to Vajda's question. This is what Polanyi meant by saying that socialism involves subordination of the self-regulating market economy to democratic society (see the epigraph to this chapter). A democratized mixed economy that subordinated the capitalist institutions of private property, market-based allocation and the profit motive to social control would 'not submit to the primacy of the economic'. Its civil society would help preserve the 'freedom of the individual' as well. Moreover it should expand freedom by extending the right to participate in decision-making to everyone. Consequently:

> There cannot be *more* freedom than the right and the possibility of equal participation in decision-making processes in terms of the democratic concept of freedom. But there can be considerably less. In terms of the democratic concept of freedom the more everyone has the right and the possibility to participate in every decision-making process, the freer people are. Liberation can thus be conceived as a lengthy process in which everyone has the right and the ever increasing 'equal possibility' for participating. And this is what democratic freedom is all about. (Heller, 1982b, pp. 367–8)

The Budapest School's view of a radical democracy, which by implication necessitates a mixed economy, is consistent with the focus on freedom characteristic of Western mixed economy theorists. For example, as Preston (1982, p. 25) argues, the 'seemingly contradictory ideological aspect of the mixed economy is its dominant concern with freedom. Corresponding to a principle of legitimacy of government intervention is a principle of legitimacy of private economic activity whether it be by firms, or trade unions'. The Budapest School's concept of democratic decision-making is not one that opposes the freedom of private economic activity. It is, however, at odds with the liberal notion of freedom that serves to allow those with the greatest amount of economic resources to assert their interests disproportionately to the rest of the population. 'Democratic freedom', based as it is on the divisibility of freedom, constrains the freedom of private economic activity in an effort to create more freedom through democratic decision-making.

The separate sphere of civil society in a radical democracy preserves private economic power in an effort to preserve individual freedom. This concern of the Budapest School is also consistent with the mixed economy literature. Grossman argues:

> At this stage, it may be worth noting that a 'mixed economy' is often said to serve a political purpose, above and beyond its economic performance. Thus, in a plural society dedicated to democratic values, the diffusion of 'economic power' that goes with the mixed economy acts as a check against any tendencies towards concentration of 'political power' that might subvert the democratic system. (Grossman, 1974, p. 18)

In other words, private economic power in a mixed economy is necessary as a check against state encroachments on individual freedom. This is clearly another conclusion the Budapest School draws from the history of soviet societies.

The checks and balances argument for separate spheres of state and civil society is supported by the experience of soviet societies. The separation of spheres in the Western mixed economies has preserved a pluralism of power that is absent in soviet societies. 'Without a pluralism of power, society becomes unambiguously divided into two parts', that is, into leaders and followers (Vajda, 1981, p. 77). As Heller states, 'All those who want to replace formal democracy with the so-called substantial one and *thereby reunify state and society in a total way, surrender democracy as such*' (Heller, 1978b, p. 868, my emphasis). The implication of her statement is that 'direct democracy' is meaningless when, as in the case of soviet societies, the state swallows civil society. Democracy is necessary to protect divergent but private economic interests, and if the state absorbs the private economic sphere, there is no longer any basis for democracy.

A non-capitalist civil society in a radical democracy does not surrender democracy. It essentially implies the 'development and transformation of civil society' and the mixed economy of the West. A radical democracy then

> means further development and transformation of civil society. Right as a legal category presupposes legal subjects and their autonomous possibilities, the private and public spheres, guaranteed by the state. If the state swallows society, there are no spaces left where these rights could be applied or be realized in any way at all. (Heller, 1978b, p. 871)

Therefore a separate sphere of civil society opens up opportunities and areas in private and public life where rights can be applied. The protection of civil society is consequently a check on state power. This is the point made by the dictatorship over needs.

However, a radical democracy's separate economic sphere would also be a self-managed society.

> *A self-managed society can and should be a civil society at the same time, preserving its priority with regard to the state, a* society in which civil rights are the preconditions of the

164

functioning of the social body itself. (Heller, 1979a, p. 111, my emphasis)

Consequently, not only can the private economic activity carried on in civil society act as a safeguard against encroachments by the state, but it can also be organized democratically. A separate sphere of civil society can be non-capitalist by being self-managed, and thus private economic power does not have to express capitalist relations of production. Private economic activity can mean collective, co-operative and democratic economic activity if firms allow for self-management initiatives.

Vajda has also emphasized the need for civil society as protection against abuses of state power. In Vajda's terms the sphere of civil society and thus the mixed economy provide a middle road or third way between the absolute value of freedom in capitalism and the absolute value of equality in existing socialism. In his view capitalism extolls freedom at the expense of equality, while in existing socialism equality negates freedom. Consequently, a radical democracy means

> the defense of 'bourgeois' concepts of 'equality' and 'brotherhood' (i.e., collectivism) in the face of the one-sided representation of the 'bourgeois' concept of freedom [in capitalism]. And, just as the absolutization of freedom as a value, instead of establishing the values of equality and collectivism in the world, threatens their destruction ... so too the absolutization of the concept equality and collectivism [in soviet society], instead of creating a kind of 'true' freedom in the place of apparent freedom, threatens to destroy the freedom of the individual. (Vajda, 1981, p. 90)

The solution is to find a middle road that harmonizes freedom and equality. One can infer from Vajda that in a radical democracy the separation of state and civil society would provide freedom, and democratized social decision-making would provide equality of participation.

The creation of a non-capitalist civil society as a protection against state power does not mean an insignificant role for the state. Part of the state's role is to guarantee individual freedoms and rights. Thus 'without civil rights of freedom (and first of all the freedom of organization), no social democracy is able to function' (Vajda,

1981, p. 10). Yet as Heller (1979a, p. 112) argues, it is the state's monopoly on the use of force that guarantees rights. If one hypothesizes a stateless society then she concludes that such a society is characterized by a 'homogeneous will' (Heller, 1978b, p. 882). Given the unlimitedness of needs and the goal of recognition of all needs, a society in which everyone agrees to a homogeneous ensemble of needs is unlikely. Thus the state's role is to ensure 'the system of contracts which ensures that the will (and interest) of all has to be taken into consideration' (Heller, 1978b, p. 882). Since a radical democracy nurtures a plurality of needs and diversity of life-styles, the state must serve as a vehicle to protect minority tastes and preferences.

Moreover the state's role in a radical democratic mixed economy is determined by the fact that there can be no absolute freedom because there is no absolute abundance. The radical democratic state will retain the historical function of coercion characteristic of all past states. Nevertheless the state's relation to a non-capitalist civil society is one where it subordinates the institutions of capitalism to democratic decision-making. It neither nationalizes most of the means of production nor eliminates markets but rather becomes the agent of redistribution.

> Thus, the old call for socialization and nationalization reappears within this model. But this call today is not followed by the traditional argument of planning versus anarchy. It is ridiculous to think that the liquidation of the basis for calculation carried out in the elimination of symmetrical market relations would in any way promote the cause of purposive rationality. The development of a broad scale of ownership by groups, communities and the state which makes possible symmetrical market relations creates a situation where the state can and should be the administrative organ of redistribution, while still not extending over all social life. (Feher and Heller, 1977, p. 18)

Furthermore as an agent of redistribution the state does not administer the economy because it is not the owner of all the means of production. This role has the advantage of maintaining greater democratic decision-making. According to Feher and Heller, if the state owns and operates all of the economy, then its monopoly position would undoubtedly create a hierarchical system of decision-making. Without any other alternatives for meeting their needs, people would easily succumb to a state bureaucracy that chose to orchestrate production hierarchically (Feher and Heller, 1983a, p. 229).

Therefore the state's role in relation to a non-capitalist civil society is not one where it socializes all means of production. 'Exaggerated nationalizations without "checks and balances" inevitably leads to tyrannical supremacy of the state over the society' (Feher and Heller, 1982b, p. 155). Mixed forms of ownership are consequently necessary to help prevent a technocratic stratum from monopolizing decision-making processes.

In summary, a radical democracy would be composed of a non-capitalist civil society legally separated from the state. Public policies would subordinate the capitalist institutions of market, profit motive and private property but not civil society as such. Although the Budapest School has not identified these public policies, the radical reforms necessary to create a non-capitalist civil society will subsequently be elaborated. Clearly, mixed forms of ownership would be necessary in this configuration to ensure democratic control over social decision-making processes.

Eliminating the exclusive character of private property involves self-management programmes that partially separate ownership from control. However, there are still beneficial effects of private ownership and non-state collective ownership in which ownership and control are not divorced.

> The positive value of ownership in a socialist [radical democracy] model is based on two factors which have proven to be lasting achievements of mankind transcending the pre-capitalist and capitalist periods: the rational administration of property as the source of the rational satisfaction of needs, and the *direct* relation of decision-making to ownership. (Feher and Heller, 1977, p. 17, original emphasis)

Private ownership and control can be useful and efficient for meeting human needs so long as they do not deprive certain segments of the population from exercising their rights to participate in the decisions that affect their lives.

Ultimately a non-capitalist civil society implies a strong private sector characteristic of the Western mixed economies. However, what is different about radical democracy's civil society is that it is more democratic with respect to social decision-making. The series of reforms subsequently discussed in this chapter would transform the Western mixed economies by extending rights of participation in economic decision-making and by improving access to the means of economic decision-making for disadvantaged social groups. Thus the reforms that would make the mixed economies' civil society more democratic would not eliminate markets, profits, or private property but would ground them in an altered social context.

The Necessity of Markets

Radical democracy is inspired by the value of equal self-determination. It represents the theoretical alternative to both industrial capitalism and existing socialism and as such requires not only a separate sphere of civil society with mixed forms of property ownership, but the use of markets as well. In a radical democracy everyone has equal rights of participation in the social processes that govern individual self-development. Markets are necessary as a means for expressing the pluralism of needs that exists in a society dedicated to individuality, self-expression and self-determination. A basic feature of radical democracy is the democratic process of recognizing all needs (except those that use others as a means), and one convenient mechanism for this process is the use of markets. Radical democracy 'has to promote the pluralism of the forms of life. Human beings can be socially equal only if they are unequal in their tastes, inclinations, desires, talents, and interests' (Heller, 1982d, p. 313). Thus markets can be used to articulate unequal tastes and interests. However, in soviet societies this function of markets has been largely suppressed by central planning. Consequently, as Vajda states,

> the complete elimination of the market mechanism leads to anarchy in production in just the same way as does a totally self-regulating market economy. In the sphere of consumer goods production, it is only by a return to the mechanisms of the market ... to a form of competition among the units of production in which the workers decide what to produce, that the economic needs of society can be met. (Vajda, 1981, p. 126)

Vajda's point is that in soviet societies markets are used to implement decisions, but they are not used to determine decisions about what to produce. Fundamental decisions about the quantity and kind of producer and consumer goods are not made by market forces but by the planning elite. It is planners' preferences, not consumers' and workers' preferences, that determine resource allocation. Once these decisions are made, markets play a limited role in implementing them. Vajda suggests that if consumers' needs are to be articulated and met, then markets should play a greater role in determining the composition of output.

There is another reason for using markets in a radical democracy. Not only are they effective for articulating a diversity of needs, but price-determining markets are a useful mechanism for assessing the scarcity of resources relative to consumers' valuation. The basic feature of the market mechanism is its ability to determine prices that reflect the relative scarcity of resources. This allocative principle of markets is appreciated by the Budapest School, and therefore it suggests that in radical democracy's condition of relative abundance (rather than relative scarcity) scarcity pricing will be necessary as a criterion for efficient allocation. However, the role of scarcity pricing will not be autonomous in a non-capitalist civil society. Markets will be 'critically supervised' and will unite 'calculative rationality' with 'emancipated human relations' (Feher, Heller and Markus, 1983, p. 278). For instance, the allocative role of factor markets will be modified by such reforms as worker self-management initiatives, public employment programmes to ensure full employment, progressive income taxation and job retraining programmes.

In the following statement, Feher and Heller indicate that markets are necessary in a radical democracy. Additionally they suggest that mixed forms of property ownership are an integral part of radical democracy and provide a foundation for market mechanisms. These remarks are an excellent summary of their defence of the mixed economy.

Modern society is a commodity-producing society; thus, the point of departure for a model purporting to be a 'third way' is the recognition of the existence of commodity exchange as an economic necessity. Commodity exchange, i.e., the market, is the only form of symmetrical economic relations in existence. It functions as the basis of calculation for all stable industrialized societies. In a twofold sense: first, it is this basis that provides the terms to assess social wealth. Its rival could only be a system of entirely arbitrary central decisions or a 'simulated market', a totally superfluous detour either to the market or to the above mentioned subjectivistic model. Further, it is the market that allows a society to calculate scarcity and shortages of natural energy sources at a given historical moment and the finiteness of working time available in a concrete social context. This means that it is impossible to abolish property as ownership in a concrete social dimension. All sorts of property can enter into symmetrical market relations: private, exclusively owned property, collective property (owned by a group of stockholders, or a worker-owned factory), nationalized enterprises with independent economic authority, etc. In our model, the predominant place will be occupied by the property held by democratic groups and by state property authorized to take independent economic initiative. (Feher and Heller, 1977, pp. 16–17)

Retaining the use of markets for articulating needs as well as for economic rationality does not mean that markets are completely autonomous or that all of them are self-regulating. The non-capitalist civil society does not abolish either the market or profit motive but, in Polanyi's words, subordinates them to a democratic society (see the epigraph to this chapter). What the Budapest School has learned from Polanyi is that 'the market as such did not emerge with capitalism; capitalism was only unique in that it totalized society under the sign of market relations and subjected the former to the latter' (Feher, Heller and Markus, 1983, p. 278). Thus under capitalism the integrative mechanisms of markets, private property and the profit motive became largely autonomous. Radical democracy re-embeds these mechanisms by subjecting them to democratic processes.

The radical democratic economy uses both planning and markets, each serving a twofold purpose: first, to allow the maximum recognition of diverse needs, and secondly, to facilitate democratic decision-making over the processes of self-development. It means 'not replacing the market by planning, but giving to both these economic mechanisms a changed character and creating a changed interrelation between the two' (Feher, Heller and Markus, 1983, p. 94). The non-capitalist civil society will then change the 'character' of capitalism's economic mechanisms. Transforming the Western mixed economies into radical democracies 'will not destroy markets but ... will overrule the exclusively profit-regulated principles of market economies' (Feher and Heller, 1982a, p. 38). The Budapest School agrees with Polanyi's view that

> the end of market society means in no way the absence of markets. These continue, in various fashions, to ensure the freedom of the consumer, to indicate the shifting of demand, to influence producers' income and to serve as an instrument of accountancy, while ceasing altogether to be an organ of economic self-regulation. (Polanyi, [1944], 1957, p. 253)

What Polanyi means is that there are reforms available that will not destroy capitalist mechanisms but rather will re-embed them by broadening participation in social decision-making.

Recognizing Polanyi's contribution, Feher and Heller state their argument as follows:

> The appropriation process outlined here does not call for the abolition of the market, but the separation of its functions that laissez-faire capitalism sought to homogenize. We have already described the first of these functions (the market as the basis of calculation), its existence is necessary for society's purposive rationality, and it does not make sense to speak either of its expansion or contraction. As to the second function, we agree with Polanyi: the market as a general reference system will gradually recede, the autocracy of 'having' will be abolished, and Marx's great postulate – the subjugation of the economic sphere to the totality of the social life process – will be realized. Equality in this model gradually becomes identical with the equality of decision-making possibilities. (Feher and Heller 1977, p. 22)

In general a radical democracy tries to make social decision-making more democratic and recognizes the pivotal role of mixed ownership and markets in this process. Equality of decision-making is necessary for the free expression of diverse needs, but so are markets and mixed ownership.

Lessons from Soviet Experience

The four features of the Budapest School's model of soviet society provide the basis for a neo-Marxian analysis in which Eastern Europe's numerous problems and crises can be clarified. Additionally such an understanding of their problems lends support to the defence of the mixed economy by demonstrating the consequences of the elimination of civil society and the abolition of market forces. The Budapest School's model reveals three categories of problems for Eastern European societies: (1) economic inefficiency, (2) problems of motivation and (3) problems of legitimation.

With respect to economic inefficiencies, since the Budapest School implicitly accepts much of the neoclassical economic critique of soviet societies, both agree that the allocative function of capitalist markets has been abolished without replacement by comparable allocative principle. Of course according to the Budapest School the reason markets were abolished was to assure social control. In the absence of scarcity pricing the command planning system has been unable to devise a suitable substitute to measure relative costs of resource use. What has replaced scarcity pricing is the system of command planning, where various micro and macro imbalances abound. Hewett has discussed and evaluated these problems, arguing, for example, that investment funding in the Soviet Union is a key macro imbalance. Accordingly in their effort to maximize output Soviet firms desire more investment funds, yet Gosplan has to allocate funds without the benefit of scarcity prices. As a result Gosplan makes seed money available to various enterprises without any assurance of the total amount necessary to complete the projects. Many projects get started but many never get completed and resources are thus wasted. At the micro level, enterprises squander inputs to achieve plan targets, and much of this Hewett traces to the fact that costs of resources are not recognized in the process of output maximization (Hewett, 1984, pp. 8–11). Kornai and the current generation of Hungarian reform economists have consistently argued this position as well (see, for example, Kornai, 1986).

In general, Western Soviet experts like Hewett would be in complete agreement with the Budapest School's assessment of the economic dysfunctions. All would agree that command planning reduces to a process of 'groping in the dark' when applied to the production of diversified consumer goods (Feher, Heller and Markus, 1983, p. 244). Correspondingly, as Hewett (1984, p. 10) comments, 'The only "customers" that count with enterprises are the central authorities that supervise them'. Yet this is a necessity dictated by the need for social control over the population. Without markets, one 'could say that the Soviet leaders want American economic efficiency based on Russian bayonets and widespread KGB bugging technology' (Feher, 1980a, p. 13). In effect, Soviet leaders want efficient production but are unwilling to implement substantive reforms for fear of jeopardizing social control. Without greater incentives from decentralized decision-making, technological innovation is retarded.

According to both the neoclassical and the Budapest schools, the absence of scarcity pricing precipitates economic irrationalities. The Budapest School argues that forms of economic waste such as labour hoarding and enterprise cost-overstatement are integrally related to the problem of shortages of raw materials and other resources resulting from the objective of production maximization (taut planning). As Kornai argues, these are 'shortage economies' because enterprises seek maximum output without being effectively policed by financial accountability and fear of bankruptcy, paternalistic state subsidies protect them from the discipline of market-based profitability (see Kornai, 1986). In other words, scarcity and waste are two sides of the same coin. For instance, the need to fulfil plan targets requires many enterprise managers to hoard valuable inputs like labour. This makes labour a scarce resource, but at the same time it is often wasted because some hoarded labour is not needed for immediate production.

Off-plan allocation among enterprise managers and the significant role of the *tolkachi* in brokering resources between enterprises as well as the vital use of influence peddling attest to the need for these devices to ameliorate the dysfunctions of taut planning (in the absence of scarcity pricing). The Budapest School maintains that many of these economic inefficiencies derive from the third feature of their model – the contradiction between the goal of social control and that of maximizing output. They cite underproduction in agriculture and the 'simultaneous production of waste and scarcity' as examples of 'irrationality' in the Soviet Union (Feher, Heller and Markus, 1983, p. 243). The system attempts to extract maximum effort and production from workers and managers without allowing them greater control. From the Budapest School's perspective, Soviet leaders prefer inefficiency to the erosion of their power and therefore continue on a course devoted to dictating needs.

With respect to problems of motivation (incentive) there are again similarities between the Budapest School and mainstream economic theory, particularly in relation to the link between motivation and the imperatives of intensive economic growth. In Western capitalist economies the lure of economic gain and the threat of job termination or lay-off provide capitalists and workers with a kind of motivation to produce that is absent in soviet societies. Both types of society rely on the use of alienated labour; but without the structural incentives of economic gain and fear of unemployment, the Eastern European economies face a serious motivation crisis.

State paternalism, primarily in the form of employment security, is essential for legitimation reasons but drastically undermines workers' motivation when it occurs under conditions of alienation. The security of employment became an important concession to workers after Stalin's crash industrialization in the 1930s. Since that time the Soviet bureaucracy has used the right to a job as a major means to legitimize existing socialism. In describing themselves as 'workers' states', soviet societies claim that their workers, unlike Western workers, are guaranteed a job. However, when workers are guaranteed a job but have little control over working conditions, they also have little incentive to produce. The Budapest School says the motivation problems show up in 'deliberate slow-downs, absenteeism, maltreatment of machinery, constant infringement of technical regulations and rules of labour discipline, and widespread theft of material and tools' (Feher, Heller and Markus, 1983, p. 127).

Because the first feature of the dictatorship-over-needs model (alienated labour) is necessary for social control and thus the second (state paternalism) for legitimation, the motivation crisis becomes acute when these societies attempt to shift from growth based on further additions of inputs to growth based on increasing productivity. This has become apparent in the post-Stalinist period. Another complicating factor is that the post-Stalinist compromise in the 1950s meant an end to active terrorism and sought greater legitimation through assurances of increased living standards and consumer goods. If intensive growth is stalled as a result of motivation crises then legitimation from the post-Stalinist compromise is also threatened as living standards stagnate.

Although none of the three categories of problems in the Budapest School model can be analysed independently of the others, the crisis of legitimation is probably considered worse than the other two. In societies where the organizing principle is the attempt to homogenize the needs of the vast majority, where there is no 'free social articulation of needs', problems of legitimation are permanent (Feher, Heller and Markus, 1983, pp. 263–5). Part of the reason for this is that soviet societies lack the reifying effects of markets, which in capitalism help to obscure the undemocratic character of decision-making. In soviet societies it becomes easier for citizens to perceive the direct political control exercised by the state bureaucracy because markets do not serve this reifying function. Consequently for the system to appear legitimate to the broad majority of the population the ruling apparatus must continually recreate the conditions for the legitimacy of its power. It must continually take the ideological offensive and find ways to secure the foundations of its rule. It must explain away apparent contradictions between the absence of self-management and the fact that it pronounces the system a workers' state.

To create not only compliance and stability but also motivation, the soviet state cannot rely on police terror but must use ideological hegemony. Crises of legitimation originate in the fact that ideological hegemony is always precarious because the extent of social control is so pervasive. 'The extent of totalization must be controlled again and again and thus reinforced' (Feher, Heller and Markus, 1983, p. 194). There are enough contradictions between everyday reality and the official claims of freedom and democracy that the ruling apparatus must constantly guard against ideological subversion.

As a result one method of legitimating the system has been the allowance for what Feher and Markus call 'fragmented' or 'pseudo' markets. The effort to perfect a system of needs dictation was abandoned with 'war communism'. Since that time there has been some use of markets as a recognition that human needs are diverse and cannot be totally directed. Although fragmented markets play no great allocative role, they do allow the population to spend its income with some discretion. In general, these are 'fragmented markets' because they are used to implement allocative decisions rather than to make them. For the sake of legitimation the use of fragmented markets was therefore a major concession to the people and an acknowledgement that markets are a significant vehicle for articulating needs (see Feher, Heller and Markus, 1983, p. 265–71; see also Feher, 1978).

The Budapest School argues that the 'struggle for markets' is a progressive struggle and that the major expression of future crises of Eastern European nations will be related to the problems of the market. *The struggle for markets 'can reconquer virtues which are not spectacular historical novelties but indispensable for a rational conduct of life'* (Feher, Heller and Markus, 1983, p. 278, my emphasis). One virtue the Budapest School believes must be reconquered in Eastern Europe is the appreciation for the 'critical human mind' (Feher, Heller and Markus, 1983, p. 244). The struggle for markets is a struggle for greater self-expression, which brings with it the desire for autonomy and the willingness to criticize. However, so long as needs are dictated by a paternalistic system of alienated labour and political command, the system will continue to face problems of motivation, legitimation and economic inefficiency. The issue of marketizing reforms becomes pivotal here because it is the only outlet whereby direct producers can establish and expand an enclave of free space for the articulation of their needs.

The Budapest School argues that marketizing reforms can be progressive because they tend to subvert political authority and social control by allowing new forms of need articulation, as well as by engendering the demand for some civil liberties, freedom of contract and the right to organize for interest representation. Thus for the Budapest School there is an integral relationship between need articulation via the markets of Western economies and the existence of formalized civil liberties. Markets as an allocative mechanism express and allow for a greater degree of interest conflict and competition, and consequently a greater reliance on their use in soviet societies would tend to create demands and concessions for the right to organize for interest representation and freedom of contract. In other words, not only would the greater use of allocative markets be subversive because of the decentralization of need articulation, but moreover it would tend to create a context in which deference to some civil liberties now denied Eastern European populations would become necessary.

In the view of the Budapest School soviet societies only function fairly effectively in sectors like defence spending and capital goods. These industries are extensive-growth oriented and therefore need

scarcely attend to consumer preferences and demand. The ramifications of consumer needs dictation is less problematic. Even though
the rate of return would be higher in the consumer goods sector, the
planning elite invests in capital goods because control can be better
maintained there and because this sector is suited to extensive
growth, where the parameter of labour motivation is less significant
(see Markus, 1982). To legitimize their rule in the eyes of the
working population, the ruling elite needs to foster intensive
growth, a higher living standard and more diversified consumer
goods, but they are handicapped by motivation problems. The
motivation problems as well as the economic inefficiencies could be
overcome by significant marketizing reforms. These by their very
nature would not only redirect resources towards more consumer
goods but would lead to greater worker and consumer
independence.

> What is effectively accumulated outside the domain over which
> the apparatus can directly dispose, does not count as an element
> of national wealth, but constitutes a threat to the latter, because
> it can confer a degree of economic independence upon those
> who own it formally or practically. And this threat, unlike that
> of the rebirth of capitalism, is a real one. (Feher, Heller and
> Markus, 1983, pp. 67–8)

The practical relevance of marketizing reforms is not that they may
threaten the rebirth of capitalism. The soviet ruling elite resists such
reforms because they may erode social control by precipitating
greater autonomy of workers and enterprises and may lead to forms
of opposition that the state is unable to manage.

Historically such threats became manifest with the 1956 Hungarian Revolution, the 1968 Prague Spring and Polish Solidarity in
1980. Soviet societies have abolished both markets and a separate
economic sphere. 'If our yardsticks are, then, individual freedom
and the collective emancipation of labour, historical regression here
can hardly be denied' (Feher, Heller and Markus, 1983, p. 250).
Consequently, the realization of equal self-determination then not
only would solve the problem of alienated labour characteristic of
both capitalism and soviet societies, but would establish mechanisms of both markets and planning that are consonant with the
democratic articulation of the manner in which individual needs are
fulfilled. If in the dictatorship-over-needs model needs are dictated,

in capitalism they are none the less shaped and moulded by corporate interests. In neither system are they democratically determined, and thus in neither one can equal self-determination be said to exist.

Democratizing the Western Mixed Economies

A radical democracy, for the Budapest School, is the third way. It is theoretically derived from its neo-Marxian analysis of both Western capitalism and existing socialism. However, the Budapest School has not specified in any detail what policy reforms would be necessary in the Western mixed economies to transform them into radical democracies. Their model is highly schematic. The features of a radical democracy, including self-management, political pluralism, the recognition of all needs, mixed ownership forms and the use of markets, are derived ultimately from the objective of democratizing social decision-making processes in both Western capitalism and existing socialism. The right of equal participation in the processes of social decision-making is the overriding concern that governs the types of reform necessary to create a radical democracy from the Western mixed economies. The Budapest School's radical democracy necessitates a mixed economy, and consequently for the model to have practical relevance in the West there must be a consistent set of reforms that, if implemented, would convert the social democratic mixed economies into radical democratic mixed economies. Such a set of reforms would therefore create the means for democratizing the stratified distribution of control over social decision-making mechanisms now characteristic of the Western mixed economies.

Stated differently, democratizing the stratified Western mixed economies means creating a non-capitalist civil society in tandem with a democratic state through a series of what could be called radical reforms. The purpose of radical reforms is to democratize the unequal distribution of power over social decision-making processes that results from the unequal distribution of the mixed economies' resources. Democratizing the mixed economies through a series of radical reforms is then what is meant by the Budapest School's themes of radical democracy, that is, the positive abolition of private property, the realization of the principles of formal democracy, the completion of political democracy, democratic freedom, relative abundance and self-managed society.

Radical reforms would be radical in the sense that they would fundamentally redistribute power in the Western mixed economies. As the neo-Marxian views suggests, the protective response prevented capitalism from becoming the dichotomized class society anticipated by Marx. It did not democratize the mixed economy but rather created a stratified distribution of power over social decision-making. This political configuration has been largely unaltered throughout the last century despite the diversity of significant reforms that have been implemented by social democracy and the welfare state. It is this fundamental redistribution of social decision-making power that makes the radical democracy model 'radical'. On the other hand, the conversion from social democratic to radical democratic mixed economy is reform oriented, because the policies necessary to democratize social decision-making would be implemented within the given context of political democracy and mixed economy.

Each reform by itself would not be sufficient to redistribute power. The radical nature of the reforms would only result if the policy changes were implemented in a programmatic fashion. In other words, with a programmatic set of reforms the combined effect would be to democratize social decision-making and transform social democracy and the welfare state into a radical democracy. The reforms would become radical only when combined into a comprehensive agenda for democratization.

Also, since the Budapest School has not attempted to specify any such reforms, one must extrapolate from the abstract features of a radical democracy. It is in this process of deriving the reform programme that one can begin to see a convergence between the Budapest School's speculative philosophy and its theoretical contribution to the mixed economy and the more pragmatic and political contribution characteristic of Western theorists of the mixed economy. The Western literature has a long and vivid history of policy suggestions and reform measures, all intended to create a more democratic capitalism. For the United States, one can find programmatic reforms with a radical character at least as early as the Populist Movement in the 1890s and continuing through the Progressive Era and into the New deal of the 1930s. The issue of democracy has been a major theme of reform movements in the

Western nations. Particularly in the United States, where explicitly socialist movements have been marginalized and have never had a viable popular constituency or organizational base, the appeal to democracy has been the only basis around which progressive movements for reform have been able to organize and gain an audience.

In the recent literature of the Western left there are numerous excellent proposals whose call for programmatic reform of the mixed economy exemplifies and illustrates the radical reforms implicit in the Budapest School's model of radical democracy. Many of these proposals advocate a series of reforms that together would redistribute power and democratize the Western mixed economies. The major themes of a radical democracy stressed by the Budapest School are the completion of political democracy, the positive abolition of private property, self-managed society and the equal recognition of all needs. The reforms suggested by these proposals are consistent with each of the Budapest School's themes. They represent logically consistent expressions of these themes and would therefore, for example, bring political democracy to completion and create a self-managed society. In general one cannot know what a self-managed society means in concrete terms or what the positive abolition of private property means unless the policy prescriptions for these purposes are specified.

For example, we can show that the common set of radical reforms identified in Furniss and Tilton (1977), Bowles, Gordon and Weisskopf (1983), and Carnoy and Shearer (1980) would transform the social democratic mixed economies into radical democratic mixed economies and would be logically consistent and compatible with the theoretical framework of the Budapest School. Therefore what the Budapest School has provided is a neo-Marxian theoretical foundation to support the call for radical reforms advanced in each of these proposals.

Drawing on Polanyi, Furniss and Tilton argue that the welfare state is the product of problems with unregulated markets and property. In effect, like Polanyi and the Budapest School, Furniss and Tilton maintain that the mixed economy is a by-product of the protective response. Furthermore, the welfare state, much maligned by both the left and the right, has no positive theory to ground its spontaneous and organic reactions to the destructive effects of self-regulating markets. 'The welfare state has yet to develop a single

180

coherent and compelling theory to guide its political practice'
(Furniss and Tilton, 1977, p. 24). In many respects it is the Budapest
School's neo-Marxian view of industrial capitalism and existing
socialism that provides a positive theory of the welfare state. Like
the Budapest School, Furniss and Tilton ground their justification of
reforms on the value of equal control over individual self-development, that is, equal self-determination. Thus the stated leading
values are equality, freedom, democracy, solidarity, security and
economic efficiency (Furniss and Tilton, 1977, p. 38).

Instead of radical democracy, the Furniss and Tilton model is
labelled the 'social welfare state', implying that the specified reforms
would actualize such a model by democratizing economic life in the
mixed economies (Furniss and Tilton, 1977, pp. 45–7). Also like the
Budapest School, they suggest that such reforms can be radical but
not revolutionary: 'The social-welfare statist strategy is not a
revolutionary one, but relies primarily on nonviolent and parliamentary means' (Furniss and Tilton, 1977, p. 47). Sweden is a
pioneer in the implementation of many of the suggested reforms,
and although Sweden is not a fully democratic social welfare state, it
has gone further than any of the other mixed economies towards this
goal.

Furniss and Tilton's list of reform proposals entails the following
nine items: (1) maximalist full employment policies, including
government commitment to unemployment rates no higher than 2
per cent and labour market policies for job retraining; (2) a national
health service; (3) housing allowances; (4) a public pension system;
(5) a guaranteed annual income; (6) progressive taxation of income
and capital, including a lowering of corporate taxation; (7) community planning and land-use regulation; (8) termination of capitalist hegemony in the cultural sphere, including 'greater public scru-
tiny and direction of large investment decisions and the elimination
of commercial advertising on radio and television'; and (9)
expanded opportunities for public participation in politics, which
would include policies to support self-management initiatives as
well as those that broaden access to public policy-making (Furniss
and Tilton, 1977, pp. 184–205). In general, the reform proposals
seek

> greater public influence over investment decisions by a variety
> of means: increased public investment, state investment banks,

investment of public pension funds according to publicly determined criteria, experiments with novel forms of public ownership, placement of public representatives on corporate boards of directors, and restrictions on private advertising. At the level of the individual firm the social welfare state promotes experiments in industrial democracy that will secure workers' participation in the determination of their working conditions. (Furniss and Tilton, 1977, pp. 45–6)

Bowles, Gordon and Weisskopf take a somewhat different approach from Furniss and Tilton's in justifying their case for reforms, but the reforms they advocate are essentially the same. They maintain that the secular decline in US prosperity since the Second World War is ultimately traceable to the undemocratic character of the society's social relations. This explanation is compatible with the neo-Marxian view that the mixed economy is characterized by stratified power over social decision-making processes. Rather than calling for socialism, the authors suggest the need for 'democratic economics' and thus a series of radical reforms. The Budapest School's democratic economics is the policy counterpart to its radical democracy. 'A more democratic and egalitarian economy has promise because people want it, and it costs less to put people in charge than it does to keep them down' (Bowles, Gordon and Weisskopf, 1983, p. 262). Consequently radical reforms would not only create a non-capitalist civil society, but would reduce economic waste and improve productivity and efficiency.

Democratic economics involves a fundamental change in the 'rules' typical of the Western mixed economies. Instead of profit-led growth, it suggests wage-led growth; instead of exclusively relying on market-based allocation, it advocates a substantial role for needs-based allocation; and instead of a foreign and defence policy premised on militarization, it suggests 'cooperation for economic security' (Bowles, Gordon and Weisskopf, 1983, pp. 268–9). A change in the 'rules' of capitalist society implies that capitalism's economic mechanisms of profit motive, private property and markets are re-embedded in a new type of civil society.

The set of reform prescriptions Bowles, Gordon and Weisskopf designed to achieve the democratization of the US economy is summarized in an 'economic bill of rights' composed of twenty-four specific rights. The twenty-four rights are combined into four categories. The first category is the right to economic security and equity and includes full-employment legislation whereby 'the federal government should make funds available to local governments to finance guaranteed public employment' whenever a community's unemployment rate exceeds 2 per cent (Bowles, Gordon and Weisskopf, 1983, p. 277). Local governments would administer these programmes, directing them 'toward projects recommended by community planning boards' (Bowles, Gordon and Weisskopf, 1983, p. 277). Again the Swedish experience is offered as a reasonably good example of public policy for full employment. The use of 'solidarity wage policies' (based again on the Swedish experience) is suggested; wage negotiations between labour and management would seek to raise low wage-rates more rapidly than high wage-rates. Additionally the government would raise the minimum wage-rate to make it equivalent to the US Bureau of Labor Statistics' 'lower budget standard' (roughly $6.50 per hour) and support equal pay for comparable worth.

The first category of the right to economic security and equity would also include an expanded programme of public child care and community service centres, amendment of the Fair Labor Standards Act to prohibit compulsory overtime and gradual reduction in the standard work-week, and passage of congressional legislation to prohibit mandatory retirement. Also it includes a system of tax-based flexible price controls for corporations.

> If a firm's unit price had increased at an annual rate of more than two percent in the previous quarter, the price agency would automatically assess a supplementary 'price-stability excise tax' equal to fifty percent of the 'excess price increase'. (Bowles, Gordon and Weisskopf, 1983, p. 298)

Such a price control system would not include wages and would apply to the majority of US output while limiting its effect to a minority of producers.

The second category is the right to a democratic workplace and includes reforms that would help establish what the Budapest School means by self-management. This would involve repeal of the Taft-Hartley Act and passage of the Labor Law Reform Act of 1978, establishment of a Union Organizing Campaign Fund through a voluntary tax check-off system, and amendment of Landrum-Griffin to require rank-and-file ratification of all union contracts. It would also require Congress to pass a Corporate Disclosure Act so that workers' right to know about their companies would be protected. Also a 'Bargaining Rights clause which would sanction and legally protect workers' bargaining over job design, investment, and all other issues concerning the organization of production' should be added to the National Labor Relations Act (Bowles, Gordon and Weisskopf, 1983, p. 313). Additionally, as with the Swedish Meidner Plan, unions and workers should 'promote collective profit-sharing agreements' and federal legislation should be passed to support such initiatives. At the workplace there is a need to support the formation of autonomous 'worker production committees' similar to the factory councils originating in Europe at the turn of the century. Lastly, democratically run community enterprises should be fostered by subsidized loans from union pension funds and community investment boards. The essential premiss is that 'worker commitment is key to workplace productivity' and the key to worker commitment is a sense of participation and control in workplace decision-making (Bowles, Gordon and Weisskopf, 1983, p. 321).

The third category is the individual's right to participate in public policy formation geared to long-term development. This would involve the creation of a Public Planning Administration utilizing a 'needs inventory' prepared by the Census Bureau. An annual needs survey would be conducted summarizing 'the most urgent social needs and [would] rank those needs by kind and intensity of popular expression' (Bowles, Gordon and Weisskopf, 1983, p. 327). The Public Planning Administration would target production using a system similar to French and Swedish indicative planning and would

> provide investment subsidies to private firms, unions, community investment boards, and other democratically controlled investment institutions in order to encourage investment in sectors whose increased output seemed of the highest public priority. (Bowles, Gordon and Weisskopf, 1983, pp. 327–8).

In an effort to democratize investment decisions 'all banks and insurance companies should be publicly controlled', with democratically elected community investment boards helping to determine investment from insurance funds and personal savings deposits. Also unions should democratically elect their own boards to oversee the investment of their pension funds. Within the third category of rights the authors suggest that the Federal Reserve Board should be elected by the House of Representatives in an effort to make its decision-making more democratic. Plant-closing legislation should be enacted as well, thus giving communities greater control over corporate decision-making. To protect the environment Congress should

> pass a community right-to-know law requiring businesses operating in a locality or transshipping goods to make available full information on the chemical and other relevant properties of potentially hazardous substances which they use or transport. (Bowles, Gordon and Weisskopf, 1983, p. 345)

The reforms in the third category are specifically intended to broaden access to decisions that determine the nation's priorities for growth and development. For example, the proposed Public Planning Administration would respond to popular social needs that are often ignored by profit-led growth. Such a proposal would not supplant the private sector but would strengthen the public sector with the overall effect of broadening social decision-making.

The last category is the right to a better way of life and includes a whole host of reforms from reduced military spending to tax reform and national health care. Many of these policy prescriptions would simply advance the social programmes of the welfare state. They argue, for example, that military production should be socialized to reduce cost overruns and increase accountability, that a National Public Energy Corporation should be created to extract and produce non-renewable energy supplies and to promote renewable energy sources, that the Dellums National Health Service Act should be passed in Congress, that government payments for home child care should be made to single-parent households and that an excise tax on advertising should be established. Finally, under the fourth category of rights a federal tax reform package is advocated that would eliminate the corporate income tax, propose one rate on all wage and salary income up to $50,000, add a slightly higher rate on income over $50,000, provide an exemption of $5,000 per household member, eliminate all deductions except state and local taxes, and tax property income at a rate double that for incomes below $50,000. The tax reform proposal would simplify the federal tax structure while simultaneously making it more progressive.

In summary, the four categories in the economic bill of rights require a programmatic set of reforms that together are intended to make social decision-making democratic. None involves political revolution or an end to the mixed economy and the regular use of markets, yet as a whole they would create a non-capitalist civil society. The 'Economic Bill of Rights *holds together as a whole*. It is internally consistent in that its proposals are mutually reinforcing' (Bowles, Gordon and Weisskopf, 1983, p. 381, original emphasis). Thus as a whole these reforms are radical because they redistribute power over social decision-making and provide the basis for a radical democratic mixed economy.

Carnoy and Shearer's argument implicitly accepts the neo-Marxian approach of the Budapest School. The problem as they perceive it is how to transform the Western mixed economies into ones more democratic in character. 'The essence of such a transformation is economic democracy – the transfer of economic decision-making from the few to the many' (Carnoy and Shearer, 1980, p. 3). In other words, the objective of the transformation, as the Budapest School's approach suggests, is to democratize the stratified system of power in the mixed economies of the West. Rather than discussing such a transformation by referring to the necessity for radical reforms, Gorz's comparable terminology is used:

> Suffice it to say that we believe that, under certain political circumstances, it is possible in a politically democratic country like the United States to win significant structural changes in capitalist society – what French sociologist André Gorz calls nonreformist reforms – changes that substantially add to the democratic rights and power of 'average' citizens in their daily lives as workers and consumers. (Carnoy and Shearer, 1980, p. 18)

Radical reforms are therefore synonymous with non-reformist reforms, and for Carnoy and Shearer such reforms redistribute power but leave the mixed economy intact. The following statement is clearly suggestive of the Budapest School:

> What is important in economics is *control* as well as ownership. To the extent that public ownership is now advocated in Western economies, it is often presented as social ownership – that is, the owner is not always the state, but can be the workers

themselves, the community, the city or region, or a combination of public and private owners. In this view, a variety of ownership patterns in states and cities would be balanced by public control and guidance at the national level. Accountability and participation would be built into the system for all enterprises no matter what their form of ownership, and certain permissible standards of economic behavior would be set. Both plan and market would function. (Carnoy and Shearer, 1980, p. 36, original emphasis)

With this in mind, Carnoy and Shearer (1980, p. 80) advocate the creation of a new government holding company that would purchase sufficient stock shares in at least one major firm in all major oligopolistic industries to enable it to pursue 'proconsumer commercial practices and, through competitive pressure', to induce the remaining firms to follow their lead. The holding company would 'help finance and encourage new public enterprises at the municipal, state, and regional levels' and 'serve as a source of financial support and consulting talent for major experiments in worker-owned and worker/community-owned enterprises' (Carnoy and Shearer, 1980, p. 81). Also, like much of the radical reform literature, there is a proposal for a public energy corporation to foster alternative energy development.

Like the Budapest School's model of radical democracy, based as it is on the negative aspects of state ownership in existing socialism, Carnoy and Shearer state that

what we are seeking, over the long run, is not greater government ownership of the economy, but *greater democratization of economic decision-making.* Public enterprise is only a means to that end, not an end in itself. (Carnoy and Shearer, 1980, p. 85, my emphasis)

Consequently the intention of the reforms is not to transcend capitalism by absorbing its civil society into the state but to democratize its stratified distribution of power over social decision-making. Carnoy and Shearer, like the Budapest School, adopt a neo-Marxian view of the Western mixed economies by rejecting the idea that property ownership in the economic base is the exclusive source of power.

Another set of non-reformist reforms are those intended to democratize investment decisions. These would include 'the creation, from both private and public employee funds, of city – and state – owned banks staffed with trust departments competent to handle large pension fund accounts' (Carnoy and Shearer, 1980, p. 124). Also, the labour movement should establish a national advisory service to help unions use their pension funds for investments controlled by them. Additionally the federal government should purchase a healthy national bank holding company and operate it 'competitively' in the capital market. These reforms would have the effect of reducing the degree to which investment spending conforms to corporate priorities. They would allow greater public input into investment decision-making.

The next set of reforms involve democratizing the workplace and are similar to those in the second category of rights mentioned by Bowles, Gordon and Weisskopf. Citing examples of successful worker-controlled enterprises such as some of the worker-owned plywood mills in the United States, the Mondragon co-operatives in Spain and the Meriden Co-operative in Britain, Carnoy and Shearer advocate

> development of public financing for cooperatives through public banks that can use pension funds for job creation and preservation, and through direct government loans to hard-pressed industries reorganizing under worker controlled production. (Carnoy and Shearer, 1980, p. 192)

Another democratizing reform would be passage of legislation fostering experiments in workplace participation, for example, the Kennedy-sponsored Worker Alienation Research and Training Act of 1972.

Finally steps must be taken to control large corporations more directly. Again, as many activists have recognized, we can look to Sweden as a pioneer in this process. Carnoy and Shearer say that 'of all of the countries in Western Europe, Sweden has made the greatest progress in legislation to increase workers' control, both at the workplace and in broader corporate decision making' (Carnoy and Shearer, 1980, p. 261). Sweden has several pieces of legislation, such as the 1976 co-determination bill, that foster greater democratic control over corporate decision-making Carnoy and Shearer state:

> In a democratic economy, planning would not replace market relationships in *all* aspects of society. Currently, the United

States is a mixed economy – a combination of planning and market relationships – but the planning is carried out either by large corporations in their own interests or by government in the service of corporate interests. Democratic planning would produce an overall framework within which market exchanges between enterprises and between consumers and enterprises would take place. (Carnoy and Shearer, 1980, p. 275, original emphasis)

The argument that democratic planning would produce an 'overall public framework' for market relations is essentially what is meant by a non-capitalist civil society and furthermore what Polanyi meant by stating that socialism is the transcendence of the self-regulating market by 'consciously subordinating it to a democratic society' (Polanyi, [1944] 1957, p. 234; see the epigraph to this chapter).

What these programmatic reform proposals express is the common theme that democracy is the key to the transformation of the Western mixed economies. Although Bowles, Gordon and Weisskopf (1983) provide the most complete and detailed list of radical reforms, this literature suggests a common set of reforms intended to democratize social decision-making. The justification for these reforms tends to be pragmatic, because it argues that the existing mixed economies are plagued by problems that can only be resolved by the prescribed reforms. Based on historical experience, what the Budapest School has to offer these reform proposals is a more elaborate theoretical foundation for the type of mixed economy the reforms would create. The neo-Marxian defence of the mixed economy is not derived from specific analyses of such problems as unemployment, sex and race discrimination, environmental degradation and so on. On the contrary it states that, given the soviet experience and Polanyi's analysis of capitalism's evolution, a truly democratic society requires a mixed economy. Conversely the radical reform literature argues that resolving existing problems requires a truly democratic society. Thus the two groups converge around a set of reforms that not only would make Western capitalism more democratic but would preserve its mixed economic form as well.

The Mixed Economy and Equal
Self-Determination

Ultimately it is the value of equal self-determination that provides the standard by which one can measure the effectiveness of radical reforms. Transforming a social democratic mixed economy into a radical democratic mixed economy through a series of radical reforms is intended to accomplish two objectives. First, these reforms should democratize the stratified distribution of power over social decision-making. Such a process will then create the conditions for each and every individual to have equal control over the direction of his or her self-development. Equal rights of participation in the mechanisms of social decision-making mean equal control over the individual's process of needing.

Secondly these reforms not only should democratize the Western mixed economies but should allow for the maximum of need differentiation among individuals. They should create equality of control but not equality of life-style. The reforms should not only preserve the pluralism of needs found in industrial capitalism but expand it. Thus the purpose of the reforms is both to maximize democracy and simultaneously to minimize constraints on individual need articulation – to equalize control without damaging the free expression of needs. As Hegedus and Maria Markus (1976a, p. 157) have argued, 'Differentiated consumption does not only promote economic development, it also allows the many sided development of the human personality'. Likewise, as Heller (1982d, p. 321) states, 'Being rich in needs means the differentiation of the structure of needs in keeping with every personality through the appropriation of social wealth embodied in different objectivations'. It is for this reason that the 'recognition of all needs' is an important feature of a radical democracy, and an essential element of equal self-determination.

A set of radical reforms would take political democracy one step further without sacrificing the pluralism of need expression and the unlimitedness of needs. This would also involve a practice of tolerance for diverse life-styles.

The specific kinds of external authorities, norms and duties from which humankind should be liberated are the ones which enjoin us to use other persons as mere means, the norms which enjoin us to practice domination, force, and violence. The liberation of humankind is not dependent on the dismantling of any other norms, rules or duties, be they religious or this worldly. (Heller, 1982b, p. 369)

Therefore people in a radical democracy can 'perform their duties as good citizens and maybe good persons under the guidance of their own major deity' (Heller, 1981c, p. 265). Markus maintains that there is a need for a type of 'creative tolerance' that becomes necessary in a society that combines both democracy and the pluralism of needs.

If plurality of values, not orderable in one fixed hierarchy and offering a possibility of choice between various types of life-form, is posited as valuable in itself, then the unity of mankind can no longer be thought either under the category of one subject ... or under the notion of a consensus reached – on the contrary it ought to be comprehended as the continuous process of *building* a consensus, as the uninterrupted dialogue of practical solidarity and creative tolerance between different cultures and forms of life. (Markus, 1980a, p. 23, original emphasis)

The ethics of a radical democracy discussed in the previous chapter provide a common set of values from which building a consensus is possible. Making diversity of needs and life-styles a value in itself means that the Budapest School's 'moral maxims' of democratic politics are essential to social stability.

Finally, the transition from a social democratic to a radical democratic mixed economy is a democratic process itself, and with the practice of creative tolerance there are no guarantees of success. As the Hungarians realized in their revolution in 1956, so long as democratic processes are honoured and tolerance for diversity is more than a formality, there is no certainty that radical democracy will succeed capitalism smoothly and irreversibly. Creative tolerance is the essence of what Heller means by 'left radicalism' as well (see Chapter 4). Creative tolerance leaves open the door not only for a restoration of capitalism but for left Bolshevism too. Viewed historically as a counter-example the Bolshevik Revolution was a blatant violation of both creative tolerance and the principles of left radicalism. As Feher states, it is the process that counts.

On a democratic basis, socialism [radical democracy] can be and repeatedly has been defeated. An absolute guarantee can only be provided by the dictatorship that corrupts the very ideals of socialism. On a democratic basis, the labor of socialism can always begin again, whereas in dictatorships this recommencement is *practically* prevented by tyrannical authorities claiming to be the sole heirs of socialism. It is this possibility of beginning again that counts: socialism is labor and not a static condition guaranteed by coercion. (Feher, 1980c, p. 64, original emphasis)

In general the Budapest School's radical democracy model gives new content to formal democracy by extending it to include equal rights of participation in all social decision-making processes. Yet in order to be consistent with the value of equal self-determination, equality of participation in social decision-making must exist within a mixed economy of planning and markets and diverse ownership forms. The transition from the social democratic to the radical democratic mixed economy is then a matter of implementing a comprehensive set of reforms that democratize the Western mixed economy and thus create equal opportunities for participation in the decisions that affect everyone's potential for self-actualization. Ultimately, the labour of socialism, as Feher suggests, is the labour of mobilization and political activism. Democratizing the capitalist mixed economy requires a majoritarian popular movement; it requires the labour of organizing, educating and struggle inspired by the knowledge that the world can be a home for humanity.

Conclusion

This study has examined the thought of the Budapest School and has argued that its approach is neo-Marxian. Additionally it has sought to interpret this neo-Marxism as a theoretical defence of the mixed economy. In effect the Budapest School's neo-Marxism implies that Marx's thought continues to offer a viable philosophical foundation for the critique of modern social formations. The Budapest School's thought remains within the Marxian tradition because it accepts Marx's critical theory paradigm. Furthermore, it does not completely dismiss Marx's analysis of capitalism, but rather suggests that Marx's approach is economistic and must be modified to include the critical role played by the state and political sphere in the evolution of the Western mixed economy. Its interpretation of capitalism's evolution, drawing heavily on Polanyi, does not rely exclusively on an economic explanation. In general the neo-Marxism of the Budapest School and Polanyi argues that what Marx viewed as the essence of the capitalist system was only one tendency in the total unfolding of the market economy. Thus although Marx is a good place to begin for contemporary social theory, one must go beyond Marx to get an accurate perspective on modern societies.

The Budapest School's approach to existing socialism indicates the extent to which Marx's mistaken view of capitalism has served the interests of domination rather than liberation. Soviet societies are, at least in part, a product of Marx's economistic view of capitalism. Marx's economism implies that the essence of capitalism is the conflict of interests between two classes that are grounded in the autonomous economic sphere. Consequently, for the vanguard party of Bolsheviks, transcending capitalism required the state's absorption of capitalism's economic sphere. The power of the

193

capitalist, lodged in the economic base of society, could only be overcome by eliminating the separate economic sphere of capitalism.

The neo-Marxian approach reveals a 'pluralism of power' in industrial capitalism that is obscured by Marx's economism. As a result soviet societies destroyed capitalism's 'pluralism of power' along with the individual freedom that had been preserved by formal democracy and capitalism's civil society. Soviet societies did not advance the liberation of humankind in their radical break with capitalism. They are not a progressive step beyond the Western mixed economies; they are regressive, and the conclusion to be drawn from the Budapest School's analysis is that Marx's understanding of capitalism is partly to blame for this.

Another generalization of the Budapest School's approach is that social progress must be conceived of as the extension of democratic decision-making. The neo-Marxian view suggests that no clear distinction can be made between economic power and political power. It rejects the orthodox Marxian position that political power can be deduced from economic power in capitalism. Vajda's conclusion that capitalism has a 'pluralism of power' is derived from the Budapest School's belief that the determination of power relations in capitalism involves the codetermination of political and economic spheres. This shifts the focus of analysis towards a more general understanding of power as power over social decision-making processes and mechanisms. As Polanyi's analysis indicates, the social democratic mixed economies are the result of two codetermining tendencies: the protective response of society and the unfolding of self-regulating market forces. They are the by-product of both political and economic forces in which the distribution of power over social decision-making processes became stratified. Thus the social democratic mixed economies are not dichotomized class societies in Marx's sense but stratified societies. Social progress beyond the Western mixed economies involves democratizing their stratified distribution of power over social decision-making processes. Soviet societies have not extended democractic social decision-making beyond what has evolved in the Western mixed economies, and thus they do not represent social progress.

The Budapest School has argued that there is a realistic alternative to both the Western mixed economies and soviet societies. Its radical democracy alternative is consistent with the fundamental value-premiss of equal self-determination because it provides every individual with the equal right to participate in the social processes that shape need fulfilment and self-development. A radical democracy does not fulfil all needs but does allow each individual the equal right publicly to express his or her needs. For the Budapest School industrial capitalism does not recognize all needs because many needs are not profitable. Additionally many people lack the purchasing power in the market to express their needs. Soviet societies make a conscious effort to satisfy all needs, but they do so by arbitrarily limiting the spectrum of needs that are recognized. By using a totalitarian political process they dictate the needs that can be expressed and satisfied. A radical democracy is an attempt to allow people the maximum freedom to express their needs; that is, it should foster a 'plurality' of needs. However, it recognizes that there will never be sufficient available resources to satisfy all of these needs simultaneously.

Radical democracy is a theoretical model based upon the Budapest School's neo-Marxian critique of industrial capitalism and existing socialism. The critique measures and compares these two social formations against the standard of equal self-determination. Industrial capitalism has a stratified distribution of power over social decision-making, but it also has a 'plurality' of needs and a significant degree of individual freedom. However, although existing socialism has a stratified power distribution, because of its totalitarian political character it has neither the plurality of needs nor the degree of freedom expressed in the mixed economies. This judgement is a result of the Budapest School's neo-Marxism. In going beyond Marx these writers have been able to reveal more about the nature of freedom in the mixed economy than Marx's economistic approach has revealed.

By founding its approach on Polanyi the Budapest School has been able to identify more specifically the nature of freedom in the mixed economy, because Polanyi's analysis is less economistic than Marx's. Polanyi's view that the mixed economy is the result of two tendencies relating to the embeddedness of the economy in society is significantly different from Marx's. Marx's approach begins with a pre-existent, autonomous economic sphere from which all power emanates. Polanyi's view better comprehends the origin of the economic sphere as it emerged from precapitalist society, and he indicates through his explanation of the protective response how

Conclusion

power was more broadly based than Marxists have believed. The 'pluralism of power' suggested by Polanyi's analysis has been interpreted by the Budapest School to mean that industrial capitalism permits a greater degree of individual freedom than Marx's approach suggests.

The anti-capitalist nature of soviet society is derived from the Marxian belief that all power in capitalism emanates from its separate economic sphere in civil society. As a result, to neutralize capitalist domination civil society had to be absorbed by the soviet state. In doing this, soviet society also neutralized much of the individual freedom protected by capitalism's civil society.

The Budapest School's neo-Marxism has nourished a broader, less economistic understanding of capitalism, and consequently this signalled a serious reconsideration of soviet society. The most fundamental conclusion to be drawn from these views is that neo-Marxism reveals a more accurate understanding of the freedom in the capitalist mixed economies than does orthodox Marxism.

Given this understanding of freedom in the capitalist mixed economies, the Budapest School's thought leads to the conclusion that the mixed economy should not be replaced but democratized. Capitalism's separate sphere of civil society has within it both freedom and domination. By reforming the mixed economy so that its decision-making processes are more democratic, domination can be eliminated without sacrificing individual freedom.

The radical reforms elaborated in the previous chapter provide a connecting link between contemporary mixed economies and the Budapest School's theory of a radical democracy. A neo-Marxian view reveals the relation between a mixed economy and individual freedom and implies that a radical democracy can be achieved by implementing comprehensive reforms that democratize social decision-making.

In general the writings of the Budapest School are philosophical in character and often lack the kind of precision necessary to justify specific policy measures and programmatic reforms. This study has attempted to overcome some of this imprecision and to make more concrete such abstract categories as self-managed society, equal self-determination, radical democracy and equal recognition of all needs. It has sought to organize many of these pivotal yet underdeveloped themes into two fundamental features: the Budapest School's neo-Marxian approach and the defence of the mixed

196

economy implicit in its analysis of Western capitalism and existing socialism. These two features are not explicit in the Budapest School's writings but together they provide an interpretative framework that unifies the Budapest School's thought.

Additionally the specific relationship between the Budapest School's neo-Marxian approach and its defence of the mixed economy is not obvious. This study has argued that such a relationship, although not specifically developed in the group's work, does exist. Drawing on Polanyi, the Budapest School's critique of Marx's economistic method leads to an understanding that Western capitalism retains a pluralism of power largely eclipsed in soviet societies. Capitalism's separation of state and civil society and its use of markets serve to preserve a sphere of individual freedom that can be expanded only by reforms that democratize social decision-making. Going beyond Marx's economism leads to the conclusion, contrary to Marx, that the Western mixed economies can be progressively reformed.

Some Concerns and Connections

There are several topics suggested in the preceding chapters that are tangentially related to the Budapest School's thought and merit further comment. The first concerns the extent to which the radical democracy model, that is, the model of a democratized mixed economy, is applicable to Eastern European societies as they currently exist. The second topic concerns the prospects for social change in the Western mixed economies, and more specifically, it concerns the relationship between the Budapest School's neo-Marxian view of the mixed economies and the absence of a radical 'class' consciousness. Thirdly, further consideration appears necessary if one is to apply the Budapest School's defence of the mixed economy and its radical democracy model to political and economic conditions in Third World nations. A cursory view suggests that the radical democracy model may have limitations as a viable alternative to soviet and capitalist development models in the Third World. Additionally some consideration should be given to the relationship between the Budapest School's neo-Marxism and American institutionalist thought in economics. In general the neo-Marxian defence of the mixed economy suggests that it shares a close affinity to American institutionalism. The similarity between institutionalism and neo-Marxism is significant because it indicates a potential convergence of the two independent radical traditions of Marxism and institutionalism. Lastly, many of the Budapest School's categories and themes are underdeveloped in its writings, and awareness of this is a necessary requisite for a broader appreciation of the group's contribution.

Radical reform of the Western capitalist economies notwithstanding, there is also the issue of whether the radical democracy model is relevant to the prospects for social change in Eastern Europe. We have analysed radical democracy as a model that can be actualized by reforming the Western mixed economies, and we have examined it as the 'completion of formal democracy'. Although it is clear that radical democracy is a mixed economy and can be achieved by reforming existing mixed economies, such a conclusion does not mean that a mixed economy must be the exclusive precondition for the *transformation* to a radical democracy. For the Budapest School a mixed economy need not precede the construction of a radical democracy. In other words, formal democracy can be completed without necessarily beginning the transition from a formally democractic society.

Feher and Heller have argued that the popular revolution in Hungary in 1956 is one example of how a radical democracy might emerge in Eastern Europe. Although the revolution was short-lived, they maintain that it was 'one of the truly radical and most complex social occurrences of this century' (Feher and Heller, 1983b, p. 83). When the Soviet Union invaded Hungary on 4 November 1956, an embryonic but well-informed version of the Budapest School's radical democracy was emerging. It was a popular democratic revolution that sought not only national independence but the re-establishment of civil liberties and political pluralism (see Donath, 1982). It had begun to forge the basis for new types of ownership that would facilitate forms of worker self-management and democratic decision-making.

In October 1956 Imre Nagy, who had become the popular leader of the revolution, circulated a memorandum to the Hungarian people. This was part of a process by which Nagy and other reformists were attempting to draft a new constitution for Hungary. According to Feher and Heller, had this process reached fruition, the new constitution would have taken formal democracy a step

Conclusion

further towards radical democracy. In his memorandum Nagy stated:

> The members of the party and the Hungarian people as a whole do not desire a return to capitalism. They desire a regime of popular democracy which would be the incarnation of the socialist theory, a regime which would take account of working-class ideals, which would not be governed by a degenerate Bonapartist power and *dictatorship*, but by the working people itself in respect of law and order. (Feher and Heller, 1983b, p. 123, original emphasis)

Feher and Heller believe that Nagy understood, at least intuitively, that a 'popular democracy' must consist of democratic decision-making processes. The purpose of the new constitution was to allow for greater use of markets and non-state property ownership so that both the plurality of needs and democratic decision-making would be advanced. It was an attempt by the Hungarian people to create a more democratic alternative to both the Western economies and soviet socialism.

Ultimately the radical democratic character of the 1956 Hungarian Revolution was what the Soviet Union would not tolerate. After crushing the revolution, the Soviets placed Janos Kadar in power, and although Hungary never returned to the hard-line Stalinist state it had been before 1956, it has showed little sign of rekindling radical democracy. What has evolved in Hungary under Kadar is a variation of the post-Stalinist soviet model. Hungary is more liberal than many other Eastern European nations because it has implemented more marketizing reforms and has allowed intellectuals greater freedom to criticize the state (see Tökés, 1979).

For the Budapest School, Hungary shows little promise of radical change. They view 'Kadarism' as 'one of the most cynical political cultures that ever existed' because the effect of the economic reforms in Hungary (that is, the New Economic Mechanism initiated in 1968) coupled with the fear of a return to more Stalinist policies has depoliticized the population (Toma and Volgyes, 1977, p. 159). Feher and Heller state that 'the majority of the population, quite obviously hostile to any variant of communism, is clearly convinced on simple observation that *within communist systems* this is the most tolerable that they can have' (Feher and Heller, 1983b, p. ix, original emphasis). Thus the economic reforms implemented under

199

Kadar have created greater reliance on market signals and decentralized decision-making by enterprises, but this has not led to political reform. In Hungary political power has not been subverted by marketizing reforms; the people simply 'settled down into apathy' (Vajda, 1981, p. 126). For the Budapest School, although Kadarism is more liberal than other soviet policies, it is not more democratic.

However, this calls into question the relationship between Kadarism and radical democracy. Kadar, now in his mid-70s, has developed a regime in which his personal stature and authority have had much to do with legitimating the Hungarian system since 1956. His rule is clearly reaching its termination, and further examination into the exact limits of Hungary's present economic reform system might reveal the potential for significant social change in Hungary after Kadar's death. So far the Hungarian people have not asked for more political reform when they have been granted economic concessions. We must continue to watch this process unfold in an effort to judge its limits and the extent to which it has been a function of Kadar's personal authority.

Another question raised by the Budapest School's approach concerns the progressiveness of Hungary's marketizing reforms. In general a neo-Marxian approach suggests that marketizing reforms should open up more space for the plurality of needs. As enterprises respond more to consumer demand there is greater differentiation of needs and more potential for 'alternative life-styles'. With needs less dictated, then one would assume a greater potential for independence from the state apparatus. If this is the case in Hungary relative to other Eastern European nations, then how can one consider such reforms progressive if they have created a more depoliticized population? The Budapest School argues that a definite stand on marketing reforms cannot be taken. Only if they lead to greater democracy should they be considered progressive (Feher, Heller and Markus, 1983, p. 95).

The position of the Budapest School with respect to the progressiveness of Kadarism appears somewhat inconsistent. At first glance one would anticipate that the Budapest School would applaud the marketizing reforms because they allow for greater expression of needs and thus open up avenues for greater individual freedom. However, a distinction must be made between pessimism regarding the freedom that Hungarians enjoy relative to the rest of Eastern Europe and the pessimism the Budapest School feels regarding the prospects for further liberalization. Like the Hungarians themselves, the Budapest School would likely admit that Kadar's economic reforms have allowed Hungarians more freedom than their Eastern European neighbours. What the Budapest School is pessimistic about is the extent to which this type of increased economic freedom will lead to greater political freedom and greater political concessions. Kadar's marketizing reforms have not culminated in demands for political pluralism, which the Budapest School argues is also necessary for progress towards a radical democracy. However, in order to assess the potential for political reform in Hungary, it is necessary to ascertain the exact nature of the freedom the Hungarians have presently obtained under Kadar. The question is whether or not economic liberalization can persist without eventually subverting political authority.

In general the Budapest School's analysis of the 1956 Hungarian Revolution reveals that it is possible for a radical democracy to emerge out of a soviet society. However, does the Budapest School's neo-Marxism and its characterization of Eastern Europe as a dictatorship over needs speak to the prospects for social change in other Eastern European nations besides Hungary? As Eastern European exiles, members of the Budapest School scrutinize developments in Eastern Europe from the outside, but with the intent and hope of discovering progressive movements and radical opposition (see Feher, 1980a; Feher and Heller, 1983c; Szelenyi, 1979; Vajda, 1981). The fundamental generalization to be drawn from their neo-Marxism is that popular opposition and movements that appear at first glance to be 'capitalist' may have a deeper and more radical democratic thrust. Opposition – and in the case of Poland, social movements – that are anti-planning, consumerist and pro-market are not necessarily capitalist. These forms of opposition to the soviet model do not have to imply a desire for the return to capitalism. For a radical democracy to be achieved within Eastern Europe there will have to be a reduction in state property as well as an increase in the use of markets.

The developments in Poland in August of 1980 correlate very well with the Budapest School's neo-Marxian perspective. Within a year of the founding of Solidarity there was a clear consensus established regarding marketizing reforms. As a reaction to a system of dictated needs, Solidarity demanded reforms that would increase the use of markets for need articulation. At the same time it did not embrace a wholesale privatization of state property. Polish workers wanted greater participation in workplace decision-making, but like the Hungarians in 1956, they were beginning to struggle with the tough questions of property ownership. They rejected the principle of state ownership and control of the means of production, but simultaneously they did not want to turn their factories over to private individuals. It is possible that had the social movements consolidated by Solidarity not been crushed, they would have gravitated towards forms of ownership compatible with self-management. The future of popular opposition may very well reveal that the Polish people were searching for a more democratic alternative to both capitalism and existing socialism.

Feher has recently argued that the probability of a restoration of capitalism developing from opposition movements in Eastern Europe is not great. He maintains that most individuals in soviet societies are extremely anti-authoritarian, and although they are anti-socialist ideologically, they would resist capitalist forms of wage-labour as well. 'There is no physical or social impossibility of a restoration, but this disobedient and rebellious subject has to be tamed first in order to be turned into a proper subject of a restored liberal capitalism' (Feher, 1980a, p. 17). On the other hand, the Budapest School believes that the prospects for oppositional movements of any kind in Eastern Europe are not promising (Feher and Heller, 1986b). Therefore even to the extent that such movements may emerge as anti-soviet and bourgeois liberal, the Budapest School would be cautiously sympathetic. Their theory suggests that capitalism has had more to offer than soviet society, and consequently a case can be made for critical support of fledgling opposition in Eastern Europe.

Additional analysis of Eastern European opposition movements is necessary, because it is not clear how anti-soviet, anti-socialist currents within these nations could be channelled towards the goal of radical democracy. A neo-Marxian perspective has a greater appreciation for markets and private property than the orthodox Marxian view. Its perspective would look more favourably upon marketizing reforms because, as Vajda says, 'with these reforms . . . the system itself is endangered because these market mechanisms generate an increasing autonomy of the economic sphere and lead to the dissolution of the unified power' (Vajda, 1981, p. 139). Even though this may be the case (with the possible exception of

Hungary), one would want to know more specifically what type of political strategy a neo-Marxian view might suggest for opposition leaders in Eastern Europe.

A second issue suggested by the Budapest School's thought concerns neo-Marxism's interest in the absence of class consciousness in capitalist societies. Orthodox Marxism argues that the working class in capitalism, as a result of its growing 'immiserization', should at some point develop a consciousness of itself as a revolutionary subject. Additionally orthodox Marxism has maintained that the inability of workers to have their needs fulfilled should lead them to question the basic logic of capitalism. In other words, the dialectic of class struggle should ultimately result in a socialist revolution because workers would become increasingly dissatisfied with their material conditions and would realize that a radical break with capitalism is necessary if they are to fulfil their needs.

At the point where the working classes realize that all their individually experienced problems are social in nature, where workers realize that their individual liberation requires social revolution, then they have developed class consciousness as well as a socialist consciousness. Orthodox Marxism has continued to support the view that capitalism's contradictions will eventually lead the oppressed classes to this point. It has embraced the view that capitalism contains within it the seeds for class consciousness.

The neo-Marxism that began with Lukacs, Gramsci, Korsch and the Frankfurt School rejected the deterministic relation between economic classes and consciousness posited by orthodox Marxism. Neo-Marxism, or what is often called Western or cultural Marxism, has argued that class consciousness cannot be considered an epiphenomenon of the economic base of capitalist society. Neo-Marxism has focused on the causes for the absence of class consciousness in contemporary capitalism, and it has generated a rich and diverse body of explanations ranging from Reich's character structure analysis to Lukacs's theory of reification. Much of this literature developed as a result of fascism, because neo-Marxists were interested in explaining why the European working classes, who were close to a socialist revolution at the close of the First World War, became so reactionary during the 1930s.

The Budapest School's interpretation of Polanyi's double movement thesis suggests that it may have a contribution to make to the question of class consciousness. As suggested in Chapter 1 of this study, the Budapest School rejected Lukacs's theory of class consciousness primarily because it rejected Marx's conception of economic class. If capitalism never became a dichotomized class society then the absence of class consciousness is less difficult to explain. The majority of wage-workers in the Western mixed economies have not developed a radical class consciousness and have historically had only a passing interest in socialism. For the most part they have not viewed capitalist institutions as the major cause of their day-to-day problems, nor have they become more unified in the pursuit of their interests. Neo-Marxism has done much to explain this phenomenon, but the Budapest School's approach may provide additional insights.

The Budapest School's interpretation of Polanyi not only questions the concept of class when it is used as the basis for investigating the missing class consciousness, but it also reveals that capitalism, and especially the contemporary mixed economy, has significantly more freedom than orthodox Marxists have realized. Based on Polanyi's analysis their approach maintains that there is a 'pluralism of power' in industrial capitalism, and along with this there is a sphere of individual freedom protected by capitalism's separate civil society and its formal democracy. The problem of the absence of class consciousness is not only due to the absence of a homogeneous working class, but it is also due to the type of freedom experienced in capitalism. Neo-Marxism, as well as orthodox Marxism, continues to draw attention to the domination, repression and oppression that exist in capitalism. To the extent that these problems exist, it is still unclear why so few people seem to experience capitalism in this way. On the other hand, the Budapest School's theory implies that the majority of working populations may have good reason for experiencing contemporary capitalism more as freedom than as domination and exploitation.

The neo-Marxian literature that tries to explain the absence of radical consciousness in the West has not understood that its absence may be due to the fact that working-class groups tend to *experience* capitalism as freedom rather than domination. The Budapest School's view has a better explanation for the nature of freedom in capitalism and may indicate that it is this freedom that accounts for the absence of a radical consciousness.

Historically Marxism has emphasized that capitalism is a system founded on social injustice, exploitation and alienation. Neo-Marxism has addressed the obvious problem that if these are fundamental features of the capitalist landscape, then why do so few victims of these problems recognize them? By contrast, the social theory we have examined emphasizes the positive feature of individual freedom within the totality of capitalist relations. If, as Vajda maintains, capitalism's greatest achievement is individual freedom, then there is reason to suppose that the overwhelming experience one has of capitalism should be freedom, not domination. Additionally, if this is the case then it is hardly surprising that a radical consciousness has not emerged from the majority of capitalism's populations.

Additional analysis in this area might assess the extent to which the neo-Marxian literature has ignored the issue of freedom in capitalism, at least as it pertains to the absence of a radical consciousness. Moreover one would want to know more exactly how individual freedom in 'bourgeois society' obscures the undemocratic nature of its decision-making processes. Finally, the results of this analysis should be applicable to the formation of a political strategy aimed at the creation of radical democracy. The previous chapter examined the reforms necessary to democratize the mixed economy's stratified social decision-making processes. It did not suggest a viable political strategy that would lead to a majoritarian movement for such reforms. Relevant investigation regarding the relationship between the Budapest School's understanding of capitalism and radical consciousness should result in some recommendations for a radical democratic political strategy, however.

There is a third issue that warrants some comment: the applicability of the Budapest School's radical democracy model to underdeveloped Third World nations. The Budapest School argues that a radical democracy offers a third way; it is a third option that transcends the limitations of both industrial capitalism and existing socialism. As an alternative to the two dominant systems one would hope that it might offer this possibility to various Third World liberation movements that are also struggling for the option of independent development.

The difficulty with the radical democracy model is that it has been developed theoretically in the context of the industrialized world. It appears especially relevant to the Western mixed economies, where democratic traditions are solidly rooted in these nations' development. Our inquiry has attempted to demonstrate how a radical democracy might be implemented in nations that already have formal democracy and a stable political climate. Radical reforms legislated in the mixed economies would require majoritarian, popular movements, but they could be feasibly implemented using formal democracy as a vehicle. The model of radical democracy represents the 'completion of formal democracy', and as such it appears particularly appropriate for countries that have had long-standing experience with formal democracy. In the Western developed nations the political climate is stable, transitions from one government to another are orderly and non-violent, and there is no reason to suspect that with sufficient popular support the transition to a radical democracy would be any different.

However, in struggling Third World nations the political climate is unstable, and changes in government are frequently violent. These are nations that have not had hundreds of years of experience with political democracy. The practice of radical democracy requires an ethical foundation in which there is a clear consensus and acceptance of the values of freedom, justice and an end to suffering (see Chapter 5). The political practice in a radical democracy requires a genuine consensus that democratic decision-making should be respected by all participants. In many Third World nations a clear consensus on democratic decision-making and ethical behaviour would be extremely difficult to achieve. Movements with a radical democratic character may be able to assume power; yet if they are genuinely democratic, but without a consensus on values and ethics, they are vulnerable to counter-revolutionary forces that may be less democratic. The path of social change in the Third World is one characterized by mutual suspicion, distrust and hatred, and this makes the transition to a radical democracy problematic.

Polanyi stated that as long as mankind consistently upheld the value of 'creating more abundant freedom for all' then

> he need not fear that either power or planning will turn against him and destroy the freedom he is building by their instrumentality. This is the meaning of freedom in a complex society; it gives us all the certainty that we need. (Polanyi, [1944] 1957, p. 258B)

Polanyi's certainty seems appropriate for easing some of the anxieties in the transition to radical democracy in the Western developed economies, but it remains questionable whether this is all the certainty needed for democratic movements to assume power in Third World nations. Movements with radical democratic aspirations must be committed to democratic decision-making at all levels, and the process of creating a radical democracy must be democratic as well. What frequently happens, as in the case of Allende's Chile, is a paradoxical situation where the more democracy the new government attempts to create the less likely it is to survive.

As a *model* of a future society, radical democracy is no less applicable in the Third World than it is in the United States or Sweden. However, further study may reveal that the transition to radical democracy would undoubtedly be different between the First and Third worlds. The experience of post-Somoza Nicaragua suggests the problematic nature of a democratic transition to radical democracy. The Sandinistas have consistently professed the ideals of a radical democracy, yet their ability to proceed along a democratic course is constrained by fear, mistrust, counter-revolution and US foreign policy. Such a turbulent political climate would appear to be the antithesis of what is necessary for the transition to radical democracy.

A fourth tangential issue concerns the relationship between American institutionalism and the Budapest School's neo-Marxism. There are numerous parallels and similarities between institutionalist and neo-Marxist thought that should be elaborated. Beginning with Veblen's criticism of Marx, in the past eighty years the intellectual traditions of institutionalism and Marxism have frequently been at odds with each other. Marxists have often considered institutionalists to be reformist and uninterested in the practical politics of organizing for social change. Institutionalists, on the other hand, have often rejected Marxists' economistic approach to the capitalist system.

However, with the development of the Budapest School there appears to be a much stronger case for the convergence of institutionalists and neo-Marxists. One such example is the similarity between Galbraith and the Budapest School on radical reforms. Their respective positions on the type of changes needed to democratize the Western mixed economies are essentially the same. Both would agree that the distribution of power in these societies is stratified and that the Marxist view of a dichotomized class society is less applicable now than ever before. Additionally there would be little dispute among them regarding the need for both a strong private as well as a strong public sector, and there would be little disagreement about the need for both planning and markets.

Another area in which institutionalists and the Budapest School converge concerns soviet societies. The Budapest School's model of dictatorship over needs reveals that these societies are exemplary ceremonial societies. They are modernized, industrialized versions of the traditional, precapitalist ceremonial society analysed by Veblen and Ayres. It is their precise and specific ceremonial nature, captured by the Budapest School's model, that distinguishes them from capitalist societies. Further analysis could demonstrate that the Budapest School's dictatorship-over-needs framework illustrates how soviet societies rely on ceremonial rather than instrumental values for their stability and reproduction. By casting the dictatorship-over-needs model in an institutionalist framework, further parallels are likely to emerge.

Ayres and the Budapest School also hold quite similar positions on values. Ayres (1961) argues that there are five fundamental values that comprise a unified value system necessary for social progress and the good society. He maintains that freedom, equality, security, abundance and excellence are values derived from the 'life process' itself, and for this reason they are cross-cultural, with similar meanings for all peoples.

The Budapest School has also developed a similar list of self-evident values necessary for a radical democracy (see Chapter 5). It argues that a radical democracy requires an ethical foundation in which all people embrace the values of freedom, justice and an end to human suffering. Both Ayres and the Budapest School recognize that these values are human creations that can be upheld and are indispensable for humankind's progress and liberation.

In sum the Budapest School's thinking has strayed far enough from orthodox Marxism that it now has much in common with institutionalism. Clearly the greatest similarity lies in policy prescriptions for the Western mixed economies. The mix of radical reforms elaborated in Chapter 6, that is, the reforms necessary to democratize social decision-making, would be mutually agreeable to both institutionalists and the Budapest School. There are, however, differences in orientation and methodology between the two strains of thought; for example, the institutionalist dialectic between technology and institutions is somewhat alien to the Budapest School framework.

Lastly, the vagueness of many of the Budapest School's key philosophical concepts merits a comment. We have attempted to systematize many of these concepts, such as equal self-determination, social decision-making, democratic freedom, relative abundance, recognition of all needs, positive abolition of private property and radical democracy. However, even though these concepts and themes can be effectively organized in an effort to interpret the Budapest School as a neo-Marxian defence of the mixed economy, it also becomes clear that they require further examination. For example, the phrase 'democratizing social decision-making' is fundamental to the definition of a radical democracy. Although the reforms suggested in Chapter 6 are intended to indicate the basic thrust of democratic social decision-making, it is not clear simply by reference to these reforms what is meant by social decision-making in general. Which decisions in a society are social and which ones are not? Exactly what are the processes through which social decisions are made, and are these processes different from those used for private decisions?

Another key category used by the Budapest School and developed in this study is that of human needs. Equal self-determination is a standard of value by which to compare Western capitalism and existing socialism. Yet needs are the medium through which people determine themselves. Needs in both of these social formations are either distorted, limited, or dictated. Yet in the mixed economy of a radical democracy all 'non-alienating needs' are 'recognized'. This study has made the concept of needs more concrete by examining it in the context of the Budapest School's view of capitalism and existing socialism, but it has not answered all of the questions that consequently arise when such a term is used as a key category.

For example, the exact process by which needs go unrecognized or become alienated and distorted in capitalism is not specified; nor is it clear exactly which needs are recognized in a radical democracy and which are not. The exact process whereby needs in a radical democracy are no longer distorted, limited, or dictated requires further clarification in general. Additionally, it is clear that in the realization of a radical democratic, mixed economy freedom and economic security will go hand-in-hand with the transcendence of distorted and dictated needs.

Conclusion

Although, in the Budapest School's writings the relationship between needs and economic security is not fully developed, further examination might show that greater control over social decision-making and greater economic security lead to less distortion of needs. Because the processes that determine the nature of the individual's needs and desires are socially determined, further analysis of the relationship between distorted needs and economic security may well reveal that the economic insecurity that many individuals in the Western nations experience is manifested in part by an inability to understand their needs and desires. As a result they are more susceptible to advertising manipulation and their needs become distorted. A radical democracy that provides economic security and equal input into the processes of need fulfilment may provide individuals with greater time and opportunity for accurate reflection upon their needs.

Even though this analysis remains undeveloped in both this study and the Budapest School's writings, it indicates the significance of the Budapest School's thought and suggests that much wider attention be given to their work. Ultimately, their contribution concerns freedom and justice and is premised by the understanding that in order to secure and promote equal freedom in the future we must recognize the nature of the freedom that humankind has to this point achieved.

Bibliography

Andreff, W. (1983), 'Where has all the socialism gone? Post-revolutionary society vs. state capitalism', *Review of Radical Political Economics*, vol. 15, no. 2, pp. 137–52.

Ayres, C. E. (1961), *Towards a Reasonable Society: The Values of Industrial Civilization* (Austin: University of Texas Press).

Bahro, R. (1979), *The Alternative in Eastern Europe* (London: New Left Books).

Boella, L. (1979), 'Eastern European societies', *Telos*, no. 41, pp. 59–75.

Bowles, S., and Gintis, H. (1986), *Democracy and Capitalism: Property, Community, and the Contradictions of Modern Social Thought* (New York: Basic Books).

Bowles, S., Gordon, D., and Weisskopf, T. (1983), *Beyond the Wasteland: A Democratic Alternative to Economic Decline* (Garden City, NY: Anchor Press).

Carnoy, M., and Shearer, D. (1980), *Economic Democracy: The Challenge of the 1980s* (Armonk, NY: M. E. Sharpe).

Castoriadis, C. (1975), 'An interview with Cornelius Castoriadis', *Telos*, no. 23, pp. 131–55.

Donath, F. (1982), '1956 and self-management', *Telos*, no. 53, pp. 160–62.

Feher, F. (1976), 'A Hungarian out in the cold' (interview with Ferenc Feher), *The Listener*, 12 Feb. 1976.

Feher, F. (1978), 'The dictatorship over needs', *Telos*, no. 35, pp. 31–42.

Feher, F. (1980a), 'Eastern Europe in the eighties', *Telos*, no. 45, pp. 5–18.

Feher, F. (1980b), 'Hungary, 1956, revolution', *Radical America*, vol. 14, no. 1, pp. 51–62.

Feher, F. (1980c), 'Toward a post-machiavellian politics', *Telos*, no. 42, pp. 56–65.

Feher, F. (1983), 'Lukacs in Weimar', in A. Heller (ed.), *Lukacs Reappraised* (New York: Columbia University Press), pp. 75–106.

Feher, F., and Heller, A. (1977), 'Forms of Equality', *Telos*, no. 32, pp. 6–26.

Feher, F., and Heller, A. (1982a), 'Equality reconsidered', *Thesis Eleven*, no. 3, pp. 23–40.

211

Feher, F., and Heller, A. (1982b), 'Eurocommunism: the fear of power', *Thesis Eleven*, no. 2, pp. 127–61.

Feher, F., and Heller, A. (1982c), 'Antinomies of peace', *Telos*, no. 53, pp. 5–16.

Feher, F., and Heller, A. (1983a), 'Class, democracy, modernity', *Theory and Society*, vol. 12, no. 2, pp. 211–44.

Feher, F., and Heller, A. (1983b), *Hungary, 1956 Revisited: The Message of a Revolution a Quarter of a Century After* (London: Allen & Unwin).

Feher, F., and Heller, A. (1983c), 'On being anti-nuclear in soviet societies', *Telos*, no. 57, pp. 144–61.

Feher, F., and Heller, A. (1984), 'From red to green', *Telos*, no. 59, pp. 35–44.

Feher, F., and Heller, A. (1986a), *Doomsday or Deterrence* (Armonk, NY: M. E. Sharpe).

Feher, F., and Heller, A. (1986b), *Eastern Left, Western Left: Totalitarianism, Freedom, and Democracy* (Cambridge, UK: Polity Press).

Feher, F., Heller, A., and Markus, G. (1983), *Dictatorship over Needs* (New York: St. Martin's Press).

Feher, F., Heller, A., Markus, G., and Vajda, M. (1983), 'Notes on Lukacs' ontology', in A. Heller (ed.), *Lukacs Reappraised* (New York: Columbia University Press), pp. 125–53.

Fekete, E., and Karadi, E. (eds) (1981), *Gyorgy Lukacs, His Life in Pictures and Documents* (Budapest: Corvina Kiado).

Frankel, S., and Martin, D. (1973), 'The Budapest School', *Telos*, no. 17, pp. 122–34.

Furniss, N., and Tilton, T. (1977), *The Case for the Welfare State: From Social Security to Social Equity* (Bloomington, Ind.: Indiana University Press).

Galan, T. (1980), 'Thoughts on the role of public holdings in developing economies: INI's experience in Spain', in W. Baumol (ed.), *Public and Private Enterprise in a Mixed Economy* (New York: St. Martin's Press), pp. 116–37.

Grossman, G. (1974), *Economic Systems* (Englewood Cliffs, NJ: Prentice-Hall).

Haraszti, M. (1975), 'I have heard the iron cry', *New Left Review*, no. 91, pp. 9–16.

Haraszti, M. (1978), *A Worker in a Worker's State* (New York: Universe Books).

Hegedus, A. (1976a), 'The self-criticism of socialist society: a reality and a necessity', in A. Heller (ed.), *The Humanization of Socialism: Writings of the Budapest School* (New York: St. Martin's Press), pp. 161–75.

Hegedus, A. (1976b), *Socialism and Bureaucracy* (New York: St. Martin's Press).

Hegedus, A., and Markus, M. (1976a), 'The role of values in the long-range planning of distribution and consumption', in A. Heller (ed.), *The Humanization of Socialism: Writings of the Budapest School* (New York: St. Martin's Press), pp. 140–60.

Hegedus, A., and Markus, M. (1976b), 'Community and individuality', in A. Heller (ed.), *The Humanization of Socialism: Writings of the Budapest School* (New York: St. Martin's Press), pp. 91–105.

Hegedus, A., and Markus, M. (1976c), 'Tendencies of Marxist sociology in the socialist countries', in A. Heller (ed.), *The Humanization of Socialism: Writings of the Budapest School* (New York: St. Martin's Press), pp. 124–39.

Heller, A. (1974a), 'Theory and practice: their relation to human needs', *Social Praxis*, vol. 1, no. 4, pp. 359–73.

Heller, A. (1974b), *The Theory of Need in Marx* (New York: St. Martin's Press).

Heller, A. (1976a), 'Theory and practice from the point of view of human needs', in A. Heller (ed.), *The Humanization of Socialism: Writings of the Budapest School* (New York: St. Martin's Press), pp. 58–75.

Heller, A. (1976b), 'Marx's theory of revolution and the revolution in everyday life', in A. Heller (ed.), *The Humanization of Socialism: Writings of the Budapest School* (New York: St. Martin's Press), pp. 42–57.

Heller, A. (1976c), 'The future of relations between the sexes', in A. Heller (ed.), *The Humanization of Socialism: Writings of the Budapest School* (New York: St. Martin's Press), pp. 27–41.

Heller, A. (1978a), 'Is radical philosophy possible?' *Social Praxis*, no. 5, pp. 5–15.

Heller, A. (1978b), 'Past, present, and future of democracy', *Social Research*, vol. 45, no. 4, pp. 866–86.

Heller, A. (1979a), 'The Declaration of Independence and the principle of socialism: contribution to a discussion', *Social Praxis*, vol. 6, nos 1–2, pp. 109–12.

Heller, A. (1979b), 'Group interest, collective consciousness, and the role of the intellectual in Lukacs and Goldmann', *Social Praxis*, vol. 6, nos 3–4, pp. 177–92.

Heller, A. (1979c), 'Marxist ethics and the future of Eastern Europe' (interview with Agnes Heller), *Telos*, no. 38, pp. 153–75.

Heller, A. (1979d), *On Instincts* (Atlantic Highlands, NJ: Humanities Press).

Heller, A. (1979e), *A Theory of Feelings* (Atlantic Highlands, NJ: Humanities Press).

Heller, A. (1981a), 'The moral maxims of democratic politics', *Praxis International*, vol. 1, no. 1, pp. 39–48.

Heller, A. (1981b), 'Paradigm of production – paradigm of work', *Dialectical Anthropology*, vol. 6, no. 1, pp. 71–79.

Heller, A. (1981c), 'Rationality and democracy', *Philosophy and Social Criticism*, vol. 8, no. 3, pp. 245–66.

Heller, A. (1981d), 'Radical philosophy', *Thesis Eleven*, no. 1, pp. 19–28.

Heller, A. (1982a), 'The legacy of Marxian ethics today', *Praxis International*, vol. 2, no. 1, pp. 346–64.

Heller, A. (1982b), 'Marx and the "liberation of human kind" ', *Philosophy and Social Criticism*, vol. 19, nos 3–4, pp. 355–70.

Heller, A. (1982c), 'Phases of legitimation in soviet-type societies', in

Bibliography

F. Feher and T. H. Rigby (eds), *Political Legitimation in Communist States* (New York: St. Martin's Press), pp. 45–64.

Heller, A. (1982d), *A Theory of History* (London: Routledge & Kegan Paul).

Heller, A. (1983a), 'The dissatisfied society', *Praxis International*, vol. 2, no. 4, pp. 359–71.

Heller, A. (1983b), 'Georg Lukacs and Irma Seidler', in A. Heller (ed.), *Lukacs Reappraised* (New York: Columbia University Press), pp. 27–62.

Heller, A. (1983c), 'Lukacs' Later Philosophy', in A. Heller (ed.), *Lukacs Reappraised* (New York: Columbia University Press), pp. 177–91.

Heller, A. (1984), *A Radical Philosophy* (New York: Basil Blackwell).

Hewett, E. (1984), 'Economic reform in the Soviet Union', *The Brookings Review*, pp. 8–11.

Hjern, B., and Hull, C. (1983), 'Policy analysis in mixed economy: an implementation approach', *Policy and Politics*, vol. 11, no. 3, pp. 195–312.

Hungarian Party Document (1973), 'The position paper of the cultural political work collective operating next to the Central Committee of the Hungarian Socialist Workers Party on the anti-Marxist views of several social researchers', *Telos*, no. 17, pp. 134–45.

Kaldor, N. (1980), 'Public or private enterprise – the issues to be considered', in W. Baumol (ed.), *Public and Private Enterprise in a Mixed Economy* (New York: St. Martin's Press), pp. 1–12.

Konrad, G., and Szelenyi, I. (1979), *The Intellectuals on the Road to Class Power* (New York: Harcourt Brace & Jovanovich).

Kornai, J. (1986), *Contradictions and Dilemmas; Studies on the Socialist Economy and Society* (Cambridge, Mass.: MIT Press).

Laclau, E. (1979), *Politics and Ideology in Marxist Theory* (London: Verso).

Lefort, C. (1975), 'What is bureaucracy?', *Telos*, no. 22, pp. 31–65.

Lieberman, S. (1977), *The Growth of European Mixed Economies 1945–70: a Concise Study of the Economic Evolution of Six Countries* (New York: John Wiley & Sons).

Lukacs, G. (1971a), *History and Class Consciousness* (Cambridge, Mass.: MIT Press).

Lukacs, G. (1971b), 'The development of a Budapest School' (an interview with Georg Lukacs), *Times Literary Supplement*, London, 11 June 1971.

Lukacs, G. (1973), *Marxism and Human Liberation* (New York: Dell Publishing).

Markus, G. (1978), *Marxism and Anthropology: The Concept of Human Essence in the Philosophy of Marx* (Atlantic Highlands, NJ: Humanities Press).

Markus, G. (1979), 'Practical-social rationality in Marx – dialectical critique', *Dialectical Anthropology*, vol. 4, no. 4, pp. 255–88.

Markus, G. (1980a), 'Practical-social rationality in Marx – dialectical critique – Part II', *Dialectical Anthropology*, vol. 5, no. 1, pp. 1–31.

Markus, G. (1980b), 'Four forms of critical theory – some theses on Marx's development', *Thesis Eleven*, no. 1, pp. 78–93.

Markus, G. (1981), 'Planning the crisis: remarks on the economic system of soviet-type societies', *Praxis International*, no. 3, pp. 240–57.
Markus, G. (1982), 'Western Marxism and Eastern societies', *Dialectical Anthropology*, vol. 6, no. 4, pp. 291–318.
Markus, G. (1983a), 'Concepts of ideology in Marx', *Canadian Journal of Political and Social Theory*, vol. 7, nos 1–2, pp. 84–103.
Markus, G. (1983b), 'Life and soul: the young Lukacs and the problem of culture', in A. Heller (ed.), *Lukacs Reappraised* (New York: Columbia University Press), pp. 1–26.
Marx, K. ([1867] 1967), *Capital, Volume I* (New York: International Publishers).
Mouffe, C. (ed.) (1979), *Gramsci and Marxist Theory* (London: Routledge & Kegan Paul).
Nove, A. (1983), *The Economics of Feasible Socialism* (London: Allen & Unwin).
Polanyi, K. ([1944] 1957), *The Great Transformation* (Boston, Mass.: Beacon Press).
Poulantzas, N. (1978), *State, Power, Socialism* (London: New Left Books).
Preston, M. (1982), 'The nature and significance of the mixed economy', in E. Roll (ed.), *The Mixed Economy* (London: Macmillan Press), pp. 18–34.
Roll, E. (1982), 'The mixed economy', in E. Roll (ed.), *The Mixed Economy* (London: Macmillan Press), pp. 1–17.
Rowley, C. (1982), 'Industrial policy in the mixed economy', in E. Roll (ed.), *The Mixed Economy* (London: Macmillan Press), pp. 35–57.
Shonfield, A. (1980), 'The politics of the mixed economy in the international system of the 1970s', *International Affairs*, no. 56, pp. 151–72.
Smith, T. (1979), *The Politics of the Corporate Economy* (Oxford: Martin Robertson).
Szelenyi, I. (1977), 'Notes on the Budapest School', *Critique*, no. 8, pp. 61–8.
Szelenyi, I. (1979), 'Socialist opposition in Eastern Europe: dilemmas and prospects', in R. Tökés (ed.), *Opposition in Eastern Europe* (Baltimore: Johns Hopkins University Press), pp. 187–208.
Ticktin, H. (ed.) (1974), 'Repression against the Marxist in Hungary', *Critique*, no. 3, p. 108.
Tökés, R. (ed.) (1979), *Opposition in Eastern Europe* (Baltimore: Johns Hopkins University Press).
Toma, P., and Volgyes, I. (1977), *Politics in Hungary* (San Francisco: W. H. Freeman).
Vajda, M. (1975), 'Truth or truths', *Cultural Hermeneutics*, no. 3, pp. 29–39.
Vajda, M. (1976), *Fascism as a Mass Movement* (New York: St. Martin's Press).
Vajda, M. (1981), *The State and Socialism* (London: Allison & Busby).
Vajda, M. (1983), 'Lukacs and Husserl', in A. Heller (ed.), *Lukacs Reappraised* (New York: Columbia University Press), pp. 107–24.

Vardys, V. S. (1979), 'Review of *Humanization of Socialism*', *The American Political Science Review*, vol. 73, no. 2, pp. 651–562.

Young, S. (1974), *Intervention in the Mixed Economy* (London: Croom Helm).

Index

double movement 57, 58, 65, 70,
203–4
dualism 29

Eastern Europe(an)
Budapest School's evaluation 22,
96–107, 172, 197, 201
economic problems 102, 172
employment security 174
energy development 187
freedom 200–1
leftist opposition 107, 203
market abolition and
reform 125–6, 176, 200, 201
Marxian heritage 107–15
oppositional movements 202
oppression 106
prospects for change 97, 197, 198,
202
revolutions 114
societies 2, 31, 96, 122
state property 201
totalitarian nature 122–3
working conditions 21, 118
economic legislation 47, 48
Engels, F. 41
England
Chartist movement 51
Industrial Revolution 44
liberal historians 51
workers' co-operative 188
Enlightenment 3, 22, 80, 89, 91
enterprise costs overstatement 173
environmental protection 185
epistemology 14, 23
equality 14, 37, 92, 136, 165, 168,
195
essence becoming nature 30
existing socialism
alienated labour 116–17
dictatorship over needs 115–31
equality 165
freedom and democracy 133–4
inadequacy of Left
explanations 106
Marxian heritage 107–15
need for re-examination 98–107
neo-Marxian critique 96–132, 193,
195
product of economism 193
state confiscation of property 136
state paternalism 117, 174
theoretical centrality 96

undemocratic character 2
See also soviet societies
exploitation 26, 49, 56, 111, 113

factor markets 169
factory council movement 32
factory legislation 61
farmers 61
fascism
Marxist view 69–70, 71–2
Polanyi's theory 70–1
racism 75
role of bourgeoisie 72
Vajda's analysis 71–6
Feher, F.
arrest 21, 37 n.1
analysis of freedom and
equality 27, 82, 85–6
on bourgeois society 41
on class system 56–7
on command planning 172–3
critique of Marx 25, 50
on de-Enlightenment of soviet
societies 97
on East European societies 106,
201
emigration to Australia 18
emphasis on conflictual character of
history 6
example of Hungarian
revolution 198–9, 200–1
on existing socialism 96
on freedom and equality 85–6
identification of socialism and
democracy 22
'irrationality' in USSR
economy 173
'it is process that counts' 191–2
'leftist' label 5
markets 169–71, 176, 177
on Marxian–Lukacsian concept of
class 6
member of Budapest School 1
on nature of man 23
on ownership 167
protest resignation 21
reports censure of Markus 17
restoration of capitalism
unlikely 202
on socialism and democracy 22, 52
on state capitalism 102
on state as redistribution
agent 166

Index

Communist party 20, 21
Kadarism 199–201
'last Stalinist premier' 16
marketizing reforms 97, 199–201, 203
political dissidents 14, 16
reform economists 172
Revolution (1956) 16, 100, 177, 191, 198–9, 201
tractor factory 116
Husserl, E. 22–3, 29

ideology 24, 74, 75, 175
individual liberty 3, 69, 89, 92, 95, 133, 135, 147, 157, 158, 196
inequalities 112
inflation 112
insecurity 135
Intellectuals on the Road to Class Power, The 104, 105
intelligentsia 124, 136
interventionism 48
investment decisions 101, 184
Italy 72

Jacobinism 82, 108, 110, 113, 119
Jacoby, R. 13 n.1
job retraining 181
justice 147, 148

Kadar, J. 16–17, 18, 21, 198, 201
Kaldor, N. 10–11
Kant, I. 92
Karadi, E. *See* Fekete, E.
Kautsky, K. 32
Kennedy, J. F. 188
Kis, J. 16
Konrad, G. 16, 104, 105
Korcula letter 17
Kornai, J. 102, 172, 173
Korsch, K. 2, 4, 41, 72, 108–9, 203
Kortars 17

labour hoarding 173
labour market 160
Labriola, A. 4
Laclau, E. 32–3, 58, 75
laissez-faire 46–7, 171
land use 181
laziness 108
Lefort, C. 7, 8–9
left radicalism 5, 114
legislation 47, 48, 61

legitimation 174, 175, 176–7
Lenin, V. I. 20, 50, 108–9
Lieberman, S. 10
living standards 91, 174
Lukacs, G.
 anti-positivism 22
 Budapest School's relationship 1, 4, 31–7
 concept of class-consciousness 71
 economism 33
 History and Class-consciousness 32, 33, 35
 on human essence 30
 member of Galilei Circle 41–2
 method seen as essence of Marxism 2, 4, 36
 opposes Lenin's authoritarianism 108–9
 rejection of determinism 32
 on renaissance of Marxism 19, 34
 'soul' 27
 students 1, 15, 21–2, 34
 theory of reification 203
 The Times interview 15
 universal Marxist perspective 4
 on workers' councils 31–2
Luxemburg, Rosa 57, 108–9

Macaulay, Lord 51
mandatory retirement 183
Marcuse, H. 19
market(s)
 as allocative mechanism 169, 175, 176
 automaticity 47
 exchange 105
 forces 39, 46
 fragmented 175
 in mixed economy 1
 necessity 168–71
 needs articulation 201
 reifying effects 175
 simulated 170
Markovic, M. 37 n.3
Markus, G.
 application of critical theory 23–4
 on consciousness 29
 on creative tolerance 191
 on essence and existence 31
 excluded from *The Humanization of Socialism* 18
 on existing socialism 98, 107
 expelled from party 18

221

Index

Szelenyi, I.   16, 17, 42, 105, 201. *See also* Konrad, G.

taxation   181, 185
technocrats   18, 19, 110, 167
teleology   29
television advertising   181
tension   147
terrorism   174
Theory of History, A   79
Third World   197, 205, 206–7
Thompson, E. P.   52, 56
Tilton, T.   *See* Furniss, N.
Times, The (London)   15
Tökés, R.   17, 124, 199
tolkachi   173
Toma, P.   199
totalitarianism   2, 121, 135, 175
totalization   73, 131, 175
trade unions   61, 73, 74, 163, 183, 184, 188
transitional society theory   100, 102–4
tribalism   56
Trotsky, L.   102
Trotskyists   7, 13 n.2
Tsarist Russia   112

unemployment   112
Union of Soviet Socialist Republics
  abolition of private property   136, 141–2
  agricultural underproduction   173
  Bolshevik Revolution   2, 72, 82, 95, 99, 121, 136, 191
  Bolsheviks' 'pessimism'   108
  expression of equality of needs   136
  industrialization   174
  invasion of Czechoslovakia   17–18
  invasion of Hungary   198
  investment funding   172
  social control   173–4
  post-Stalin period   130
  state as monopoly capitalist   101
  working conditions   174
United Kingdom   11, 47
United States of America
  child care provision   185
  Corporate Disclosure Act   184
  Declaration of Independence   52–3
  Dellums National Health Service Act   185
  economic decline   183
  Fair Labor Standards Act   183

Federal Reserve Board   185
institutionalist economics   197–8, 207–9
mixed economy   11, 95, 179, 188–9
National Labor Relations Act   184
New Deal   74
Populist movement   179
reform prescriptions   182–6
Taft-Hartley Act   183
Worker Alienation Research Act   188
worker-owned factories   188
'us-them' relationships   59, 116, 123
utopia(nism)   20, 47, 57, 82, 86, 93, 139, 148

Vajda, M.
  analysis of fascism   71–7, 78
  on abolition of class differences   79
  on anti-positivism of Budapest School   22–3
  on bourgeois democracy   74, 81–2
  on class-consciousness   34
  contributor to *The Humanization of Socialism*   16
  definition of state   48
  on elimination and reform of market   111, 168–9, 202
  expulsion from the Party   18
  on freedom in civil society   79–82
  on Marx's method   5, 6–7, 98
  member of Budapest School   1, 15
  on mixed economy as middle road   165
  on pluralism of power   54, 164, 194
  on politics and society   38, 48–9
  on proletariat   33, 55
  student of Lukacs   1, 15
  on subordination of the economy   66, 162
  'Truth or Truths'   23
  on wage-labour roles in individual   161
value commitment   36
Vardys, V. S.   16
Veblen, T.   19, 207, 208

wage-bargaining   115–16, 183
war communism   175
waste   173, 182
Weber, M.   52, 56
Weisskopf, T.   *See* Bowles, S.

225

welfare state   3, 180–1, 185
Western economies
  democratizing   162, 171, 178–92,
    205–6
  development (1879–1929)   70
  markets   176
  pluralism of power   164
  private sector   167
  reform proposals   162, 186–9
  separation of spheres   164
  unplanned nature   135
  workers' insecurity   135

See also   capitalism
Western Eurocommunist parties   106,
  107
work   28
worker-controlled enterprises   170, 188
workers' councils   3, 32, 184
world communications   83
World War 1   72, 74, 106
World War 2   13 n.2, 182

Young, S.   10
Yugoslavia   17